Deshbandhu Chitranjan Das

Deshbandhu Chitranjan Das

Series Editor
M.A. Seewan

Editors
Saud Akhtar **R.K. Singh**

Himalaya Books Pvt. Ltd.
'Ramdoot', Dr. Bhalerao Marg, Girgaon, Mumbai - 400 004
Tel : (022) 23863863. Fax : (022) 23877178
Email : himpub@vsnl.com

Edition : 2016

Published by : **H.B.P.L.**
"Pooja Apartments", 4-B, Murari Lal Street, Ansari Road,
Darya Ganj, New Delhi-110 002
Phones: 23270392, 23278631 Reliance : 30180392 to 396
Fax: 011-23256286 Email : hphdel@vsnl.com

Sole Distributers : **HIMALAYA PUBLISHING HOUSE PVT. LTD.**

Branch Offices :

Mumbai : "Ramdoot", Dr. Bhalerao Marg, Girgaon, Mumbai - 400 004.
Phone: 022-23860170/23863863, Fax: 022-23877178
E-mail: himpub@vsnl.com;
Website: www.himpub.com

Nagpur : Kundanlal Chandak Industrial Estate, Ghat Road, Nagpur - 440 018. Phone: 0712-2738731, 3296733; Telefax: 0712-2721216

Bengaluru : Plot No. 91-33, 2nd Main Road Seshadripuram, Behind Nataraja Theatre, Bengaluru-560020.
Phone: 08041138821, 9379847017, 9379847005

Hyderabad : No. 3-4-184, Lingampally, Besides Raghavendra Swamy Matham, Kachiguda, Hyderabad - 500 027.
Phone: 040-27560041, 27550139

Chennai : New-20, Old-59, Thirumalai Pillai Road, T. Nagar, Chennai - 600 017.
Mobile: 9380460419

Pune : First Floor, "Laksha" Apartment, No. 527, Mehunpura, Shaniwarpeth (Near Prabhat Theatre), Pune - 411 030.
Phone: 020-24496323/24496333; Mobile: 09370579333

Lucknow : House No 731, Shekhupura Colony, Near B.D. Convent School, Aliganj, Lucknow - 226 022.
Phone: 0522-4012353; Mobile: 09307501549

Ahmedabad : 114, "SHAIL", 1st Floor, Opp. Madhu Sudan House, C.G. Road, Navrang Pura, Ahmedabad - 380 009.
Phone: 079-26560126; Mobile: 09377088847

Ernakulam : 39/104 A, Lakshmi Apartment, Karikkamuri Cross Rd., Ernakulam, Cochin - 622011, Kerala.
Phone: 0484-2378012, 2378016; Mobile: 09387122121

Bhubaneswar : 5 Station Square, Bhubaneswar - 751 001 (Odisha).
Phone: 0674-2532129, Mobile: 09338746007

Kolkata : 108/4, Beliaghata Main Road, Near ID Hospital, Opp. SBI Bank, Kolkata - 700 010, Phone: 033-32449649, Mobile: 7439040301

Printed at : Infinity Imaging System New Delhi. On behalf of HPH.

Preface

Biography, is now a form of literature, very much in vogue. In fact, biography is a description or account of someone's life and the times, which is usually published in the form of a book. A biography is more than a mention of personal facts (life, education, work, relationships and death), it also portrays the subject's experience of events. Technically speaking, a work is biographical, if it covers, all of a person's life. Biography writing has a long history. A biography is real. Ancient Greeks developed the biographical tradition, which we have inherited, although until the 5th century AD, when the word 'biographia' first appeared, in Damascius' "Life of Isodorus," biographical pieces were called simply "lives". It is quite likely that the Greeks were drawing on a pre-existing eastern tradition. Certainly Herodotus' "Histories" contains more detailed biographical information on Persian kings and subjects. The earliest surviving pieces, which we would identify as biographical are Isocrates' "Life of Evagoras" and Xenophon's "Life of Agesilaos," both from the fifth century BC. "Parallel Lives" by Plutarch, a Greek writing under the Roman empire, is a series of short biographies of eminent men.

The Golden Age of English biography emerged in late eighteenth century, the century in which the terms "biography" and "autobiography" entered English lexicon. The classic works of the period were Samuel Johnson's "Critical Lives of the Poets" and James Boswell's "Massive Life of Johnson". Generally American biography followed English model. By World War I, cheap hardcover reprints had become popular. The decade of the 1920s witnessed a biographical 'boom'. Later, biographical writings developed a lot and today biographies are written and compiled in the finest form of the genre. In India too, biography, as a form of literature has been evolved, cultivated and polished over the years. Here is an effort to promote this tradition further.

This series of biographies of great men, great women and celebrities in all walks of life is an adventurous academic endeavour, in its own right. A team of researchers and compilers has worked for a good period of time to accomplish the project. For this purpose, hundreds of books by eminent authors and editors have been consulted and referred to. We have benefited from various works, liberally, in order to illustrate and enrich this effort of ours. Present book is devoted to the great personality of Deshbandhu Chitranjan Das.

An important personality in Bengal, during the time of the noncooperation movement, Deshbandhu Chitranjan Das started the boycott of British and other western dresses. He was elected the mayor of Calcutta Corporation and also became President of Congress. A lawyer by profession, he went on to play a very important role in Indian struggle for independence. He acquired his higher education from England. His career in law kicked off, when he successfully defended Aurobindo Ghosh in the Alipore bomb blast case. He set an example for others in adopting the hand made desi khadi garments. He later set up the Swaraj Party to propagate his non-moderate views with Motilal Nehru. He also launched a newspaper, named 'Forward' to spread his message to the public and fight the British Raj, but later rechristened it as 'Liberty'. Deshbandu was continuously ill, throughout his political life. But despite this, he showed spunk and unwavering determination in opposing the foreign rule. Chitranjan Das advocated the adherence to constitutional ways in order to attain independence for India. He preached communal concord and supported the cause of national education. Subhas Chandra Bose was his staunch follower. Fondly, Das was called Deshbandhu (the friend of the country).

This is a compact and comprehensive account of the above mentioned great life, which is bound to attract the attention of scholars, researchers, students and the general readers, alike. Let's hope this humble effort would receive a warm welcome and due applause.

— *Editors*

Contents

1

Introduction

Great freedom fighter Chittaranjan Das (C.R. Das) (popularly called Deshbandhu— "Friend of the country") (November 5, 1870 - June 16, 1925) was an eminent Bengali lawyer and a major figure in the Indian independence movement.

Deshbandhu Chitranjan Das belonged to the famous Das family of Telirbagh, in Bikrampur, Dhaka (now in Bangladesh). He was the son of Bhuban Mohan Das, and nephew of the Brahmo social reformer Durga Mohan Das. Some of his cousins were Satish Ranjan Das, Sudhi Ranjan Das, Sarala Roy and Lady Abala Bose. His eldest grandson was Siddhartha Shankar Ray and his granddaughter is Justice Manjula Bose.

Educated in England, where he became a Barrister, his public career began in 1909 when he successfully defended Aurobindo Ghosh on charges of involvement in the previous years Alipore bomb case. He was a leading figure in Bengal during the Non-Cooperation Movement of 1919-1922, and initiated the ban on British clothes, setting an example by burning his own European clothes and wearing *Khadi* clothes.

He brought out a newspaper called *Forward* and later changed its name to *Liberty* to fight the British Raj. When the Calcutta Corporation was formed, he became its first Mayor. He resigned his presidency of the Indian National Congress at the Gaya session after losing a motion on "No Council Entry" to Mahatma Gandhi's faction. He then founded the Swaraj Party, with veteran Motilal Nehru and young Huseyn Shaheed Suhrawardy, to express his immoderate opinions.

He was a believer of non-violence and constitutional methods for the realisation of national independence, and advocated communal harmony and championed the cause of national education. His legacy was carried forward by his disciples, and Notable by Subhash Chandra Bose.

He is generally referred to by the honorific Desh Bandhu meaning "friend of the nation." In 1925, Das's health began to fail and in May he withdrew to a mountain home in Darjeeling, where Mahatma Gandhi visited him. On 16 June 1925, with a severe fever, he died. The funeral procession in Calcutta was led by Mahatma Gandhi, who said:

> "Deshbandhu was one of the greatest of men... He dreamed... and talked of freedom of India and of nothing else... His heart knew no difference between Hindus and Musalmans and I should like to tell Englishmen, too, that he bore no ill-will to them."

2

An Illustrious Life

Native Place

Chitranjan Das belonged to the famous Das family. He was the son of Bhuban Mohan Das. Vikrampur has been for many centuries a centre of learning and culture in Eastern India. In the twelfth century the capital of King Ballal Sen and King Lakshman Sen of Bengal was situated in Vikrampur.

It was the home of Dipankar who went to Tibet in the tenth century with the message of the Buddha. In the middle ages this was the seat of Kedar Roy who defied the might of Imperial Delhi for many years. In more recent times it has been the home of some of the leading men of Bengal. Jagadish Chandra Bose came from this pargana and also Chittaranjan Das.

Vikrampur (which is now in Bangladesh) is washed by the waters of many rivers and streams. The mighty Padma flows along its western boundaries, and on the eastern side flows the Meghna. The flow of these rivers leads to constant erosion and formation of new land. The rivers have given the area a good climate but they have also compelled the local people to seek their livelihood by struggle against nature. Lord Carmichael who visited Vikrampur in 1915 described it in the following terms: "Vikrampur seems to resemble in some ways my native land of Scotland, for many of the best of her sons seek employment far beyond her borders and, indeed, like Scotsmen in the British Empire, take a large share in the administration of the affairs of the people, and like Scotsmen, they arc always proud of the land from which they come and their children are proud of the connection with the home of their forefathers." Telirbag is a village of Vikrampur located on the northern bank of the Padma.

Chittaranjan was born in a family of Vaidyas hailing from this village. The Vaidyas are physicians by profession and have been noted for their progressiveness and love of learning. The community has for many years been remarkable for the encouragement it has given to education among all its members. In fact, in women's education the community has always been in the forefront in India.

Family Background

Chittaranjan was born with the virtues and characteristics of his birthplace and his community. He showed from early life a spirit of adventure, great devotion to causes and a determination to excel. He inherited from his great-grandfather, Chandra Nath Das, the generosity which was such a marked characteristic of his nature. Chittaranjan's grandfather, Kashishwar Das, was a Government pleader of Barisal and had three sons, Kali Mohan, Durga Mohan and Bhuban Mohan, who were all *vakils* (lawyers) in the Calcutta High Court. The eldest Kali Mohan, rose high in the profession and was a man of remarkable courage. He was also a little short-tempered and often came into conflict with authority. In those days it was rare for a lawyer to challenge a judge, particularly a judge of the High Court. Kali Mohan Das was once pulled up by Mr. Justice Louis Jackson while arguing a case. He retorted: "I am surprised, my Lord, that though you have been a District Judge of so many years' experience, I cannot make you understand what even a student of law can very easily follow."

The judge was naturally annoyed and drew up proceedings against him. Many of his friends advised Kali Mohan Das to apologise, but he refused to do so.

The matter was referred to the full Bench of the High Court and Sir Barnes Peacock, then Chief Justice, gave a decision in Kali Mohan's favour in the following words: "No doubt Kali Mohan Babu was intemperate in his language but the principle of law he was arguing was right. So no action is called for."

Durga Mohan Das was a great social reformer and an ardent Brahmo. He refused to give his eldest daughter in marriage to the Maharaja of Cooch Behar as she had not then attained the age of sixteen, the minimum fixed by the Brahmo Samaj for the marriage of girls. He collaborated with Ananda Mohan Bose, Shib Nath Shastri and others in working for the equality of the sexes and the abolition of *purdah.* His three sons also joined the legal profession and became Barristers-at-Law. One of them, Satish Ranjan Das, became the Advocate-General of Bengal and later Law Member in the Viceroy's Executive Council.

Father: Chittaranjan's father, Bhuban Mohan, was both a vakil and an attorney of the Calcutta High Court. A man of great culture and wide sympathies, he was generous to a fault. He was fond of poetry, loved music and composed verses and hymns which he used to sing every morning. He was also a good writer with a simple, chaste and direct style. As editor of the *Brahma Public Opinion,* he attained a high position among the journalists of Bengal because of his sincere and forceful writing. Like his brother, Kali Mohan, he also came into conflict with authority on many occasions. Chittaranjan inherited many of the qualities of his father but perhaps it was his mother who had greater influence on him. She was large-hearted and hospitable and possessed a fine sense of justice. She did not receive high education but had great natural gifts and endowments. She needed them to overcome the difficulties which the family had to face because of her husband's impetuous and generous nature. He was extravagant himself and in addition always willing to incur debts to help others. In the end, he was declared an insolvent and the family was in distress because of the debts and the claims made on it by many dependants. Nistarini Devi shouldered these responsibilities with courage and common sense. Neither adversity nor wealth had any effect on her character and she faced both with equanimity. It was natural that Chittaranjan should be deeply devoted to her and ready to face any risk for her sake.

Birth and Early Life

Chittaranjan Das was born in Calcutta on Saturday, the 5th of November 1870. He was the second child in a family of eight. He had an elder sister, four younger sisters and two brothers. Early in his life Chittaranjan came in contact with Bipin Chandra Pal, one of the well-known political leaders of India and a renowned orator. Chittaranjan was from his infancy fond of patriotic poems and used to recite them with great fervour.

Education

Early Education

He entered school at the age of nine and passed the Entrance Examination of Calcutta University in 1886. Soon after, he joined the Presidency College which has produced some of the most prominent figures of India in the last hundred years. In fact, Presidency College men used to say, "Anybody who is anybody in public life is somebody from Presidency College" Among Chittaranjan's contemporaries were a number of men who distinguished themselves in public administration, politics and literature. Chittaranjan was strong in English but weak in Mathematics. He was very fond of Bengali literature and immersed himself in the writings of Bankim Chandra Chatterji. He also studied Rabindranath Tagore and was an admirer of Keats, Shelley and Browning. He was a keen debater and became secretary of the Students' Association which was often addressed by Surendra Nath Banerjea who soon became one of the eminent leaders of the Indian National Congress. Das wanted Bengali to be introduced as a second language for University examinations and saw the Vice-Chancellor of the University. His plea was not accepted as the Vice-Chancellor thought that it might detract from the prestige and importance of Sanskrit.

Higher Education

In 1890 Chittaranjan was sent to London to qualify himself for the Indian Civil Service. Along with him went J. N. Gupta who had been a friend in college and later became a distinguished member of the Indian Civil Service. In London Chittaranjan came in contact with Prof. Carveth Reade who took a great liking for him and taught him philosophy and literature.

Chittaranjan sat for the Civil Service Examination in 1892 but did not take all the papers because he felt he might not do well. His friend J. N. Gupta entered the service and went to Oxford but Chittaranjan remained in London. Prof. Carveth Reade had formed a high opinion of his young pupil and wished to encourage him in every way. He advised him to think out problems on his own and go through textbooks only after he had formed his own views. This meant hard work, but Professor Reade told him that it would develop in him the power of independent thought and expression.

Chittaranjan took the ICS Examination in 1893 and felt that he had acquitted himself well. He communicated his hopes to his father by cable. Another competitor. Albion Banerji, wrote to his friends that Chittaranjan was sure to succeed. Ultimately, however, it turned out that instead of fifty as formerly announced, only forty-two persons were to be recruited that year and Chittaranjan was placed forty-third in the list.

Political Activities

It was then said, and many believed it, that Chittaranjan had lost his place in the service because of his political activities. He was from early childhood a patriot and had given evidence of his love of home-made goods. In London, he used a heavy gold chain which attracted the attention of his teachers. When asked why he used such an unfashionable article, Chittaranjan replied that he preferred an inelegant Indian chain to the most fashionable chain manufactured in Britain.

Chittaranjan had also become involved in political activities on behalf of India soon after he sat for the Civil Service Examination for the first time. There was a Parliamentary election in 1892 in which Indian sympathies were with the followers of Gladstone. The political enthusiasm of students had been roused by a series of incidents starting with the agitation against the Ilbert Bill in

1883. Surendra Nath Banerjea was imprisoned the same year and Lord Ripon received a warm and enthusiastic farewell from the people while the British elements were glad to see him go.

Congress on the Scene

The first session of the Indian National Congress was held in 1885 in Bombay under the presidentship of Mr. W. C. Bannerji. The second was held in Calcutta with Dadabhai Naoroji as the president and the third in Madras under Badruddin Tyabji. Intellectual classes responded enthusiastically to the Congress but the British authorities were disturbed and angry. Lord Dufferin referred to the members of the Congress as a microscopic minority but all this had only the effect of creating a stronger spirit of nationalism among the youth of the country.

In 1889 the Congress held its fifth session in Bombay which was attended by Charles Bradlaugh, a Liberal member of the British Parliament. On his return, Bradlaugh introduced a Bill for reforms in India, but although it had passed the second reading it could not become an Act because of his serious illness which ultimately ended in his death. Lord Cross, then Secretary of State for India, brought a Bill which was passed as the India Council's Act, 1892. It provided for nominated, not elected, legislatures in spite of the advice of Lord Northbrook, Lord Ripon and Lord Sandley in the House of Lords and Mr. Gladstone in the House of Commons.

It was only natural that the 1892 election should pay some attention to the Indian question. Some of the opponents of Indian Home Rule made derogatory remarks about Indians in their speeches. This provoked a strong reaction among the Indian students in Britain. Chittaranjan took a leading part in this political campaign and even though a candidate for the Civil Service, he spoke strongly at Exeter and elsewhere in favour of Indian reform. His speeches attracted the notice of important Liberal leaders including Gladstone. In the end, the Liberals won the election but Chittaranjan, as already mentioned, was not among the successful candidates for the Civil Service. He felt that he had lost his place in the Service because of his political activities and cabled to his father: "Failed. One Place Out. Jobbery:"

The family was greatly distressed not only because of his failure but also because they feared that in his disappointment he might adopt some desperate course or refuse to return to India. Bhuban Mohan wired to his son that he should study for the Bar and followed up with a letter that the family traditions equipped him for the legal profession. An extract from a letter which Sir. Richard Garth ex-Chief Justice of the Calcutta High Court, wrote to Bhuban Mohan is of interest in this connection:

> "I tried my best, but the fiery speeches of your son at Oldham have spoiled everything. I could not persuade the India Office."

Chittaranjan joined the Inner Temple and was called to the Bar in 1893.

Career as Lawyer

Chittaranjan was sworn in as an advocate of the Calcutta High Court before Mr. Justice Sale in December 1893. Like many other young lawyers, he also had to struggle hard and face many disappointments in his early career. The outlook indeed looked gloomy for him. His father was over head and ears in debt. This was bad enough, but his financial difficulties became even worse when he stood for election to the Calcutta Corporation and was defeated at the polls. In those days barristers used to give themselves airs and many of them considered in *infra dig* to travel by tram or on foot. Chittaranjan used to go to the High Court by tram and walk back across the Maidan on foot.

Chittaranjan's father had incurred heavy personal debts. In addition he had incurred obligations on behalf of others because of his generous and impetuous nature. He had stood surety for a person at the request of his clerk. When the man absconded, Bhuban Mohan became liable to pay back a sum of Rs. 30,000. When Chittaranjan began to practise, bonds for the repayment of two debts were renewed in the names of both father and son.

Some creditors went to court for realisation of their debts. Bhuban Mohan and Chittaranjan were declared insolvent and their estate and effects vested in the Official Assignee on the 16th of June 1896.

For four years or more, Chittaranjan had to struggle hard for bare survival. His father had practically retired from the profession and Chittaranjan had to support a large family, while he was yet a declared insolvent. These difficulties did not discourage him, however, but made him struggle harder to build up his career.

Chittaranjan had, of course, a great advantage in the traditions and connections of his family. His grandfather Kashishwar had been a Government pleader. His uncles were also well-known lawyers. The family has produced three High Court Judges and one of them, Sudhi Ranjan Das, became Chief Justice of India. Chittaranjan's own younger brother. P. R. Das, rose to be one of our leading lawyers.

Civil practice on the original side has attracted some of the best legal brains in the Calcutta High Court but building a practice on the Original side usually takes a long time. Situated as he was, Chittaranjan could not wait and had to depend on criminal practice which often took him away to the *mofussil* courts. He was so hard up that he often accepted fees which were much lower than was customary for barristers of his standing. The Maharaja of Natore, who was an intimate friend of Chittiranjan, relates an incident which gives us a picture of Chittaranjan's condition at the time. Once when he had gone to Chittaranjan's house he found him dejected and sitting all by himself. When he met Chittaranjan again after some time, he found that he was in a better mood as he received a case which would bring him a fee of Rs. 300. The Maharaja was surprised at the smallness of the figure but Chittaranjan had accepted it gratefully as there was no money in the house even for the bare necessaries of life.

Soon Chittaranjan's reputation began to rise. He proved specially successful in cross-examining witnesses and turning the evidence to his client's advantage. He was greatly helped by his friend Sarat Chandra Sen who was a successful *vakil* at the Alipore Criminal Court. As Chittaranjan's reputation came to be recognised, he began to concentrate on practice in the city. This also gave him an opportunity to turn his attention to the Original side and he slowly but steadily built up a reputation in civil cases.

Success as Lawyer

The year 1907 marked a turning point in Chittaranjan's career as a lawyer. He had by this time established himself as a successful lawyer in both civil and criminal law. He now emerged as a great patriot and defender of national workers. Brahma Bandhob Upadhyaya was accused of sedition before the Chief Presidency Magistrate, Calcutta. Chittaranjan defended him as well as Bipin Chandra Pal.

A case which attracted still greater attention was the famous Alipore Bomb Conspiracy Case in which one of the accused was Shri Aurobindo Ghose who later became famous as the seer and philosopher of Pondicherry. This case deserves a somewhat more detailed discussion as it has become a part of the story of the Indian national struggle.

The Chief Presidency Magistrate of Calcutta, Mr. Kings-lord, had become very unpopular because of the severity with which he punished persons accused of political offence's. He had passed severe sentences on the editors and printers of nationalist newspapers. In one case he sentenced a young boy of fifteen to whipping, which caused indignation even among the British. Lord Morley, who was then Secretary of State for India, was shocked by some of his judgements and wrote to Lord Minto, the Viceroy, in the following terms:

> "I must confess to you that I am watching with the deepest concern and dismay the thundering sentences that arc now being passed for sedition, etc. We must keep order, but excess of severity is not the path to order. On the contrary it leads to the path of the bomb."

The leaders of the revolutionary movement in Bengal decided that Mr. Kingsford must be made to pay for his actions with his life. That would also serve a warning to other officers. A bomb was sent to him by post. He did not open the parcel and was providentially saved. A second attempt was made on his life after he was transferred from Calcutta and became the District Judge of Muzaffarpur. Two young men, Khudiram Bose and Profulla Chaki, were sent to do away with him, but the bomb they hurled killed two innocent women instead.

The murder of Mrs. Kennedy and Miss Kennedy of Muzaffarpur shocked public opinion and there was great indignation among all sections of the people. Khudiram was arrested on the 1st of May 1908 at the Wani railway station. Profulla Chaki was also captured at Mokama railway station, but he shot himself with his own revolver. Khudiram was eventually tried and sentenced to death by hanging.

The Government decided that the conspiracy behind these murders must be exposed. There was a search at 32 Murart-pukur Road and twenty-six members of the Jugantar Party, a revolutionary group, were arrested. Later Shri Aurobindo Ghose was taken into custody from his residence at 48 Grey Street. A preliminary enquiry was held on the 19th of August 1908 and the accused were charged with sedition and conspiracy. It was alleged that after the partition of Bengal in 1905 the accused had preached sedition through the Bengali weekly *Jugantar* and had conspired together to wage war against His Majesty's Government. It was also said that they sought to overawe the authorities by violence and had collected arms and made extensive preparations for manufacturing bombs. Among the other charges were that they had attempted to wreck the train by which the Lieutenant-Governor Sir Andrew Fraser was travelling, had thrown a bomb into the residence of the Mayor of Chander Nager, fired at Mr. Allen the District Magistrate of Dacca and sent Khudiram and Profulla to murder Mr. Kingsford.

One of the accused, Narendra Nath Goswami, turned approver during the enquiry and eight more persons were arrested as a result of his disclosures. Goswami, however, did not live to enjoy the benefit of his betrayal Two of the accused, Kanai Lal Dutta and Satyendra Nath Bose, shot him dead in the Presidency Jail hospital. They were tried for murder and sentenced to death. All this evidence was put together and the surviving accused were committed to sessions.

The regular trial began on the 19th of October 1908 before Mr. Beachcroft Additional Sessions Judge of Alipore. The prosecution was conducted by the famous lawyer, Mr. Eardley Norton, while Shri Aurobindo was at first defended by Messrs. B. Chakraborty and K. N. Chowdhury.

Shri Aurobindo had voluntarily embraced poverty and public subscriptions were raised for his defence. The amount, however, was soon spent and a time came when there was no one except Chittaranjan left to defend him. After his acquittal Shri Aurobindo expressed his gratitude to Chittaranjan in the following terms:

> "He came unexpectedly, a friend of mine. . . . You have all heard the name of the man who put away from him all other thoughts and abandoned all his practice, who sat up half the night day after day for months and broke his health to save me—Srijut Chittaranjan Das. When I saw him I was satisfied."

Chittaranjan worked hard in defence of his client. He devoted all his thought and energy to the case and studied up all the available case law to strengthen his brief. For ten months, Chittaranjan devoted himself exclusively to Aurobindo's case. Not only did he do so without any fee but he had to sell his carriage and horse and borrow money on personal bonds. His earnings came to an end while his expenses continued as before. When the case was over, he was in debt to the extent of about Rs 50,000.

Chittaranjan worked heart and soul to defend Aurobindo but even then his anxiety for his client would not allow him to compromise his dignity. Once when Chittaranjan was arguing about the admissibility of some evidence, the judge dismissed his argument as nonsense. Das immediately reported: "It is a pity that you are on the bench and I am at the bar.

If you had said this somewhere else. I could have given you the proper reply." The judge realised that he had erred, and the matter came to an end with his apology. Though there were a number of accused in the conspiracy ease, the Government's real target was Shri Aurobindo. Mr. Beachcroft himself observed in his judgement:

> "Aurobindo was the accused whom more than any other the prosecution were anxious to have convicted, and but for his presence in the dock, there was no doubt the case would have been finished long ago."

The trial continued for 126 days. Over two hundred witnesses were examined; 4,000 paper exhibits and about 500 material exhibits in the form of bombs and explosives were filed. Chittaranjan's concluding address continued for nine days, and the peroration with which he ended will rank among the classic of legal addresses.

An item of evidence produced by the prosecution was a letter which Aurobindo had written to his wife in 1905. In this letter Aurobindo said:

> "At present I have no work of my own. I am always busy with His work. My mind has undergone a radical change. I do whatever I am commanded by Him to do. I have no will of my own. God will also be kind to you and He will show you the true pain. You are my wife (Sahadharmini). won't you help me in my mission?
>
> Divine energy (Brahmatej) is necessary for the salvation of the country."

The prosecution interpreted this letter as evidence of conspiracy and argued that Aurobindo was asking his wife also to join him in the work. Chittaranjan, on the other hand, regarded it as a statement of deep spiritual faith and submitted that it was the language of total self-effacement and resignation. He pointed out that the cardinal doctrine of Hinduism was to regard oneself as a tool in Clod's hand. It is Divine Will that acts through man. The religious spirit of the letter is found even in the use of the word *Sahadharmini*. The term means one who is a fellow worker in the attainment of the religious ideal. Similarly, the use of the word *Brahmatej* or divine energy indicates that human arms are insignificant in comparison with divine force.

Another item of evidence advanced by the prosecution was that Aurobindo had attended a meeting held on the 28th of March to honour Bipin Chandra Pal on his release from jail. Chittaranjan pointed out that Bipin Chandra Pal had suffered imprisonment for the sake of Aurobindo. It was natural, therefore, that Aurobindo should attend the meeting out of a sense of obligation. He maintained that this could not be construed as an act of conspiracy.

Das dealt in a similar manner with the other arguments put forward by the prosecution. He displayed great legal acumen in arguing that confessions of other accused could not be admitted as evidence against Aurobindo. The approver's evidence was expunged and Das's masterly analysis of the facts of the case convinced the assessors. The words with which Das concluded his speech will always have an appeal for those who love freedom and human dignity.

Das first interpreted Aurobindo's thought in the following manner:

> "If it is suggested that I preached the ideal of freedom for my country and that this is against the law, I plead guilty to the charge. If that is the law here, I say I have done that and I request you to convict me, but do not impute to me crimes I am not guilty of, deeds against which my whole nature revolts and which, having regard to my mental capacity, is something which could never have been perpetrated by me. If it is an offence to preach the ideal of freedom, I admit having done it. I have never disputed it. It is for this that I have given up all the prospects of my life. It is for this that I came to Calcutta, to live for it and to labour for it. It has been the one thought of my waking hours, the dream of my sleep. If that is my offence, there is no necessity of bringing witnesses into the box to depose different things in connection with that. Here am I and I admit it. If that is my fault, you can chain me, imprison me, but you will never get out of me a denial of that charge. I, however, venture to submit that it is no offence in the eyes of the law to preach the ideal of freedom. With regard to the crimes with which I have been charged, I submit there is no

evidence on the record and it is absolutely inconsistent with everything that I thought, that I wrote and with every tendency of my mind discovered in the evidence."

Das then made the following submission to the Court:

"My appeal to you, therefore, is that a man like this, who is being charged with the offence with which he has been charged, stands not only before the Bar of this Court, but before the Bar of the High Court of history. My appeal to you is this: that long after this controversy will be hushed in silence, long after this turmoil, this agitation, will have ceased, long after he is dead and gone, he will be looked upon as the poet of patriotism, as the prophet of nationalism and 'a lover of humanity. Long after he is dead and gone, his words will be echoed and re-echoed not only in India but across distant seas and lands. Therefore I say that the man is not only standing before the Bar of this Court but before the Bar of the High Court of history.

The time has come for you. Sir, to consider your judgement and for you gentlemen (addressing the assessors) to consider your verdict. I appeal to you. Sir, in the name of all the traditions of the English Bench that form the most glorious chapter of English history. I appeal to you in the name of all that is noble, of all the Thousands of principles of law that have emanated from the English Bench, and I appeal to you in the name of the distinguished judges who have administered the law in such a manner as to compel not only obedience but the respect of all those in the cases in which they had administered the law. I appeal to you in the name of the glorious chapter of English history and let it not be said that an English judge forgets to establish justice.

To you gentlemen I appeal in the name of the very ideal which Aurobindo preached and in the name of

> the traditions of our country. Let it not be said that two of his countrymen were overcome by passions and prejudices and yielded to the clamour of the moment."

The assessors gave their opinion in favour of Aurobindo and on the 6th of May 1909 Mr. Beachcroft delivered his judgement in which he accepted the assessors' view and acquitted Shri Aurobindo Ghose. He however, sentenced Aurobindo's brother, Barindra Kumar Ghose, and another accused, Ullasker Dutta, to death. There was an appeal against this judgement before the Chief Justice, Sir Lawrence Jenkins, and Mr. Justice Carnduff. Das had again to take up the case. For 48 days he pleaded for his clients with great skill and persuasiveness.

The ground on which Das argued his case may be briefly mentioned as an example of his wide knowledge of law and great forensic ability. Barindra Kumar and Ullaskar had been charged with the offences under Sections 121, 121 A, 122 and 123 of the Indian Penal Code. For prosecution under these sections it is absolutely necessary to have the sanction of the Government under Section 196 of the Criminal Procedure Code. Complaints under these sections can be made only on the basis of that sanction. Das pointed out that Government sanction for prosecution had been asked for offences under Sections 121 A, 122 and 123 of the Indian Penal Code but not under Section 121. There was thus no sanction for prosecution under this section nor could there be any valid complaint in the circumstances. Death is the extreme penalty under Section 121 of the Indian Penal Code but since there was no regular sanction for the charge under this section, Barindra and Ullaskar must be acquitted of offence under that section.

The judges accepted the cogency of Das's argument and' dropped the charge under Section 121. Barindra and Ullaskar were thus saved from the gallows and convicted tinder Section 121A of the Indian Penal Code. Their sentences were accordingly reduced from death to transportation for life.

The Chief Justice was greatly impressed by Das's presentation of the case and his masterly handling of the intricate and voluminous evidence. He placed on record his appreciation in the following words incorporated in his judgement: "I desire in particular to place on record my high appreciation of the manner in which the case was presented to the court by their leading advocate, Mr. C. R. Das." With this case, Das came to the forefront in the Calcutta Bar. His reputation as a patriot and a lawyer spread throughout the country. Many in fact began to look upon him as perhaps the best advocate in the whole of India.

If the Alipore Bomb Case established his reputation as one of the greatest lawyers on the criminal side, the famous. Dumraon was equally eminent as a practitioner of civil law. When he took up the case it was regarded as a lost cause, but Das was able to achieve victory for his client by hard work and sheer brilliance. The facts of the case may be briefly stated:

> The Maharaja of Dumraon, Sir Radhaprasaid Sinha, died without any male issue. His first daughter died shortly after marriage to the Raja of Mandar without any issue. Sir Radhaprasad's second daughter was married to the Raja of Rewa. In March 1889 the Maharaja., by a registered document granted his wife the power of adopting a boy after the Maharaja's death from the Ujjaini family of Dumraon, Buxar or Jagadishpur. The document was registered in Calcutta. In 1890, when the Maharaja made his will, he confirmed the power of adoption in that will. In 1894 the Maharaja died and Maharani Beniprasad Koeri, on the 12th of December 1907, just a day before her death, adopted Jang Bahadur Singh, the son of Joyprasad Sinha of Jagadishpur. He was the heir apparent to the Dumraon *gadi* and was named Maharaj Kumar Sriniwas Prasad Sinha. After the death of the Maharani, the estate came under the management of the Court of Wards.

Babu Keshabprasad Sinha, next agnate of Maharaja of Dumraon, had somehow or other incurred the displeasure of the Maharani. The Maharani had all along wished to give the estate to her second daughter, the Rani of Rewa. But the Maharaja had not liked the idea that his ancestral property should thus be transferred to an altogether different line. Desiring to adopt the nearest agnate, Keshabprasad, he had made a proposal to Keshabprasad's father, Babu Rajeshwari Prasad, to this effect.

But Rajeshwari Prasad did not agree to the Maharaja's proposal. After that Keshabprasad could not even get permission to see the Maharani who being prostrate with serious illness, adopted Jang Bahadur with the help of Manager Sheosaran Lal, Muntajin Lachhmiprasad and her son-in-law, the Raja of Mandar. After her death, Babu Keshabprasad tiled a suit for setting aside the adoption as illegal and void and claimed Rajgarh as his due.

Keshabprasad had consulted eminent lawyers who, however, considered his case a hopeless one. He then engaged Das as his counsel. Against him were engaged Mr. Garth, a famous barrister of Calcutta, and Mr. Hasan Imam of Patna. Das was engaged at a fee of Rs. 10,000 per month with a promise that if he won the case he would be given property which would fetch Rs. 50,000 a year. Das won the case and fulfilled his part of the contract, but his client did not keep his promise.

Das based his argument on the fact that adoption could not oust the claim of an heir who enjoyed legal rights according to time-honoured custom. The right that had vested in Keshabprasad after the Maharaja's death in terms of Mitakshara Law could not be divested by a later adoption. The judge accepted Das's argument and held that the adoption was invalid and Keshabprasad was the legal heir to the estate.

There was an appeal against the judgement which was heard by a Special Bench of the Calcutta High Court consisting of the Chief Justice, Sir Lawrence Jenkins, and Justices Ashutosh Mookerjee and Sir John Woodroffe, There was a compromise in terms of which the judgement of the lower court was upheld, but it was agreed that Srinibash would be given a property with an annual income of Rs. 48,000 a year.

There was a second Dumraon Case in 1914 when the Rani of Rewa brought a suit against the new Maharaja. Maharaja Keshabprasad did not this time engage Das but in the end he had to seek his help for arriving at a compromise by which the Rani of Rewa gave up her claim in exchange for a property with an income of Rs. 48,000 a year.

There was a third Dumraon Case, between 1917 and 1920, when Das again came to Maharaja Keshabprasad's rescue. Some property had been purchased in Burma by the Dewan of the Maharaja and he, the Dewan, claimed that this had been given to him as a gift. Das's cross-examination turned on the interpretation of a Persian word which could be read as *anjani* or *ayamat.* Das held that the correct reading was *anjani* and meant that the Maharaja had given the money to the Dewan for purchasing the property on behalf of the State. The judge was impressed by Das's argument and accepted his contention that the Maharaja had advanced the money not as a reward to the Dewan but on behalf of the State.

There was an appeal against this judgement, which came up before the Patna High Court in 1924. Das was approached but as he had in the meantime decided to give up his practice, he did not accept the brief.

It was in political cases, however, that Das was seen at his best as a lawyer. In the Dacca Conspiracy Case of 1910 Das defended Pulin Behari Das, leader of Anusilan Samity, and his colleagues. The Anusilan Samity was formed in 1905 after the partition of Bengal and it was alleged that it was a secret organisation for overthrowing the British Government by unlawful means. Das challenged not only the jurisdiction of the court and the legality of the whole proceedings but also argued that the Anusilan Samity was intended to develop the mental, moral and spiritual qualities of its members. In spite of Das's able advocacy, three of the accused were sentenced to transportation for life and another 33 to different terms of imprisonment. In his appeal to the Calcutta High Court, Das was able to get the sentences substantially reduced. The sentences of transportation for life were changed to six years' rigorous imprisonment and the conviction of only eleven people was upheld.

Shortly after this, Das took up the defence of the accused in the Delhi Conspiracy case. This was another political trial which attracted wide notice throughout India. The Government had charged fourteen persons with conspiracy and overt acts for the overthrow of the Government culminating in the attempt on the life of Lord Hardinge, Viceroy of India, in 1912. After protracted enquiry the case was committed to a Court of Sessions presided over by Mr. Harrison, I.C.S., Sessions Judge of Delhi. The prosecution was conducted by Sir John Alston, Advocate-General of U.P. The local lawyers for defence proved no match for him. Some of them came to Calcutta and requested Das to take up the defence. Das was at that time heavily engaged in Calcutta and found that even if he went to Delhi for two days, he would suffer a loss of at least Rs. 6,000. At the same time he felt that the young men implicated in the case should be properly defended. He finally decided to take up the case though it meant heavy financial loss for him.

Das appeared in the court at Delhi in May 1914 and argued that the prosecution's case lacked in legal validity and factual evidence. The judge conceded that there was force in Das's contention, but this was challenged by Sir John who at one stage characterised one of Das's observations as untrue. Das protested in such strong language that the judge was taken aback and asked him to apologise to Sir John. Das insisted that there was no occasion for apology and he was not prepared to offer one. In the end Das won his point and the judge who till then had been somewhat harsh on the defence lawyers, changed his attitude and treated prosecution and defence in exactly the same way. The local lawyers of Delhi were delighted and felt greatly encouraged in their conduct of the case.

Another well-known political case in which Das was able to save five young men convicted of political crime is popularly known as the Alipore Trunk Murder Case of 1918. The prosecution story was that five young revolutionaries had murdered one of their fellow members who was suspected of being a spy. The body was than packed in a trunk and sent by railway parcel. It began to decompose within a day or two, and nobody appeared to take delivery. Das was engaged on behalf of one of the accused, a young boy named Panchanam, who was heir to one of the biggest estates in Calcutta. In fact, however, Das defended, all the accused and after 28 days' sittings the accused were all acquitted. The Advocate-General of Bengal complimented Das on his handling of the case.

A somewhat unusual case was Kutubdia Detenu Case in which seventeen internees under the Defence of India Act were prosecuted for leaving their place of detention and going to Chittagong. Das took up the defence of these *detenus* without any fees and in addition spent his own money to assist them. He spent almost a fortnight in Chittagong in conducting the case and pointed out that the *detenus* had not absconded but gone to the District Magistrate to place before him their legitimate grievances regarding food, drinking water, accommodation and allowance.

As such, they could not be charged with any intention to defy the law or any legal order. In spite of Das's eloquent plea the judge found the accused guilty. He sentenced them, however, to only two months' imprisonment.

This brief account of Das's success as a lawyer may be concluded with a reference to the *Amrita Bazar* Patrika Contempt Case of 1918, A Bench of the Calcutta High Court had held that the Calcutta Improvement Trust could not acquire private land at will. At the same time, another judge of the High Court, in an analogous case on the Original side, had held that the Improvement Trust had the power of such acquisition.

In order to reconcile these two conflicting decisions a Special Bench of the High Court was formed with the Chief Justice. Sir Lancelot Sanderson, Justice Sir John Woodroffe and Mr. Justice Chitty. The *Amrita Bazar Patrika,* a well-known daily of Calcutta, commented editorially on the Constitution of this Special Bench and suggested that an Indian judge owning land should have been taken in place of Mr. Chitty. The Chief Justice issued notice to show cause why the *Patrika* should not be prosecuted for contempt of court. The matter came up for hearing before a full Bench of the High Court.

The *Amrita Bazar Patrika* encaged almost all the luminaries of the Calcutta Bar including Messrs. Jackson. Norton, Chakraborty and Chittaranjan Das. The case was naturally opened by Mr. Jackson, but from the beginning there was altercation between him and the Chief Justice. Mr. Norton then tried to argue the case. He also found the judges unsympathetic. Nor did Mr. Byomkesh Chakraborty fare better and it seemed that the case was going against the accused.

Das then rose to plead for his clients and approached the question from an entirely new angle. He submitted that there had been no intention to cast any reflection on the High Court. Some of his expressions were unfortunate, but his real intention seemed to be that the matter should be heard by a full Bench. As such, the article might be improper, but it did not constitute contempt of the court. Das further drew a distinction between civil and criminal liability and placed his case with such great analytical skill and erudition that the judges were convinced and decided in favour of the *Patrika.*

After Das's death, both the Bench and the Bar paid eloquent testimony to his skill, courage and integrity as a lawyer. It was pointed out that the secret of his success lay in the extreme care with which he hunted up all references and weighed all facts. Statements by witnesses, as well as documents and circumstantial evidence were analysed with the utmost care and ingenuity. In addition he had an iron will and never yielded ground either to judges or to adversaries. There was not the slightest trace of sycophancy in his pleading nor the faintest suggestion of fear in the presence of authority. He stood up like a man and spoke with a sincerity and conviction which influenced even judges who were initially hostile.

Mayor of Calcutta

Barrister C.R. Das was involved in India's freedom movement. He led Bengal in the Non-Cooperation Movement. He was the first Mayor of Calcutta Corporation. In 1924 Calcutta Corporation election, the Swarajists won by a huge margin and Chittaranjan Das became the Mayor of Calcutta (Now Kolkata). Netaji Subhas Chandra Bose was appointed as the Chief Executive Officer of Calcutta Corporation. During his tenure in Calcutta Corporation, Chittaranjan Das handled various welfare projects with efficiency.

After he became Mayor of Calcutta, one of the Councillors wanted begging to be stopped in the city. Das promptly remarked that then the Mayor would be the first accused as he was the greatest beggar in Calcutta at the time. On another occasion the Chief Executive Officer of the Calcutta Corporation admired a table in the Mayor's room and remarked that it was a thing of beauty. Das retorted: "But to me it is not a joy for ever."

Career in Literature and Journalism

It was natural that a man of strong feeling and imagination like Das should be attracted to literature and poetry. From his early childhood he was deeply influenced by the Vaishnav poets. Their sincerity and utter simplicity made a profound impression on him which lasted throughout his life.

This influence was reinforced by the life and precepts of Shri Chaitanya. Born in a Brahmo family in which the major emphasis was on rationalism, Das perhaps experienced the emotional currents of the Vaishnavism of Bengal the more strongly. He was also influenced by Bankim Chandra Chatterjee who, in spite of his strong intellectual bias, showed a strain of devotion and mysticism in his writings.

As a Poet: The first book of poems published by Das was *Malancha,* a book of lyrics. This consists of devotional poems and lyrics of Nature. There are also poems which indicate Das's deep sympathy with the underdog in society. A poem entitled "The Harlot" raised a storm of protest in the Brahmo Samaj and even led to some trouble at the time of his marriage. Das, however, did not allow this opposition to impair his deep sympathy with human suffering. He would not submit to the dogmas of any society and believed that faith and devotion were the cardinal virtues of man.

Das's poetic work included other books like *Mala, Sagar Sangeet, Antaryami* and *Kishore Kishori.* These attracted wide appreciation and the great oriental scholar, Mr. John Alexander Chapman, spoke highly of them. Mr. Chapman even translated some of Das's poems, while Shri Aurobindo Ghose translated many others. In discussing one of Das's poems, Mr. Chapman observed: "In Deshbandhu's mind singing and living were one. Song is life and life is song. Certainly song is as old as human life and is the proof of the divinity of mankind. If a man lived as he should, he would sing as he should. The imperfection of song is the imperfection of life."

Mala was published in 1904 and is marked by a deeper religious spirit. Its poems revealed Das's growing concern with religious faith and belief in the unknown and unknowable.

If *Malancha* introduced Das as a poet, *Sagar Sangeet* made him famous. It was written in November 1910 when he was returning from England by sea. The poems are remarkable not only for the novelty of subject but their beauty of thought and literary grace. In feeling and movement *Sagar Sangeet* is deep like the sea and a happy fusion of devotion and thought.

This growing yearning for God is seen even more clearly in his *Antaryami* and *Kishore Kishori. Antarymi* reveals a calm and peaceful spirit which remain unruffled in the midst of difficulties as a result of prayer and meditation. The same concern with personal life is seen in *Kishore Kishori* where Das sings of the eternal love of Krishna and Radha.

As a Journalist: If Das's deep personal faith found expression in his Ivric poems, his concern with social and political affairs led him to the service of Bengali literature through journals. He brought out in 1914 the famous Bengali monthly *Narayana,* Apart from essays, stories, poems and songs by the editor, the journal published contributions from renowned writers like Brojendra Nath Seal. Bipin Chandra Pal, Hari Prasad Shastri. Rakhaldas Banerjee. Suresh Chandra Samajpati and many others. It was, however, a little unfortunate that *Narayan* came to be regarded as a kind of counterblast to *Sabujnatra.* This latter journal was edited by Pramatha Choudhury under the pen name Birbal. Conducted under the inspiration of Rabindranath Tagore, it reflected his mood at the time which was influenced to a large extent by Ibsen. Some of the stories of Tagore like "Bostami" and "The Wife's Letter" provoked the more conservative elements in Bengal. *Narayana* was intended to be a reply to these new ideas propagated through literature. In one of his essays, Das wrote as follows:

> "Rabindranath has imported many things from the West. That no doubt has added to the rich variety and wealth of Bengali literature but has not helped to develop and preserve Bengal's individual culture and its national genius. Under no circumstances should

we suffer ourselves to be led by the glamour of the West. All critics would not perhaps accept this criticism of Tagore but there is no denying that the publication of serious and thoughtful writings and devotional songs based on India's own traditions helped to check the forces of modernism which were sweeping many of the younger writers off their feet. That Das himself had felt the impact of these forces is seen from his poems like "The Harlot" or stories like "Dalim" and "Prana-pratishtha", which show how women who have sinned against society can be redeemed through love and devotion.

As a Writer: It would be wrong, however, to think that Das was always living on the high peaks of feeling and devotion. His lyric poems rise to great heights, but his stories and serious essays show a keen intellectual perception. Humour was an equally strong element in his character and revealed itself in both his speech and writing. Indians are credited with being always serious but Das had an inexhaustible stock of genial humour. Even the dullest company was enlivened by his light-hearted sallies. His humour often stood him in good stead in his professional career.

It is difficult to give a full idea of Das's humour in an English book, as much of it depended on Bengali quips, puns and allusions. Once a senior pleader, Kishoripati Ray, was brought to jail in a small litter as he could not walk. When Das asked him about his health, Mr. Ray said that he had come in a chariot as he could not walk. Das retorted that was how Kishorinati (Vishnu) always came.

During; elections to the Bengal Legislative Council, Das was supporting Satkari Roy against his own cousin, Mr. S. R. Das. A gentleman whose name was Surya (Sun) came and reported to Das that another friend Bidhu (Moon) was working for Mr. S. R. Das. Das retorted that if Bidhu could do something for S. R. Das, Surya should do ten times as much for Satkari.

Das used to argue that the Vaidyas — the community to which he belonged — were in fact Brahmins. Mrs. Das once asked what evidence there was for his statement. Das replied at once:

"The evidence is that I have married a Brahmin." Every one burst out laughing.

During the Gaya session of the Congress, Das and some of his friends were talking among themselves informally. An outsider who was present asked in impatience, "Sir, when will the proceedings begin?" Das retorted, "As soon as you stop."

Once a gentleman remarked that if there was no difference between the Independents and the Swarajists he could not understand why the Independents did not join the Swaraj Party. Das replied, "They will then lose their independent title!"

Last Phase

Deshbandhu Das was suffering from fever when he returned to Calcutta (Now, Kolkata) on the 5th of May 1925. This time he did not stay in his own house but with a friend. Everyone who came in contact with him noticed that there was a marked change in his attitude. The present writer used to see him almost everyday during this period. Deshbandhu Das had always been a fighter and never postponed for tomorrow what should be done today. All this had changed. If anyone asked him to do something, his reply invariably was, "Please wait for a few days. I shall attend to your request when I return from Darjeeling."

One day he said to one of his friends that Mahatma Gandhi had no enemy, while his own enemies were many. He thought that perhaps this was due to the fact that Mahatma had no ill feeling for anybody while he himself had not been able to expel such feelings completely from his heart. Differences which divided men hurt him more and more and he repeatedly said that we must look at all questions from a broader point of view. He also began to express his sense of the futility of life and struggle. He developed a philosophic vein in which honour and popularity seemed trivial things in comparison to self-realisation and union with God.

Deshbandhu Das also became more and more indifferent to luxuries and material comforts. He told Satkaripati Roy, then Secretary of the Bengal Provincial Congress Committee, that he had given up all his wordily goods and was now shorn of everything. When Satkaripati Roy said that he would have material poods in abundance after the battle for freedom was won, Deshbandhu Das was offended that Roy should talk of material goods and wealth. He declared that he himself would readily give up even the few material possessions that still belonged to him and only wished that the Congress would build him a small cottage by the Ganges where he could live a simple life.

While Deshbandhu Das became resigned in his personal affairs, his patriotism remained as strong as ever. Satyaranjan Bakshi and Saroj Dutt once asked him what would happen if the Government refused to listen to the national demand. Deshbandhu Das replied that the only way of achieving national independence was to arouse national consciousness among the masses. It was on this issue that he wanted elections to be fought in the coming year. Once the people were aroused, civil disobedience would become inevitable. If civil disobedience was started on a sufficiently large scale, no civilized government could withstand the movement.

Deshbandhu Das started for Pabna on the 11th of May. Formerly he had assistants and servants to look after his luggage and do whatever was needed on the journey. Now he was alone with his wife and felt quite helpless. Prafulla Chakraborty, one of the editors of the paper *Forward*, was going by the same train and came forward to take charge of Deshbandhu Das's luggage and look after him. Deshbandhu Das stayed at Pabna for three or four days and greatly enjoyed his stay on the banks of the river Padma. He kept away from the town but many people came to see him and he spoke to them about the urgent need of village organisation. The three or four days' stay rested him considerably and on the 15th of May he started for Darjeeling.

A large number of people, including the Raja of Narajole, were waiting for him at the Darjeeling railway station on the morning of the 16th to give him a hearty welcome. They were disappointed as Deshbandhu Das travelled by a car sent for him by the Maharaja of Dighapatia. At Darjeeling he stayed in *Step Aside,* which belonged to Sir Nripendra Nath Sircar, later Law Member in the Viceroy's Executive Council. Sir Nripendra Nath wrote to the present writer on the 19th of February 1926 as follows:

> "In spite of Mr. Das knowing that my views were opposed to his views, he always entertained a kindly

feeling for me. One day I looked him up and was shocked to find his condition. His legs were thin, he was looking depressed. I suggested to him that he should visit Darjeeling and be my guest and I was willing to place one of my houses at his disposal. He said he was thankful but he must bear his own expenses. I put it to him whether he would have allowed me to pay my own expense if I occupied a house of his as his guest. He ultimately agreed and wrote to me a very touching letter, but the contents of that I cannot expose to the public gaze.

"While at Darjeeling he used to write to me from time to time. His last letters were very cheerful."

Sir Nripendra Nath had made all arrangements for Deshbandhu's comfort and his health soon began to improve. At first he had to move about in a rickshaw, but after a few days he began to walk a little. Dressed in a Kashmiri overcoat and wearing a red silken cap, he looked like venerable 'sanyasi'. Anup Goswami, who had been charged by Sir Nripendra Nath to look after Deshbandhu Das, said to the present writer that two thing in Deshbandhu Das attracted him deeply. The first was his robe of renunciation and the second was his sweet smile and serene look. There was also a strange magic in his voice. Whoever came in contact with him was swayed by it. In spite of the apparent improvement in his health, the fever did not leave him completely and he used to get attacks at least once a week.

Prafulla Chakraborty, who saw him in the last week of May, has recorded his impression in the following words:

"I shall never forget Deshbandhu's figure reclining on a sofa in the corridor in *Step Aside* talking gently — with a winsome smile but a compelling look — to those who called to see him. The country was uppermost in his mind. I saw him last on the 26th of May. I called on him about 8-30 P.M. I found him in bed reclining on a pillow. His last words to me were: 'Prafulla, you had better go now. I want to say my prayers.'"

(Ami Ektti Nam Karbo).

Mrs. Besant saw Deshbandhu Das on the 29th of May in connection with the Commonwealth Bill of India. He went over the clauses of the Bill with her and assured her that he would discuss the matter further with his colleagues as soon as he returned to Calcutta (Now, Kolkata). Such political discussions, however, excited and also exhausted him. In fact his emotional nature was so strong that ones he was moved, he could not regain his composure for a long time. Asked to listen to *Kirtan* songs, Deshbandhu Das said that such songs touched him too deeply. If he listened to them, he would be so moved by the words and music that he would not be able to sleep for several nights.

Gandhi's Visit: Mahatma Gandhi was at that time touring Bengal. Deshbandhu Das wrote to him: "Please remember you are under my jurisdiction; I am the Chairman of the Reception Committee. You have to include Darjeeling in your tour. This is my command." The Mahatma wrote:

> "There will be a Working Committee meeting at Calcutta. Programme for other places has also been fixed up. It will not be possible now. Please do not mind."

Deshbandhu Das wrote in reply:

> "Then bring the whole Committee here. I shall arrange for their accommodation. The B.P.C.C. shall pay the fares of members. I am writing to Satkari accordingly."

There was no reply and after the Working Committee meeting, Mahatmaji prepared himself to go to Darjeeling to see his friend. He wrote that he would stay for two days only. Deshbandhu made all arrangements for his comfort and supervised the details personally in spite of his poor health.

Mahatma Gandhi arrived at Darjeeling on the 4th of June. Deshbandhu Das was overjoyed and took upon himself the responsibility of looking after him. He had even secured five goats from Jalpaiguri in order to provide goat's milk for Mahatma Gandhi. They spent four days together and Mahatma Gandhi was delighted to see the improvement in Deshbandhu Das's health. The Mahatma had originally intended to stay for two days but, at Deshbandhu Das's insistence, he stayed for five days in all.

The two friends often talked about the British attitude to India. Deshbandhu Das had been impressed by Lord Birken; head's gesture and felt that the presence of Lord Reading in London would further help in advancing Indian interest. It was then generally held that Lord Reading was trying to get the Minority Report of the Muddiman Committee accepted by Parliament. Deshbandhu Das expressed the belief that Lord Birkenhead was a strong man and would do something for India. He said that he preferred always to deal with strong men.

But Mahatma Gandhi had grave doubts and he said that much as he wished, he could not agree with Deshbandhu Das. He pointed out that there was no unity between Hindus and Muslims. In fact, there was friction everywhere. Bengal was divided into many parties. In this situation, Mahatma Gandhi held that nothing could be expected from the British. They had never yielded to weakness and it was therefore the duty of Indians to make themselves strong.

Deshbandhu Das brushed aside such doubts and said that Mahatma Gandhi was arguing like a logician. He himself would be guided more by his intuition. He had an inner feeling that something big was about to happen.

Mahatma Gandhi felt that he should not question such strong faith and remained silent. He later said that he did not argue with Deshbandhu Das, as he felt a deep respect for Deshbandhu's robust faith. He also hoped that Englishmen would realise what a great friend they had lost in Deshbandhu Das.

Mahatma Gandhi was also influenced by the consideration that Deshbandhu Das had already worked wonders by his faith. Later he wrote: "Though I knew Englishmen would not do anything at that stage and we had no data to expect anything from Birkenhead, I must acknowledge we owe a duty to the dead man — Deshbandhu — who is one of the parties responsible for making English politicians think of India more than they did before."

When Mahatma Gandhi and Deshbandhu Das had reached agreement, Deshbandhu Das wrote a letter to Mrs. Besant, in which he conveyed to her their views about the Commonwealth Bill. He also wished to be informed of the steps she visualised in case the Government rejected the Bill. After his death, Mrs. Besant wrote, "His medical advisers counselled a trip to Europe at the end of the cold weather. I spent several hours with him in Darjeeling in three long interviews on the 29th and 30th of May. He was much changed in manner and outlook as was indeed seen in his Faridpur speech. His old aggressiveness had disappeared and he was very calm and gentle."

Deshbandhu Das discussed with Mahatma Gandhi all questions relating to Indian politics. The major part of their talks was devoted to *Charkha, Khadi* and village organisation. Deshbandhu Das had already framed a scheme of village organisation for which he collected over a hundred thousand rupees. Mahatma Gandhi advised him that the spinning wheel should be the centre of all his activities. He also suggested that this organisation should be independent of politics and be placed in charge of an expert. Mahatma Gandhi suggested that Satishchandra Das Gupta be placed in charge of the work. Deshbandhu Das agreed and it was decided to set up a small committee consisting of Satishchandra Das Gupta, Satkaripati Roy and one other member. Deshbandhu did not name the third man but wanted to select him after due consideration.

Deshbandhu Das had begun taking lessons in spinning at Patna with a teacher sent to him by Dr. Rajendra Prasad. He did not make much progress at the time, but at Darjeeling he began doing a fair amount of spinning. He laughingly told Mahatma Gandhi that he lacked manual skill and his wife knew how helpless he was. Basanti Devi confirmed that it was so and Deshbandhu Das had to call on her even for unlocking his despatch box. Mahatma Gandhi humorously retorted that it was all a part of feminine wile and that Basanti Devi kept her husband completely helpless so that she could have mastery over him.

In referring to this incident, Mahatma Gandhi later wrote, 'The whole house seemed to come down with Deshbandhu's ringing laughter. He had the capacity for weeping and laughing heartily. His weeping he did in secret, but he could laugh before hundreds of people and cover them with the sunshine of his laughter."

One day Deshbandhu Das told Mahatma Gandhi that he wished he could live like a peasant in a small cottage in a village. Mahatma Gandhi remarked that religion was playing a more prominent role in Deshbandhu Das's politics than ever before. Deshbandhu Das replied that he had taken to politics as he regarded it as part of his religion. Mahatma Gandhi said that this might be so, but spirituality was much more prominent in his character at this period.

Pramotha Chowdhury, who was at Darjeeling during these days, wrote,. "I can fully bear out from my personal experience the truth of what Mahatma Gandhi has said. Nobody who came in contact with him at Darjeeling could have failed to notice that his nature had acquired a sweetness which added a fresh charm to his naturally masterful character. I also never heard a harsh word escape his lips. Although we did not see eye to eye in many matters, our occasional discussions about those subject; which were dear to his heart never generated heat.

Deshbandhu Das was worried about developments in the Calcutta Corporation. A difference had arisen about the burial of a Muslim Pir inside the Municipal Market. Deshbandhu Das told Mahatma Gandhi, '"I have been greatly worried about the Pir affair. Neither Suhrawardy nor Subhas had any authority to allow the Pir to be buried in this manner in the Hogg Market. A wrong has been committed but we cannot wound the feelings of the Musalmans. A wrong has no doubt been done but it will be a greater wrong, to exhume the body."

Deshbandhu Das also discussed the Tarakeswar affairs with Mahatma Gandhi. They signed a joint statement and later Deshbandhu Das asked Mahatma Gandhi to examine for himself the accounts of the Swarajya Party in Bengal. When Mahatma Gandhi said that he had seen the accounts, but the chief complainant was Sir Surendra Nath Banerjea, Deshbandhu Das remarked with sadness that there was a great deal of jealousy among public men in Bengal. He requested Mahatma Gandhi to meet Sir Surendra Nath and also Shyamsunder Chakravarty and try to bring about a solution among the different sections of the Congress. If he succeeded, it would be a great service to Bengal.

There were also discussions in a lighter vein between the two leaders. On one occasion Mahatma Gandhi sat in a chair next to the bed on which Deshbandhu Das was reclining. Das knew that Gandhi liked to sit cross-legged. He had a pillow placed on the bed and a hand-spun rug arranged to make a *gaddi* for Gandhi. Deshbandhu then asked him to sit on this.

Mahatma Gandhi asked Das:

> Do you know what this reminds me?
>
> Deshbandhu—What please?
>
> Mahatma—My memory goes back to forty years ago. It was thus my wife and I sat together when we were married. The only thing lacking is the hand-clasp.
>
> Then, turning to Basanti Devi, he said, "I wonder what Basanti Devi has to say to all this."

The whole house again rang with a laughter, alas, soon no more to be heard.

Another day, Das asked if the five goats brought for Mahatma Gandhi were giving milk regularly. Anup Goswami was in charge of Gandhiji's food and he replied. "Of the five only two give some milk but the other three refuse to do so. However much we coax them they stretch themselves on the ground."

Mahatma Gandhi remarked that he was glad to see that these goats had self-respect. Das retorted that three had non-cooperated and ought to be put in jail. The two loyal ones should be rewarded with titles by Mahatma Gandhi. They both burst out laughing.

The Charkha hummed at Darjeeling throughout the five days. Mahatma Gandhi, Mahadev Desai and others spun for many hours daily. Basanti Devi was also a good spinner, and even Deshbandhu Das occasionally spun. One day, Das suggested that they should have a photograph taken of their entire group plying the Charkha. There were many photographers present and Gandhiji remarked, "Too many cooks will spoil the broth, but it is good to have the whole of *Step Aside* converted into a spinning class."

Mahatma Gandhi and Deshbandhu Das accompanied by Mahadev Desai used to go out for occasional walks. They made an impressive group with Mahatma in his loincloth and warm *chaddar*, Mahadev Desai with his Khadi cap and Deshbandhu Das in long robe and silk headdress.

Indira Devi Chaudhurani described the scene vividly:

> "Those last days of Chittaranjan at Darjeeling when we sometimes met in his house or out of doors! Mahatma Gandhi was staying with him at the time and I remember how Chittaranjan insisted on pulling up the warm rug that always kept falling off Mahatmaji's shoulders. He himself used to wear a sort of long *chupkan* fastened at the side which he must have devised himself or had copied from some Indian fashion." Mahatma Gandhi left Darjeeling on the 9th June. The two friends did not meet again.
>
> It has been mentioned earlier that Deshbandhu Das had benefited by Dr. D. N. Roy's treatment. He had an attack of fever on the night of the 9th of June and went to sec his physician on the 12th. When Dr. Roy discussed with him the nature of the fever, Deshbandhu Das remarked that the thought of another attack made him shudder. He also remarked that homoeopathic medicine would be effective only after the allopathic poison had been eliminated from the system. On the same day he also visited Sir Jagadish Chandra Bose. Lady Bose was his cousin and at her request he listened to Kirtan songs for some time.
>
> About this time, he wrote a letter to Pandit Motilal Nehru who was his closest friend, associate and colleague in his public life. This letter is perhaps the last time when Deshbandhu Das put in writing his inmost thoughts about Indian political affairs.

After some personal enquiries, he said:

> "I am getting better, but very slowly. The only complaint is an attack of fever once every week I get it on the

> 6th day besides this weakness. I am determined to stick here till I am really better,
>
> "The most critical time in our history is coming. There must be solid work done at the end of the year and the beginning of the next. All our resources will be taxed but we are both of us ill. God knows what will happen.
>
> "Something may come in July or August or even later. I believe something may come out of the Birkenhead-Reading conversations; ....Something tells me that they will make some kind of a proposal to us, whether it will be of any real value to us is another matter. But I do not wish to complicate the issue by any Commonwealth Bill or any such thing in the meantime. If nothing acceptable comes, the next Congress at Cawnpore must give a clear political lead."

About this letter Pandit Motilal Nehru wrote Hater:

> "On the 12th June, the day I returned to Dalhousie from Chamba, I found on my table a long letter of five closely written pages all in his own handwriting. When we parted at Patna in April, for ever as it now turns out, it was agreed not to trouble ourselves with politics during the brief rest we were allowing ourselves and had not written to each other since. I value this letter as the last will and testament of our departed chief."

Deshbandhu Das sent for a close associate on the evening of the 13th of June. He was with him till the early hours of the 14th of June. During his evening meal, Deshbandhu Das talked about art, politics and economics. He remarked that a real artist is true to the kindred points of heaven and home, He then brought out a book of Bengali poems and recited with feeling passages from Chandidas and Vidyapati. As he read about Shri Chaitanya, his voice was choked with emotion and tears came to his eyes.

Deshbandhu Das then said that it was the day when he expected an attack of fever and would therefore take very little food. Every five minutes he asked to feel his pulse. He was very happy when told that there was no sign of fever. It was at 10 p.m. that his temperature generally rose but that evening he had no fever even at that hour. He felt very happy and so did everyone else present.

The other members of the household went upstairs after dinner but Deshbandhu Das detained his friend, for he wanted to discuss certain things. He told him, "I shall finish my business with you. This Pir question has annoyed me a good deal. A wrong has indeed been done, I cannot flout public opinion nor I can hurt the sentiments of Muslims. If other Councillors raise the proposal for exhuming the body and the Muslim members then resign, I shall also resign with them. But if any sect among the Muslims claims the body and have it removed for burial at some other place, then all troubles will be over. You go and see Sarat and ask him to speak to Suhrawardy so that everything may be smoothly done. Unless the thing be satisfactorily settled I can't remain in peace." He also wrote a letter to Sarat Chandra Bose to that effect.

He went on talking till midnight. He seemed to be in the best of spirits and was extremely cheerful. Basanti Devi went upstairs about midnight but soon returned and said, "It is now post-midnight and you should retire." Deshbandhnu Das told her not to worry; the fever had been checked and he would have no more fever. He felt cheerful in body and mind. Nobody could then know that this was the last flicker of the lamp before it went out.

A friend, who slept downstairs just below Deshbandhu Das's room. Early in the morning, he woke up as I heard some noise upstairs. There was movement and also sound of groaning. At about 5 a.m. he was informed that Deshbandhu had an attack of high fever at 3 o'clock. Das was shivering and this could not be stopped even with blankets piled on him. He rushed up and heard Deshbandhu Das ask in a weak voice, "Who is that?"

He replied in a broken voice, "Hemendra." Deshbandhu Das said, "Hemendra, you told me that I would not get fever again."

His heart was rung by his piteous words he could not say anything in reply. He sat by him and kept pressing his legs, shoulders and arms. He complained that there was intense pain not only in his shoulders and arms but also in the legs and waist. The associates applied hot fomentations but they gave him little relief. He suddenly said, "Inform Mahatma Gandhi about my condition. I do not think I will be able to write to him."

After a little while he said to his close associate, "You should now go, you must get back to Calcutta and meet Suhrawardy and Sarat Bose." Then he turned to his wife and asked if food had been prepared for his associate. He was reluctant to leave Darjeeling but he knew how anxious Deshbandhu Das was over the question of the burial of the Pir in the New Market he had therefore no option but to leave tor Calcutta. When he was about to leave, Deshbandhu asked him, "Do you think you will be able to go to Pabna on your way to Calcutta?" Before he could reply, he himself remarked, "No, you should go to Calcutta directly."

In fact, he wanted he to go to Pabna to meet his son, but public duty had always precedence over personal affairs so far as he was concerned. Most reluctantly and sadly the man took leave of Deshbandhu Das and left Darjeeling at 9 a.m. on the 15th of June, he did not then realise that he would never see him again. He had attacks of fever every week and, like others, he also thought that there would be a remission on Monday. In fact, no one then thought that his condition was so serious. As he was leaving, Deshbandhu Das said, "Send me a telegram as soon as you reach Calcutta."

He later heard, that there was inflammation of his left leg in the afternoon. Soon this spread to the right leg as well, and the temperature rose steadily. There was extreme pain above the ankle and the physicians thought it might be filariasis. Examination of his blood however showed no trace of the disease and after 8 o'clock at night, the temperature began to come down. However, he could not sleep, and slowly he began to lose strength.

On Tuesday, the 16th of June 1925, the temperature had fallen below normal and was going down. Dr. Roy, the homoeopath, told Mrs. Das that he was worried about the case and advised that an allopathic physician might be called in. Hearing of it, Deshbandhu made it clear that he did not wish to change his physician.

After a little while, Deshbandhu Das was given oxygen but it did not do him much good. At one o'clock in the afternoon his condition took a sudden turn for the worse. His eyes lost their lustre and there was difficulty of breathing. He gradually lost consciousness. Telegrams were sent to Calcutta to Deshbandhu Das's son-in-law asking him to come immediately with some physician from there. Dr. Roy kept watch till 4 p.m. and then he left, Deshbandhu Das never regained full consciousness.

The Demise

At about 4:45 p.m. he muttered the name of God and his life came to an end. The news spread throughout Darjeeling. Friends and relations and men, women and children of all communities and races came to pay their tribute of respect to the illustrious leader. Streams of people came from far and near. Some of the hill people walked fifteen miles to have a last glimpse of him. It was a dark night and a high wind was blowing among the pines. There was darkness inside the house as well, and Basanti Devi sat by the body of her husband till long after midnight.

Sir Jagadish Chandra Bose advised that the body should be taken to Calcutta for the last rites. In the meantime Dr. J. M. Das Gupta and Surendranath Haldar had arrived from Calcutta. The Bengal Government instructed the Railway authorities to make all necessary arrangements for the last journey to Calcutta. There was an immense crowd at the Darjeeling railway station. When the hearse arrived in Calcutta next morning, an immense crowd had collected. From Sealdah station right up to the cremation ground, which was five or six miles away, it was one vast sea of humanity. In fact, at every station from Darjeeling to Sealdah, huge crowds had come to express their grief and pay their homage to the departed leader.

Mahatma Gandhi was in Calcutta when the dead body arrived. He was among those who held the bier, but the rush was so great that he was swept off his feet. Volunteers had to lift him up on their shoulders to save him from being crushed. Not only were the streets full of men and women, but every roof, every window and every door was crammed with grieving women and children. All shops were closed. All vehicles stopped moving. The entire city of Calcutta was hushed in silence. There was grief throughout the country. The universal regard Das commanded was evident in the manner in which hundreds of Europeans mustered to pay him their last respects.

The funeral procession moved like a giant python uncoiling in its pent-up sorrow. About half a million people accompanied the bier. It took full eight hours before it could reach the cremation ground at Keoratala. It was almost evening by the time the funeral pyre was lit. Mahatma Gandhi sat with silent, sad eyes, as the flames consumed the mortal remains of Deshbandhu.

There was a condolence meeting, where Mahatma Gandhi was the only speaker. Overcoming his emotions with great difficulty, and indeed breaking down once, the Mahatma said:

> "Deshbandhu was one of the greatest of men. I have had the privilege of knowing him intimately for the last six years and when I parted from him only a few days ago at Darjeeling, I said to a friend that the closer I came to him, the more I came to love him. I saw during my brief stay at Darjeeling that no thought but that of the welfare of India occupied him. He dreamed and thought and talked of freedom of India and of nothing else. And I may tell you that up to the last moment I was with him in Darjeeling, he was asking me to stop longer in Bengal, to bring all the different parties together so that the energies of all may be concentrated to one purpose He was fearless. He was brave. His love for the young men of Bengal was boundless and even his adversaries admitted, there was no other man who could take his place in Bengal. His heart knew no difference between Hindus and Musalmans and I should like to tell Englishmen, too, that he bore no ill-will to them.
>
> "The body that held Deshbandhu has perished, but his soul will never perish. Not only the soul, even the name of him who has served and sacrificed so much will remain immortal. His service and sacrifice were matchless. May the memory ever remain with us and

> may his example inspire us to noble effort. Everyone who follows his example to ever so little an extent will help to perpetuate his memory. May his soul rest in peace."

Deshbandhu Das was a great admirer of Robert Browning and often used to recite the following lines:

> One who never turned his back, but marched breast forward. Never doubted clouds would break; Never dreamed though right were worsted, wrong would triumph; Held we fall to rise, are baffled to fight better, Sleep to wake. This is the best epitaph for Deshbandhu Das.

The Legacy

A few years before his death Das gifted his house and the adjoining lands to the Nation to be used for the betterment of the lives of women. Today it is a huge hospital called Chittaranjan Seva Sadan and has gone from being a women's hospital to one where all specialities are present including the treatment of cancer. Chittaranjan Park is a locality in South Delhi, Adjoining Greater Kailash II, named after him. This locality houses many Bengalis, who settled in Delhi during partition days.

[The Biographical account is based on the material penned and recorded by *Mr. Hemendranath Das Gupta,* a noted author.]

3

In Political Arena

Early Political Life

Deshbandhu Chitranjan Das was interested in politics even during his student days. In fact he and his friends felt that it was on account of his political activities that he had not been appointed to the Indian Civil Service. In his professional life also politics played an important part and some of his outstanding successes as a lawyer were in political cases. Patriotism was the guiding force also of his literary work. Almost everything he wrote was imbued with his deep love for the country and respect for its traditions. It was this sense of social obligation which led him to start his journal *Narayana*. Thus he was a nationalist first and a lawyer and a literary figure after that.

When Das came to the arena of politics, he brought with him all the qualities that had marked him out as a lawyer and a literary figure. He had great powers of eloquence and persuasiveness. His legal training enabled him to analyse the different aspects of a question and also gave him a strong sense of realism. This capacity for objective analysis was combined with the furore and passion of a poet. Naturally, from his earliest days in politics he fought for Swaraj for the masses and not for a handful of upper class men and women. His country recognised his great qualities and gave him the loving title of Deshbandhu or "Friend of the Country."

The beginnings of modern Indian politics may be traced to the first meeting of the Indian National Congress in Bombay in 1885. At that stage the Congress was mainly a petitioning body. The partition of Bengal shook it out of its mildness. The resolutions and the language in the Congress sessions became more forceful but it would be a mistake to regard the Congress at this stage as a revolutionary body in any sense.

In 1905, however, new forces rose within the Congress. Bipin Chandra Pal became the spokesman of the younger generation and his paper *New India* voiced their aspirations. Das was closely associated with Bipin Chandra Pal and opposed the mendicant policy of the Moderates who still controlled the Indian National Congress. Bipin Chandra Pal, in speaking of this time, wrote as follows:

> "At this time another movement was slowly gathering strength in our policies. The *New India* was started in 1901. From its very birth, Chittaranjan was very intimately associated with it. When the original proprietors found it difficult to bear its burdens, Chittaranjan came forward to save it. A joint stock company was formed to finance it and Chittaranjan, though unable to join the Board of Directors of the Company owing to his insolvency, induced his friends to put their names and money into this enterprise. In 1905, with the birth of our new nationalist movement, our old intimacy and comradeship grew more intimate still. For nearly twenty years Chittaranjan and myself were really co-partners in the service of our common motherland. While I worked, he found the means of my subsistence. And he bore my burdens with a deep and abiding sense of sacred duty which made it possible for me freely to accept his help without hesitation or humiliation."

A Swadeshi Mandali was formed in Das's house in 1904.

It was a group of chosen friends whose object was to propagate ideas of self-help and Swadeshi. In a speech delivered at Darjeeling on the 16th of October 1905 Das declared as follows:

> "The chief reason for which this Swadeshi movement is desirable appears to me that it provides the first step towards the path of self-reliance of the Bengali nation. For the same reason it is my firm conviction that our national progress depends upon the success of this movement. The histories of the world have proved that no nation can help another. As every person has to work out his future through his personal exertion, so is the case with a nation. It has to depend upon its own strength for achieving freedom. But if you depend on another nation, even in thousands of years you will not find the path of real freedom."

Das spoke mainly in terms of Bengal in this meeting but his was a broad nationalism which included the whole of India. He had even begun to think in terms of an Asian federation. He was influenced in this by Okakura, a famous poet of Japan, and also by Sister Nivedita. He was greatly moved by Okakura's book *Ideals of the East.* Sister Nivedita had written in the Introduction: "Asia is one, the Himalayas divide only to bring closer the two mighty civilizations of the East—one of India and the other of China."

Das and his friends began to feel at this time the need of a national system of education. Certain developments gave further strength to their desire to start a national college. In October 1905, a circular was issued by the Government of Bengal which prohibited students from taking part in politics.

Students were fined and sometimes even flogged by the headmasters of some schools at the instance of the Inspectorate. Das learnt that Shri Subodh Mullick, a rich philanthropist of Calcutta, was willing to make a handsome donation in case a national college was started. Das immediately took up the project of a national university and secured from Shri Mullick the promise of one hundred thousand rupees. The project was announced on the 9th of November 1905.

This was the beginning of the National Council of Education which later developed, into the Jadaypur Engineering College, It is today a statutory university with a special bias towards technology. Das asked Aurobindo Ghose to give up his post as vice-principal of the Gaekwar College of Baroda and come to Calcutta for serving the nation. When the National Council of Education was formed, Aurobindo Ghose joined it as its first principal.

The year 1906 was another important date in Das's political career. At the Bengal Proving! Conference which was held at Barisal with Mr. A. Rasul as its president, Das drafted the main resolution. He advocated the policy of self-reliance in place of petitions and appeals which till then had been the chief instruments of political activity. The Conference, however, could not complete its deliberations peacefully as the open sessions were broken up by the police. Volunteers and students were beaten up for shouting the slogan *Bande Mataram.* Surendra Nath Banerjea was arrested and convicted. Even the Moderate leaders were shocked and they predicted that this was the beginning of the end of British rule in India. In June 1906, within six weeks of the break-up of the Conference, Lokamanya Tilak came to Calcutta and organised the Shivaji Festival. Tilak's message on the occasion, "Swaraj is my birthright", became the slogan of Indian nationalism. He and other Maharashtrian leaders were Das's guests during the Calcutta session of the Congress, and their association gave a further impetus to the growth of the nationalist party.

The Congress came under the control of the Moderates after its session at Surat in 1907 was disrupted. Das remained aloof from active politics but his services as a lawyer in important political cases enabled him to maintain his contacts. In April 1917, he was invited to preside over the Bengal Provincial Conference in Calcutta. In proposing his name, Surendra Nath Banerjea declared that he would soon be one of the most trusted and beloved leaders of India.

Since this was Das's first major political pronouncement, it would be proper to give some quotations to indicate the trend of his political thought at the time:

> "I feel a peculiar pride in calling myself a Bengali. The Bengalis have a mission of their own. They have their own valour, culture, literature, religion and practices. They have a history and a future before them. And so I can declare with confidence that he knows not my Bengal who describes the Bengalis as wanting in discipline ... "We seldom think of Bengal. We have lost our touch with the general mass, hence all our political agitations have become fruitless and empty. The country does not consist only of the educated class but of all classes, sects, and creeds..."

Das blamed our political assemblies for their failure to call on the common people, the tillers of the soil, to join them. It was purely a *bourgeois* policy and not based on an all-embracing democratic principle. Our political agitation was unreal as it was divorced from intimate touch with the people who formed the backbone of the country. In his address, he showed how, with the progress of British rule, we had imitated some of the worst European vices, sacrificed our former life of simplicity and vigour and in its place adopted love of ease and luxury. In his opinion it was Bankim Chandra "to whom the true nature of the Mother was first revealed. It was he whose eyes were first blessed by the blessed vision of the motherland." Das declared:

> "I have found out the true soul of Bengal. I have learnt to appreciate the real history of Bengal. The images of Buddha of the Buddhists, of Siva of the Saivas, of Sakti of the Saktas and of the devotional love of the Vaishnavas rise up before my vision. I think of the immortal songs of Vidyapati and Chandidas and feel myself glorified by the glorious life of Shri Chaitanya. The songs of Jnanadas, Govindadas and Lochan Das vibrate in my heart's core. The devotional songs of Ramprosad Sen melt my heart.
>
> We then saw our mother and Bankim's song touched our heart through the ears. I can appreciate the message of Shri Ramakrishna and Keshab Chandra.

> I feel inspired by the words of Vivekananda. I can realise that a Bengali, whether a Hindu, a Muslim or a Christian, is after all a Bengali. He has an individuality of his own. He has his own culture, and if he means to realise himself he will have to be a true Bengali.
>
> The Bengalis have a place to call as their own under the sun. They have their own duties and mission in this world. A Bengali must be a Bengali at heart. The Bengalis have some distinction from the rest of the creation, a special aspect of the Eternal manifestation of the Creator's will."

He not only analysed the present condition of the country and the causes of economic and political decay but also offered a constructive plan for the reorganisation of villages which form the backbone of India:

- We must reconstruct our villages and take all steps for the rehabilitation of the people.
- We must give sufficient food to cultivators to enable them to labour all round the year.
- We must remove water scarcity, dig new tanks, clear old ones.
- We must clear jungles.
- We must establish Panchayats and cooperative credit societies enabling the cultivators to get loans at low interest, and start cottage industries.

One may sum up Das's message as a call to self-reliance. He was no enemy of the West but he felt that unless India could meet the West as an equal, there could be no permanent friendship between them. He was not against such friendship between Britain and India provided each developed itself to its highest capacity. He spoke of the old days of India when her granaries were full and the people had enough to eat. There was joy in village life and the peasant returned home after his toil with a smile on his lips. He held that our weakness was due to disunity. He condemned the blind imitation of the West in manners, customs and habits of speech, dress, food and drink. In his book *The Heart of Aryavarta,* Lord Ronaldshay has referred to Das's speech in the following terms:

> "Mr. Das spoke indeed with all the ardour of a missionary. He smote in pieces the golden calf which he set up as symbolical of the ideals of Europe and with the fervour of a seer he promised the way to a promised land."

In 1916, Mr. Asquith desired to have the advice of representative Indians on the attainment of self-government by India. His Secretary of State was Mr. Austen Chamberlain who wished to make declaration in this behalf. The elected members of the Viceroy's Legislative Council prepared a memorandum which was adopted unanimously by both the Indian National Congress and the Muslim League. This joint scheme came to be known as the Congress-League Scheme, but this was not accepted by the British Government. Instead a scheme prepared by Mr. Lionel Curits who came to Delhi in 1917 and suggested a dyarchical form of Government seemed to find official favour. Ultimately, on the 20th of August 1917, Mr. Montagu, who had become Secretary of State for India, made an announcement in Parliament pleading for the progressive realisation of responsible government for India.

Mrs. Annie Besant was then the most vocal spokesperson of self-government for India. She had formed the Home Rule League which attracted many of the leading Indian politicians of the day. The Government disapproved of her activities and she was soon interned under orders of the Governor of Madras. Das fully supported her views and had already joined the League. He protested vigorously against her internment. At a meeting of the Indian Association in Calcutta, he said:

> "I do not think the God of Humanity was crucified only once. Tyrants and oppressors have crucified humanity again and again. Every outrage on humanity is a fresh nail driven through his sacred flesh."

Das was anxious that Mrs. Besant should preside over the next session of the Indian National Congress at Calcutta in December 1917. The reception committee voted in her favour but

Shri Baikuntha Nath Sen, the chairman of the reception committee, held that the election was invalid. Surendra Nath Banerjea, who was the leader of the Provincial Congress Committee, wanted to have as President the Raja of Mahmudabad. He wished that the election should be decided by the All-India Congress Committee in which he had a majority. In the meantime, six other Provincial Congress Committees in addition to Bengal had already voted in favour of Mrs. Besant.

Das took his stand on the principle of democracy within the Congress organisation. He expressed great regard for Shri Baikuntha Nath Sen, who was a friend of his father, but he felt that Shri Sen had gone against the wishes of the majority in the Bengal Provincial Congress Committee. He therefore moved that Rabindranath Tagore should be elected chairman of the reception committee in place of Shri Sen. A crisis seemed unavoidable when Sir Chandra Madhab Ghose, a retired Judge of the Calcutta High Court and once its acting Chief Justice, intervened and brought about a settlement. It was agreed that Mrs. Besant would be elected President of the Congress while Rabindranath Tagore and Shri Sen should both resign from the reception committee. After their resignation was accepted. Shri Sen would be re-elected chairman of the committee. Tagore immediately resigned his seat and Shri Sen remained the chairman.

The meeting of the Congress proved a great success—Mrs. Besant was received by the people with great enthusiasm. After the session Das started a tour of the province and repeatedly declared that what he was working for was "neither self-government for Hindus alone nor for Muslims alone nor, for the landlords and merchants alone, but self-government of the people of India where the interests of all will be protected."

The Secretary of State for India, Mr. Montagu, after his announcement on the 20th of August 1917, came to India in November and met Das and other national leaders during his tour. In an interview with Das, which lasted for three hours, the following conversation was reported to have taken place:

"Mr. Montagu—Yes, Mr. Das, what are your views towards the reforms that Lionel Curtis suggests?

Das—The reforms suggested by Curtis cannot succeed. Provincial autonomy is essential.

Montagu—But I understand you were for the Dyarchical Scheme as suggested by Lionel Curtis.

Das—Yes, I was, as a concession to weakness, for the sake of unity. I had hopes that Anglo-Indians would join us. I therefore toned down my demand, but their militant attitude has sent me back to my original ideal.

Lord Chelmsford remarked, probably with disgust: "Is it not premature to speak of provincial autonomy? Some reforms may be given as a trial. If you work satisfactorily, you will also get further rights in time."

Mr. Montagu has left a record of his impressions in the following words:

> "In December 1917, I had a talk with C. R. Das, an extremist, but a most sensible fellow. He originally was an advocate of the Curtis Scheme. Now he absolutely repudiates it. His demand is complete responsibility at once for local government. Das argued very strongly. I argued with him. I implored him. I saw him privately and he added: The halfway house is no good: there is no intermediate stage possible between Responsible Government and complete responsibility.' He attracted me enormously. But his distrust is for the police and the way in which the C.I.D. is used.
>
> "Das further added: 'Well, give us Standing Committees, a new electorate, decent Legislative Councils and no powers for five years, promising us it all in five years in your House of Parliament. I would rather have this than steps that I know will not work.'"

The Calcutta session of the Congress in 1917 was one of the turning points in the history of the organisation. Till then the Congress had been controlled by the Moderate elements among political workers. After the death of Gokhale and the retirement of Sir Pherozeshah Mehta, Surendra Nath Banerjea became the most important leader of the organisation. Among his chief lieutenants were Bhupendra Nath Bose and Ambica Charan Mozumdar, who also were Moderates. The election of Mrs. Annie Besant was the first successful challenge to Surendra Nath's leadership. The ascendancy of the Moderate elements began to wane. A new leadership consisting of Bal Gangadhar Tilak, C. R. Das, Byomkesh Chakraborty, Mohammad Ali Jinnah and Hasan Imam came into power. Mrs. Besant's Home Rule League became the controlling authority of the Congress and as one of her chief lieutenants, C. R. Das became one of the foremost personalities in the political and national life of India.

Surendra Nath Banerjea delivered a powerful speech on self-government at this session of the Congress but this was his last speech from that forum. He never again spoke from the platform of the Congress and was virtually replaced by Das.

In a speech during this period, Das referred to the terrorist movement which had then captured the imagination of a large section of young men in Bengal and had admirers in other parts of India. Das did not himself believe in terrorism and secret societies, but he could not help being attracted by the idealism which was displayed by them. He said:

> "Being thwarted in their zeal for freedom, they grow impatient and believe in revolution. They see before their eyes that all nations, big and small, are eager for freedom. These liberty-loving young men smarting under foreign rule have become impatient for freedom. You give them freedom, you tell frankly that you will change the Constitution, that you will administer the country for their good and you will find all anarchism will be extirpated. You want soldiers, I shall give you. If you give us liberty, I shall give up my practice for six months and shall raise an adequate army from the country."

The rift between the two sections of the Congress soon became still wider. A draft resolution on reforms was published on the

8th of July 1918 over the signature of the Secretary of State of India and the Governor-General after their report received the assent of the British Government. A special conference of the Bengal Provincial Congress Committee was held three days after the announcement. The Moderates found themselves in a minority at this conference which regarded the reforms as disappointing.

A final decision was however left to the special session of the Indian National Congress to be held in Bombay on the 29th of August 1918. Surendra Nath Banerjea accepted the report while Das considered it thoroughly inadequate. The elections had given a clear majority to supporters of Das in both the A.I.C.C. and the various Provincial Congress Committees.

Surendra Nath Banerjea now left the Congress and started the Liberal League with himself as the President. With his retirement, Das became the chief figure in the Bengal Congress and the brunt of the work of the Congress organisation fell on him. It was mainly through his efforts that the site in Bombay was chosen and Syed Hasan Imam was elected President of the special session. He himself contributed about Rs. 10,000 towards the expenses of the session. With his characteristic generosity and desire to carry as large a section of the people as possible with him, Das felt that the Moderate elements should be given another opportunity to participate in the activities of the Congress. He was largely responsible for the following resolution passed at the special session:

> "The Congress appreciates attempts on the part of the Right Hon'ble the Secretary of State and His Excellency the Viceroy to inaugurate, a system of responsible government in India and while it recognises that the proposals constitute an advance, it holds that the proposals as a whole are disappointing and unsatisfactory."

The annual session of the Congress met in Delhi in December 1918 under the Presidentship of Pandit Madan Mohan Malaviya. The Congress reaffirmed the Bombay resolution relating to self-government and expressed the view that full responsible government should immediately be introduced in the Provinces of British India. The resolution was moved by Shri B. C. Chakraborty and seconded by Shri Vithalbhai Patel.

Mrs. Besant, Shri Srinivasa Sastri, Shri B. N. Sharma and a few other Moderate leaders attended this session and moved certain amendments. Shri Sastri argued that the words 'disappointing and unsatisfactory' be omitted from the text of the resolution. He did not also wish to fix any time limit. Mrs. Besant felt that the Bombay resolution should be repeated as it was settled as a compromise between the Nationalist group and the Moderate group but she also did not like a time limit. She advised the delegates to advance steadily and cautiously and uttered a warning against precipitate action.

Das thanked Mrs. Besant and Shri Sastri for attending the Congress but said he could not accept their point of view. He argued that India was being ruled by a bureaucracy, and self-government would mean the end of bureaucratic rule. It was therefore hardly likely that the Civil Service, which was the real ruler of the country, would consent to introduce self-government quickly and thus end its own supremacy unless a time limit was fixed. He also took objection to Shri Sastri's move to delete the words 'disappointing asked the delegates to put their hands on their hearts and answer the question for themselves whether they were satisfied or disappointed.

Shri Sastri had pleaded that the Congress should not press for provincial autonomy as the country was committed to the Curtis Scheme. Das replied that nobody in India had accepted the scheme, and he was lustily cheered by the whole audience.

Das then turned to deal with the arguments advanced by Mrs. Besant. She had emphasised the need of compromise but Das retorted, "Mrs. Besant is out of court here. Who were the parties to the compact? The Moderates as a party have not joined the Congress. Therefore it is the Moderates who have broken the compact and he that breaks the compact has no right to insist on the performance of the compact by the other party. I again ask—"

Mrs., Besant—"I said nothing about a compact. I said it was a compromise."

Das—"I stand corrected. Mrs. Besant says she did not use the word compact but compromise. Well what I ask is this: Between whom was that compromise? Compromise means two parties—Moderates and Nationalists. If some of the Moderates joined, who are those Moderates? What right have they to barter away the rights of the people? So far as I am concerned, I entered into that compromise upon a surrender of points by us when I hoped that the Moderate party as a whole would join us. The Moderate party has not joined us. Are we still to go by that compromise and sell our birthright because the Moderate party does not join us? (Cries of No, No). Since the Congress session held in Bombay, the country has declared its opinion in Bombay, Madras, United Provinces, Bengal and elsewhere. Is it your personal right that there can be a binding compact or compromise or agreement? And because you have chosen this compromise must you stand by it for ever and ever? I say such a principle is pernicious and I refuse to follow it. The whole of the country demands it and I call upon you to do your duty and reject the amendment in toto."

In the sequel, all the amendments were lost and the resolution was accepted by an overwhelming majority. This result was largely due to the eloquence of Das. Prof. Jitendra Lal Banerjee has left on record the following account of discussions in the sub-committee meeting which preceded the opening session:

> "After the second day's sitting of the Congress, the Subjects Committee met at the appointed hour. Discussions and debates dragged on till midnight. The whole discussion was about the Reforms. Deshbandhu was our leader. We were to oppose the Reforms. On the other side were ranged many distinguished personages. Mrs. Besant. Srinivasa Sastri and the President himself, Pandit Madan Mohan Malaviya. Mr. Das rose after noon and by his wonderful eloquence he tore into shreds the arguments of his opponents. The victory was his. When we were coming out after the dissolution of the meeting we found the veteran old Dewan of Travancore, Mr. V. P. Madhav Rao, in spite of his old age and severe winter

> of Delhi seated there leaning against the outer wall. He asked me to sit down and listen to him. He said: "How beautifully Das fired up ! I never saw anything like it." The change in the temper of the Congress may be inferred from the fact that Lokamanya Bal Gangadhar Tilak was elected by the Congress to represent India before the Joint Parliamentary Committee in London.

Rowlatt Act

A series of events happened in quick succession in the" year 1919 which changed the course of Indian history. The first incident of note was the passing of the Rowlatt Act on the 18th of March 1919. It gave extraordinary powers to the Government of India for the suppression of the political movement and any other action aimed against the State. It authorised arrest and detention of persons without trial. It nullified the provisions of the Indian Evidence Act under which confessions made to a police officer could not be admitted as evidence.

There was great opposition throughout the country to the passing of the Rowlatt Bill. Mahatma Gandhi led the agitation against the Bill and declared that the country should observe Satyagraha on the 6th of April, the second Sunday after the Act received the assent of the Viceroy, Lord Chelmsford. Mahatma Gandhi looked upon Satyagraha as a religious movement intended for self-purification and penance. He declared that if a Satyagrahi or civil resister considered a law to be unjust, it was his duty to defy it. He should therefore break the law and suffer the penalty.

Hartal was observed throughout India on the 6th of April 1919. Not only was Das moved by the political aspect of this call but he also found in Mahatma Gandhi an embodiment of the principle of spiritual force. Addressing a mammoth meeting in Calcutta on the evening of the 6th of April, he said:

> "Satyagraha is spiritual force. It is the power of love. With love we shall conquer the self. We shall give up selfishness, hatred and envy and shall be self-controlled. This is no doubt the message of Mahatma

> Gandhi but it is the time-honoured message of India, the message of Prahlad, Meera Bai and Vasishtha. The Rowlatt Act is an obstacle to the movement for freedom. We cannot attain freedom unless we remove the obstacle. For that we have to enkindle love for our country, we have to be Satyagrahis and give up hatred and envy. Rise, brothers prepare yourselves and rest assured that the goal cannot be attained by persons of weak mettle."

He further said:

> "As the Bills are subversive of the principle of liberty and destructive of the elementary rights of individuals, in the event of these Bills becoming Law and until they are withdrawn I shall refuse civilly to obey these laws and other such laws and I further affirm that in this struggle I shall faithfully follow truth and refrain from violence to life, person and property."

Mahatma Gandhi was at the time in Bombay. He started for Delhi on the 7th of April with the intention of going to Lahore. The Punjab Government detained him on the way and banned his entry into the Province. He told the authorities that he wanted to go to the Punjab in response to the invitation he had received and assured them that he was going there not to foment unrest but to allay it. The Government refused to be convinced.

Martial Law in Punjab

The action of the Government led to further excitement among the people. The Government resorted to repressive measures which ultimately culminated in the tragedy of Jalianwala Bagh and the proclamation of martial law in the Punjab.

Jalianwala Bagh brought about a total change in the attitude of the ordinary Indian towards the Government of the day. Till this time, the majority of the people had a kind of faith in the *bona fides* of the Government. The massacre of innocent persons followed by public flogging and other humiliating measures shocked the entire nation. General Dyer had passed barbarous sentences even on loyal citizens and the support he received from the Lieutenant-

Governor of the Punjab further infuriated the people. The All-India Congress Committee expressed the horror and consternation of the people at this barbarous measure. The Committee demanded a Royal Commission to enquire into the incident but the Government of India set up instead an Enquiry Committee with Lord Hunter as chairman. There were two Indian members on the Committee, Sir Chimanlal Setalvad and Pandit Jagat Narain.

It was at first decided that Das should attend the sittings of the Committee and lead the cross-examination of the witnesses. This was not allowed by the Punjab Government. It was then proposed that Lala Harkissenlal, Pandit Rambhuj Dutt, Dr. Saifuddin Kitchlew and others who had been arrested should also be allowed to lead evidence before the Committee. This was a reasonable request, as Sir Michael O'Dwyer, General Dyer and Col. Johnson had also been asked to tender evidence. The Government did not accept even this request. Das and Motilal Nehru then proposed that these Punjab leaders should at least have their statements recorded, but this request was also refused. Nor did the Government of India or the Secretary of State for India, to whom representations on the point were made, agree. The Congress leaders then felt that there was no option but to boycott the Hunter Enquiry Committee.

The A.I.C.C. then set up an independent Enquiry Committee under the chairmanship of Mahatma Gandhi and with Das, Motilal Nehru, Abbas Tayabji and Dr. Jayakar as members. Membership of this Committee involved great personal loss and sacrifice to all the members and in, particular to Das and Motilal Nehru. They had to give up their practice for more than three months and a half. Das spent about Rs. 50,000 from his own pocket for his expenses, as he lived, in the words of Mahatma Gandhi, "like a Prince". Das showed all his extraordinary skill in analysing evidence and exposing the defects in the martial law. He could not agree with Mahatma Gandhi on all points, but like a true democrat he said, "I may not agree with you on all points but I shall bow to the decision of the majority." Jawaharlal Nehru has left on record his impression of Das in the following words: "This was the first occasion I had of working with him and under him. I valued that experience much and my admiration for him continually grew."

Montford Reforms

Soon after, Congress decided to send a deputation to London to lay India's claim before the Joint Parliamentary Committee which had been set up under the chairmanship of Lord Selbourne. Lokamanya Tilak was a member of this deputation which met Mr. Montagu and other prominent British politicians. The Indian Reforms Act, popularly known as the Montford Reforms, was passed on the 24th of December 1919 while Tilak was on board the ship on his return voyage. Mr. Montagu appealed to the people to work the Reforms and gave an assurance that the political prisoners would be released in order to create the proper atmosphere.

Congress Session at Amritsar

Congress met at Amritsar within a few days of the passing of the Act. Motilal Nehru was the President, and the session was attended by all the leading figures of the organisation. Tilak, Gandhi, Das and Madan Mohan Malaviya were there, and so were Ali brothers. Dr. Kitchelw, Lala Harkissenlal, Pandit Rambhuj Dutt and others who were released in terms of the amnesty proclaimed on the passing of the Government of India Act 1919. On the eve of the session, Motilal Nehru appealed to the Moderate leaders to come back as "the lacerated heart of the Punjab called to them." But they did not respond to the request, for they had already decided to work the Reforms.

Das moved a resolution which declared that the Reforms were inadequate, unsatisfactory and disappointing. It called on Parliament to take early steps to establish full responsible government in India in accordance with the principle of self-determination. The resolution was supported by Tilak and Bipin Chandra Pal and accepted by the subjects committee.

When the resolution came up before the open session Mahatma Gandhi objected to the word 'disappointing'. He argued that if they considered the Reforms disappointing they should not discuss them at all. He therefore moved an amendment that the people should cooperate to work the Reforms in order to secure an early establishment of full responsible government.

Das regarded Gandhiji's amendment as a climb-down and objected to it vehemently. He felt that the Reforms should be rejected and a new Act demanded. Tilak was of the same view. Gandhiji, on the other hand, was supported by Madan Mohan Malaviya and Mohammad Ali Jinnah.

The discussion! continued for two whole days. Finally a compromise was reached by which the words inadequate, unsatisfactory and disappointing' were retained but a clause was added that, "Pending establishment of full responsible government, the Congress trusts that so far as may be people will so work the Reforms as to secure an early establishment of full responsible government; and this Congress offers its thanks to the Hon'ble E. S. Montagu for his labours in connection with the Reforms."

Gandhiji has given an account of how the compromise was effected.

> "I felt that the Reforms, though defective, could still be accepted. Deshbandu Chittaranjan Das, on the other hand, adhered firmly to the view that the Reforms ought to be rejected as wholly inadequate and unsatisfactory. Lokamanya was more or less neutral. I framed my resolution and with a trembling heart undertook to move it. Pandit Malaviyaji and Mr. Jinnah were to support it. I could notice that although our difference of opinion was free from any trace of bitterness and although our speeches too contained nothing but cold reasoning, the people could not stand the very fact of a difference. It pained them. They wanted unanimity.
>
> Even while the speeches were being delivered, efforts to settle the difference were being freely exchanged among the leaders for that purpose. Malaviyaji was leaving no stone unturned to bridge the gulf. Just then Jairamdas, a delegate from Sind, handed over his amendment to me and pleaded in his sweet manner to save the delegates from the dilemma of a division. His amendment appealed to me. On seeing this, Lokamanya said, 'If Chittaranjan approves, I will have

> no objection.' Chittaranjan at last thawed and cast a look towards Sri Bipin Chandra Pal for endorsement. Malaviyaji was filled with hope. He snatched away the slip of paper containing the amendment and before Deshbandhu had even pronounced a definite 'yes', shouted out: 'Brother Delegates, you will be glad to learn that a compromise has been reached. What followed beggars description. The *pandal* was rent with clapping of hands and the erstwhile gloomy faces of the audience lit up with joy."

The Amritsar Congress thus marked a triumph as much for Das as for Mahatma Gandhi. It also revealed clearly Das's; view about obstruction and non-cooperation with the legislative councils.

The non-official Punjab Disorders Enquiry Committee met again at Banaras on the 20th of February 1920. The members were unanimous in their findings that brutal atrocities including outrage on women had been committed. The Committee demanded the resignation of Lord Chelmsford, the recall of Sir Michael O'Dwyer, the punishment of General Dyer and the return of fines realised during the period of martial law.

Even the official Hunter Committee could not absolve the officials concerned. The majority report by the three British members minimised the misdeeds but the minority report submitted by Setalvad and Jagat Narain tallied with the findings of the Congress Enquiry Committee.

Some people in the United Kingdom and a large section of the British in India organised demonstrations in favour of ' General Dyer and Col. Johnson. The Government of India rejected the findings of the non-official Enquiry Committee and also the minority report of the Hunter Committee. It accepted instead the majority report and absolved General Dyer of the charges preferred against him. This shocked Mahatma Gandhi who now termed the Government as 'satanic'.

There was another question which worried Mahatma Gandhi greatly. During World War I, Turkey had fought on the side of Germany and Austria and against the Allies. The Muslims of India supported the Allied cause on the assurance that no injustice would be done to the Turks. This assurance was not honoured, and after the war Turkey was broken into several fragments. There was a proposal to remove the capital from Constantinople to Asian soil. Many of the sacred places of the Muslims passed under Christian domination. All this led to great excitement among Indian Muslims and a movement known as the Khilafat movement was begun by the Ali brothers, Maulana Abul Kalam Azad, Hakim Ajmal Khan and others. In a conference on the 30th of May 1920, a resolution was passed adopting a policy of non-cooperation with the Government.

Gandhiji supported the cause and wrote to the Viceroy pleading for justice being done to Turkey. This was ignored and the affront added fresh fuel to the fire. A sub-committee of the Congress was formed which recommended a boycott of educational institutions and law courts as a protest against the Punjab atrocities and the injustice to Turkey. There was no suggestion about boycott of legislative councils in the sub-committee's report, but Mahatma Gandhi insisted on its inclusion in the Congress programme. A special session of the Congress was called at Calcutta on the 4th of September 1920 to consider this momentous issue.

Lala Lajpat Rai was invited to preside over the session. Das and Motilal Nehru were at that time at Arrah in connection with the Dumraon case. From the beginning Das had been against the boycott of councils. He proposed instead that a deputation should be sent to meet the British Prime Minister. If it failed to produce the desired result, the Congress should boycott all schools and colleges and law courts. He was strongly in favour of boycott of educational institutions and establishment of national schools and colleges but he felt that boycott of the councils would be detrimental to the national interest.

Bipin Chandra Pal moved an amendment on the question of council entry. In seconding the resolution, Das urged strongly that in no circumstances should the councils be boycotted. He did not attach too much importance to the sending of a mission. He would not himself hesitate to give up his practice. He was also prepared to advocate the boycott of schools and colleges, but he considered it a great mistake to give up the struggle within the councils.

In pressing his point of view, he said:

> "These are not gifts of the British Government. Reforms have been wrung out of the hands of the British Government. I want to make the councils an instrument for the attainment of Swaraj and to use the weapon which is in the hollow of your hands to bring about full, complete Swaraj. What you have earned through toil and struggle, for the last thirty-five years, you should not give up by entirely shutting yourself out."

He declared emphatically:

> "I yield to none in my demand for full self-government. I wanted the same thing in the Bombay special session of September 1918, out in order to give full scope to the Moderates to remain with us, I toned down our demands. The Moderates left and the demand was raised a little higher in Delhi. Then the Punjab affair and injustice to the Khalifa intervened. Why should the demand be lowered today? I am the last man for that item." Jawaharlal Nehru has described the scene in the following words: "Mr. C. R. Das led the opposition not because he disapproved of the spirit behind the resolution, for he was prepared to go as far, or even further, but chiefly because he objected to the boycott of the new legislatures."

In spite of his opposition, the special session accepted tentatively the programme of boycott of councils but left the final decision till the Nagpur session. Das felt greatly worried as he was in favour of direct action for improving the political situation of the country and at the same time he considered the boycott of Councils highly injurious. He spoke to various groups of people in Bengal and Assam and made it clear that he supported Council entry not to help but to embarrass the Government, particularly by exercising their vote in such a way that the appointment of Ministers would become impossible.

In the meantime, elections to the councils had been held in October 1920. The Nationalists did not contest any seat, and the elections were won by Moderates. This itself, in Das's opinion, was an example of the harmful consequences of the council boycott policy. The Moderates who were returned to the legislature cooperated with bureaucracy and gave it the camouflage of popular support.

Das also felt that the preliminary measures for non-cooperation had not proved successful. The special session of the Congress had been held in September but by November hardly any lawyer had given up practice. Nor had students responded in any large scale. Maulana Mohammad Ali's attempt to convert the Aligarh College into a national university did not succeed. A similar fate met the attempt to transform the Banaras Hindu College. Even the National School at Calcutta, opened "by Mahatma Gandhi himself, was soon closed.

In a press conference on the 30th of November 1920 Das said:

> "Non-cooperation is our only chance. A complete programme of non-cooperation with renunciation of titles and honorary offices at one end and refusal to pay taxes at the other should be at once adopted and worked out within the shortest possible time. The programme of non-cooperation is an organic whole. Work should be undertaken in all directions so that a call for the enforcement of the complete programme may be made within the shortest time.
>
> I was not for boycott of the councils as I wanted to work out the principle of non-cooperation from within the councils but in obedience to the Congress resolution we withdrew our candidatures and the matter has no practical importance now."

It was against this background that the Nagpur Congress was held in December 1920. Many people expected a trial of strength between Mahatma Gandhi and Das. When they found that about four hundred delegates from Bengal accompanied Das, this expectation was further strengthened. Mahatma Gandhi decided to forestall any open conflict and invited Das for a heart-to-heart discussion on the eve of the session. He also realised that Das, with his spirit of sacrifice and earnestness, could give a great impetus to the movement. Their difference was only on the question of boycotting the councils. In all other matters their views were similar if not identical.

Das proposed during their discussions that the country should undertake a programme of five years' preparation before launching the non-cooperation movement Mahatma Gandhi argued that the present was the most opportune time. The Punjab wrong and the Khilafat question and the refusal of the Government to redress either of these offered an opportunity which could not be neglected. In order to meet Das's point of view, Gandhiji agreed to omit the clause on the boycott of councils from the main resolution. The were already over must also have weighed with him. Maulana Mohammad Ali worked hard to bring about a settlement between Gandhiji and Das. In his own words, he "moved like a shuttlecock between these two mighty persons".

The resolution drafted by Das and accepted by Mahatma. Gandhi was considered to be more practical and effective than the one passed at the special session in Calcutta. It did not demand the boycott of councils. Instead, it called for the resignation of the Moderate leaders who had been returned unopposed. The resolution also declared that boycott of schools and colleges and law courts should not be gradual but immediate. It advised the people to withhold payment of taxes.

Das moved the resolution himself and announced that he would give up his own legal practice. There was wild enthusiasm and the entire audience gave evidence of a new spirit, strength and energy. In fact not only Nagpur but the whole-country was astir with a new life.

Renunciation of Legal Practice

Das's renunciation captured the imagination of the whole country. When he gave up his practice in 1920, he was at the top of the legal profession in India. His enormous income enabled him not only to live in comfort but also to exercise power in all spheres of social life. Das loved to have literary discussions and also devotional soirces in his home in the evenings but he now devoted himself wholeheartedly to the political struggle. Along with his practice he gave up the religious and devotional gatherings.

Journey to Jail and Trial

Deshbandhu Das was removed to the Presidency Jail on the 10th of December 1921. On the 12th, Mr. Kyd, one of the Deputy Commissioners, came to see him in the jail. Deshbandhu asked him to show the warrant, but Mr. Kyd replied that he had not been arrested under any warrant but on suspicion under Section 54 of the Criminal Procedure Code.

Deshbandhu Das wanted to know if there had been any amendment of the law since the time he gave up his practice. Somewhat surprised, Kyd asked him the reason for this question. Deshbandhu Das replied that Section 54 of the Criminal Procedure Code applied only to cognisable cases. Persons connected with voluntary organisations could not be arrested under that section. Mr. Kyd had to beat a hasty retreat.

Later, on the same day, Deshbandhu Das was produced before the Chief Presidency Magistrate. The case was adjourned till the 20th of January 1922. The court also passed an order that the trial should be held inside the Civil Jail as there was an unprecedented rush of people who had come to watch the proceedings. The police had found it difficult to control the crowd and there had been friction when they dealt harshly with the people.

A few days after Das's arrest, there was a move on the part of the Government which, if properly handled, might have turned the course of Indian history. The complete success of the 'hartal' in Calcutta had deeply impressed the Government.

The way the voluntary organisations had worked and, still more, the signs of disaffection among the police had made the bureaucracy nervous. On the other hand, the powerful lead given by Deshbandhu Das had inspired the country with a new hope and energy. The Government was particularly anxious to avert a 'hartal' on the 24th of December when the Prince of Wales was to arrive in Calcutta.

About a week before the Prince's arrival, Lord Reading went to Calcutta. He perhaps felt that there should be another attempt to come to terms with the Congress so that the Prince's visit to India might end successfully. Pandit Madan Mohan Malaviya visited the Central Presidency Jail and had several conversations with Deshbandhu Das and Maulana Abul Kalam Azad. Das was also allowed facilities of telephonic communication in order to discuss matters with his colleagues and particularly with Mahatma Gandhi.

On the 19th of December 1921, Deshbandhu Das and Maulana Azad agreed provisionally that a settlement with the Government might be effected on the following terms: The Congress would call off the 'hartal' of the 24th of December 1921 and would stop the despatch of volunteers for picketing and boycott. Government, in its turn, would release all persons arrested under the Criminal Law Amendment Act or Seditious Meetings Act. There would be a Round Table Conference which would discuss important questions regarding Swaraj, Khilafat and the Punjab wrongs.

Deshbandhu Das exchanged telegrams with Mahatma Gandhi and asked for his approval before these terms were finalised, Mahatma Gandhi wanted to know about the date and composition of the conference. He also insisted that the Ali brothers and the other Fatwa prisoners must be released.

Deshbandhu Das informed him that the conference would be held in January 1922 and about 20 representatives of the Congress including Mahatma Gandhi, Deshbandhu Das, Ali brothers, Pandit Motilal Nehru and Maulana Azad would take part in the conference. Regarding the Fatwa prisoners, they would be released in course of time.

Mahatma Gandhi did not at first agree and telegrams continued to be exchanged between the two leaders. When he finally gave his consent, it was too late. His last telegram was received at a time when the Viceroy had already left the city and the Viceregal Council had concluded its session in Calcutta. The Prince had arrived in Calcutta only to be greeted by a total 'hartal'. Although Deshbandhu Das was glad about the success of the boycott, he felt that a grand opportunity for settlement had been missed.

When the trial was held inside the Civil Jail on the 20th of January 1922, not only the public but also Press reporters were refused admission. Only lawyers could go inside the Jail and even they had difficulty in doing so. When the trial began, Deshbandhu Das asked the magistrate whether it was a public trial or a trial in camera. The magistrate said that it was a public trial but he had no reply when Das pointed out that even the members of the Bar were being refused admission.

Charges were framed against Deshbandhn Das under Section 17 (2) of the Criminal Law Amendment Act and it was decided that on the next day of hearing the trial would be in public court. On the 24th of January Deshbandhu Das had an attack of influenza. The fever abated after a few days but he rapidly grew weaker and emaciated. Finally, on the 7th of February, Deshbandhu Das was produced before the Chief Presidency Magistrate who asked him if he wished to say anything. Deshbandhu Das refused to make any statement or cross-examine witnesses or lead any evidence in self-defence during the trial. The magistrate then sentenced him to six months' simple imprisonment.

All eyes turned to Deshbandhu Das who remained completely unaffected while the whole court was moved with deep emotions. After the judgement had been delivered, Deshbandhu Das made a statement to the effect that it was utterly futile to defend oneself in such circumstances. He pointed out that three of the signatures for which he was being convicted were not his, even though the manifestos had been issued under his instructions. He rejected the evidence of the handwriting expert who had sworn that they were his signatures, which, he said, only proved that the bureaucracy could send anybody to jail if it wanted.

Deshbandhu Das was removed to the Central Jail where he found many of his friends and followers. His son Chira Rajan Das was already there. So were Subhas Chandra Bose, Hemanta Sarkar and Birendranath Sashmal. Maulana Abul Kalam Azad was also in the same jail and came to see him.

Deshbandhu Das began to suffer from fever and loss of sleep. On the 15th of March, the Government issued a communique about his health which stated that he had fever every afternoon but there was no other complication. Sir Abdur Rahim, then a member of the Executive Council, intervened and ordered that Deshbandhu Das should be provided with home-made food and be treated by Dr. D. N. Ray, a famous homoeopath of the city. Deshbandhu Das, however, continued to lose weight and soon developed symptoms of diabetes.

Deshbandhu Das was the President-elect of the Congress session which was to be held at Ahmedabad. Since he was in jail, he sent his Presidential address through his sister Urmila Devi. Basanti Devi also sent a short and touching message. Deshbandhu Das's address was read in the open session by Shrimati Sarojini Naidu, and Hakim Ajmal Khan acted as President in his absence.

After the session of the Congress, Mahatma Gandhi proposed a mass civil disobedience movement at Bardoli in Gujarat. The programme consisted of refraining from payment of land revenue and other taxes. Before the movement could be launched, an untoward incident happened at Chauri Chaura in Gorakhpur district when a number of policemen were killed. Mahatma Gandhi immediately called a meeting of the Working Committee and suspended *sine die* the projected mass civil disobedience movement at Bardoli. He also directed the Congress organisations of all Provinces to stop the activities of the volunteers and suspended all meetings and processions. He suggested that instead of these activities, all members of the Congress should take to spinning.

Deshbandhu Das was greatly upset by this decision. He told his associates, "Whatever justification Mahatmaji had in stopping mass Civil Disobedience at Bardoli, he had none in stopping the work of volunteers in Bengal which had practically paralysed the work of the Government and this was the second instance when Mahatmaji bungled the situation."

Subhas Chandra Bose has also left on record how upset Deshbandhu Das was: "Deshbandhu was beside himself with sorrow and anger at the way Mahatma was repeatedly bungling. The Bardoli retreat came as a staggering blow."

Apart from Deshbandhu Das, other leaders of the Congress were also unhappy at the decision taken by Mahatma Gandhi. Maulana Abul Kalam Azad told the present writer that it was impossible to expect that the whole of India would be non-violent. He commented that it was too much to punish a whole Province for the fault of a particular village.

Pandit Motilal Nehru and Lala Lajpat Rai were still more vehement in their protest. Lala Lajpat Rai wrote a seventy-page letter in which he observed: "The whole of the country has been punished. Is it proper to inflict punishment on the people living on the Himalayan border for the misdeeds of the people of Cape Comorin?"

The whole country was demoralised by the sudden reversal of Congress policy. Government now felt sufficiently strong to strike at Mahatma Gandhi himself. He was arrested on the 10th of March 1922 for certain articles published in *Young India* and sentenced to six years' simple imprisonment. The condition of the country can be easily imagined. From the wild enthusiasm of recent months, it fell into the depth of despair and dejection.

When Deshbandhu Das was sentenced, the jailor asked him if he would like to be classed as a European-class prisoner. It will be remembered that in those days certain special facilities were offered to prisoners who were classed as Europeans. Without a moment's hesitation, Deshbandbu Das rejected the suggestion and said he wished to be treated as an Indian pure and simple.

He spent his time in prison reading, writing and discussing issues with his friends. His reading consisted of history, politics, philosophy and economics. Mornings he used to devote to a book on the history and philosophy of Indian nationalism which he was writing at the time.

One of his diversions in prison was to talk together. He recalled the pleasure with which he had seen Sir Henry Irving and Ellen Terry act on the London stage. He also suggested to the other political prisoners that they might produce a play inside the jail. *Profulla,* a social drama by the well-known Bengali dramatist Girish Chandra Ghosh was selected for the purposed. Rehearsals and preparation for the stage kept all the political prisoners busy and in due course there was a regular performance. This was the first time that a drama had been staged inside an Indian jail.

It was, however, in discussions with his friends and fellow workers that Das revealed his inmost thoughts. His simplicity and sincerity impressed all who came in contact with him, while his genial humour enlivened whatever subject he touched.

One day there was a discussion about the attitude of the Congress towards entry into the legislatures. One of the workers said that Council entry would interfere with the non-cooperation movement. Deshbandhu Das denied this. He asserted that one could non-cooperate both from inside and outside the legislature. In fact the Reforms could be wrecked more successfully by opposition from within the legislature and the bureaucracy would, he said, feel quite helpless.

When asked what the programme should be inside the Councils, Das replied that Congressmen would obstruct the Government in every one of its acts. They would demonstrate to the country and to the world outside that no substantial good had been achieved by the Reforms. They would mend or end the existing Constitution.

When a critic maintained that it was already known that the Reforms were a sham, Deshbandhu Das retorted that such an assertion was completely useless. The bureaucracy was doing whatever it liked and yet it could act under cover of approval by the legislature. All the repressive laws were being passed by the Councils. He then mentioned what Lord Ronaldshay had told him—that the Government was acting according to the advice of the elected representatives of the people and as such the British had no responsibility for such measures. Deshbandhu Das said that it was necessary to demonstrate that the present members of the Councils were not true representatives of the people.

The critics were not yet convinced. They wanted to know if there would be an end to all repression once the Congress captured all the legislatures.

Deshbandhu Das said that it would be too optimistic to expect any such development. It would, however, have the effect that action by the Government would no longer have the stamp of popular consent. There would be two parties within the legislatures—the Government party and the people's party. The bureaucracy would perhaps still do whatever it wished, but it would then have to act on its own. This would rouse the people and make it easier to carry on the national struggle.

One of the workers asked if membership of Councils would not be against religion. Deshbandhu Das was amused but he contented himself by the reply that it was no more against religion than civil disobedience was.

One of the workers remarked that the Government would in that case take away what the country had already gained. Das replied that the Government had in reality given almost nothing. No real good could come from the bureaucracy. In fact, under the dyarchical system, the bureaucracy did not take the Ministers into confidence. Whatever little had been given was simply because the Government had no other alternative.

One of the questioners asked if it was Deshbandhu Das's view that every governmental measure, whether good or bad, should be opposed. Das's reply was that he did not believe that the bureaucracy could do any real good. He admitted that there may be temporary benefits like the establishment of charitable dispensaries but such measures could not really serve the people and certainly could not bring about Swaraj.

Asked if he would accept ministership, Das emphatically said 'not'. He pointed out that acceptance of office would be another name for cooperation. He would, however, be willing to accept office provided all the departments were brought under popular control. As a practical politician he realised that the country might have to begin with provincial autonomy.

Questioned whether Council entry would secure Swaraj, Das replied that the British Parliament would be compelled to think of compromise if the popular party captured the Councils and expressed the people's point of view at every stage. In this way the objective might be reached even without civil disobedience.

Deshbandhu Das's observation surprised some who wanted to know if his statement meant that he was not in favour of civil disobedience. Das pointed out that his action in the last year or two proved that the question was beside the point. His main object was to achieve Swaraj for the people and civil disobedience was merely an instrument. Before resorting to civil disobedience, it was necessary to gain in strength by resisting specific acts. He added that if, through the support of the people, provincial autonomy could be secured through legislative action, he for one would not insist on civil disobedience which was in any case a last weapon.

Some of the workers asked if he would take the oath when he became a member of the Council. Deshbandhu Das replied that he saw no objection. After all even those who believed in non-cooperation were using stamps issued by the Government and in other ways using facilities created through Governmental activity. He believed that the purpose was to end the bureaucratic rule of the country and bring about a change in the system of Government. In his view there was no obligation to wage war against the King or Parliament and as such he did not see any objection to taking an oath in the name of the King.

Some extremists were most satisfied with these answers. They asked Deshbandhu Das if he did not desire complete independence outside the British Commonwealth. Das's reply was that he wanted independence and was not concerned with what form it took. He wanted Swaraj which was in every way full independence for the Indian people to work out their destiny. The question of severing connection with the British Commonwealth had not yet become a live issue but should the Congress adopt such a decision Deshbandhu Das said that he would stand with the Congress and fight for it.

The Bengal Provincial Conference was held that year at Chittagong with Shrimati Basanti Devi as president. In her address, she referred to the question of Council entry and observed that the Congress might have to consider a change in tactics and adopt a policy of non-cooperation within the legislature. This was interpreted as an indication of Deshbandhu Das's own views and gave rise to bitter controversy and opposition both inside the jails and outside. Many even among Deshbandhu Das's friends and followers reacted violently and opposed the move.

Das remained in Calcutta and spared no pains to make the boycott of the Prince's visit complete and peaceful. The whole city presented a deserted look. All the shops and bazars were closed. Schools were closed and courts did no work. Only cars and carriages which had the label "On national service" were able to move about in the streets.

The 'hartal' in Calcutta was so successful that papers like *The Englishman* and *The Statesman* found fault with Government for having practically abdicated and allowed the Congress volunteers to take control of the city. Consultation were held at Government House, Calcutta, on the 18th of November. Soon after, a legal petition was filed by the Bengal Chamber of Commerce, an organisation of British merchants, alleging that people had been forced and intimidated during the 'hartal.' This was not true, but Government decided to strike.

The people of the city were shocked to learn on the morning of the 19th that the police had raided nearly all Congress and Khilafat offices in the city between midnight and 3 a.m. *The Statesman* and *The Englishman* also published sensational headlines to the effect that all volunteer organisations of the Congress and the Khilafat in Calcutta and the suburbs would be declared illegal. Public meetings were prohibited and the Criminal Law Amendment Act was revived.

Das was about to start for Surat for a meeting of the Congress Working Committee. He told his co-workers that the Government had moved because of the success of the 'hartal'. He feared that there would be more repression and Sashmal and Subhas Chandra would be arrested. As already mentioned, Birendranath Sashmal was then the secretary of the Congress Committee, Subhas Bose the secretary of the Publicity Board and Mujibar Rahman secretary of the Khilafat Committee. Das advised his lieutenants to wait till his return, for he wished to decide the line of action after consultation with Mahatma Gandhi and other colleagues. Soon after Das left, the Commissioner of Police, Calcutta, issued a notification by which all public meetings, demonstrations and processions were prohibited for three months.

The Working Committee was to have met at Surat on the 22nd of November. Serious disturbances broke out in Bombay on the 17th of November. Mahatma Gandhi undertook a fast in expiation and suggested that the Committee should meet in Bombay. The meeting was held on the 22nd and 23rd of November. As a result of the deliberations, the Working Committee gave permission to each Province to start civil disobedience provided it was satisfied that non-violence in word and action would be strictly maintained.

The Bengal Provincial Congress Committee met on the 27th of November and invested Deshbandhu with all powers to conduct the civil disobedience movement. It decided that volunteers should go out on the 3rd of December to hawk Khadi in the streets. Each batch was to consist of live volunteers. They would wear no badges but would be clad in Khadi. Besides the live, another volunteer would act as a scout and watch them from a distance so that the head office could be informed in case of their arrest.

A 'hartal' was also announced for the 24th of December when the Prince was due to arrive in the city.

Ten batches of volunteers went out on the 3rd and 4th of December but no one was arrested. Das now decided to intensify the programme and also began to prepare himself for the hardships of jail life. He began to sleep on a hard bed and take prison rations in spite of the protests of his family. He explained to them that it was good to prepare oneself to the conditions of prison life, because he expected to be arrested any moment.

Lala Lajpat Rai was arrested under the Punjab Seditious Meetings Act. Das said he welcomed this direct attack and appealed to the people to observe strict non-violence in all their activities. He felt that it was necessary to insist on non-violence in thought and action in the light of what had taken place in Bombay. About 5,000 men had enlisted as volunteers in Calcutta but many of them had signed the pledge without any intention of actually participating in the movement.

Das felt that there was a fall in public enthusiasm because not enough people were coming forth to offer Satyagraha. His own son came forward at this stage and volunteered to lead a batch of "Satyagrahis. He was arrested soon after and taken to jail. When some friends of Das wanted to take to his son special food and bedding, Das remarked that he had no objection, provided all the others who had also been arrested were treated in the same way and given special food and bedding.

There was a new development on the morning of the 7th of December 1921. Basanti Devi, Deshbandhu Das's wife, and Urmila Devi, his sister, decided to take the lead in hawking Khadi, When they were doing so, a police sergeant approached Basanti Devi and asked her, "Madam, what are you doing?" Basanti Devi replied that she was selling Khadi and asking people to observe 'hartal' on the 24th of December. The sergeant then said that she was under arrest and asked her to go with him to the police station. She did so willingly. The arrest of Basanti Devi had an electric effect on the people. Immediately more than a thousand young men offered themselves for arrest. They also developed a new militancy. When the trial magistrate asked them for a statement, the young men replied that they had come to serve their country and did not think that they were guilty of any offence. Among those who courted arrest at this stage was Hiralal Gandhi, the eldest son of Mahatma Gandhi.

Basanti Devi's arrest had in fact stirred up the whole of Bengal. Muslims as well as Hindus joined the national movement in thousands. There were stirrings even among the police. While Basanti Devi and her companions were being carried to the prison, a number of police constables saluted her and vowed that they would resign their jobs. Factory workers also joined as volunteers and offered themselves for arrest. The Government was disturbed by these new developments and orders were issued that the wages of police men would be forthwith increased.

When Deshbandhu Das heard of Basanti Devi's arrest he took it calmly and advised all Congressmen to devote themselves even more resolutely to the national programme. In his heart he exulted at this evidence of the courage and spirit of sacrifice that was moving the women of India. He told some of his friends that he was now sure that the Government would be shaken to its very foundation. The Government, however, had no intention of keeping these ladies in prison. They were released at dead of night and sent home. Deshbandhu Das felt that this was an insult and became even more determined that the struggle should continue.

Basanti Devi and her companions went out again the next morning. Strong military pickets were posted in different parts of the city and many innocent passers-by were beaten up. One of the victims of such an unprovoked assault was Principal Heramba Chandra Maitra, a venerable professor and a citizen whose loyalty to the Government of the day had never been questioned. The work of Basanti Devi and her companions, however, was not obstructed.

A few days earlier, Lord Ronaldshay, then Governor of Bengal, had in a public meeting expressed his high regard for Deshbandhu Das in the following terms:

> "A gentleman of Bengal of great ability and blessed by providence with intellectual powers of a high order will shortly preside over the deliberations of a body which still, I believe, claims the name of the Indian National Congress. How splendid a niche he might carve for himself in the temple of fame, what a name he might make for himself in the passes of history, were he to come forward as a champion and apostle of the religion of goodwill ! Will he do so? His responsibility is great, for if on the other hand he urges his followers to proceed on their course down the slippery slopes of revolution, it must be obvious to the meanest intelligence that Government will have no option but to take up the challenge which is thrown down."

Disturbed by the trend of events, Lord Ronaldshay felt that he would like to have a discussion with Das to find out a basis of settlement. They met on the 8th of December and discussed matters for more than one hour.

When Lord Ronaldshay asked Deshbandhu Das to call off the 'hartal' on the occasion of the visit of the Prince of Wales, he replied that it did not rest with him. He was only carrying out the mandate of the All-India Congress Committee. Lord Ronaldshay then spoke about the volunteer organisations but Deshbandhu Das told him that the volunteers were discharging their duties peacefully and Government had no justification for arresting them. Lord Ronaldshay was not prepared to accept this position and said that there had been cases of breach of the law and the Government was bound to maintain law and order.

Deshbandhu Das said that even if there had been occasional lapses from non-violence the volunteers were by and large acting peacefully and it was not proper to condemn all volunteer organisations in Bengal as organisations of sedition and violence.

Lord Ronaldshay retorted that the Government was acting on the advice of the representatives of the people in the legislature. When Das protested that they were not representatives of the people. Lord Ronaldshay countered by saying that since the Congress had not contested the elections, it was not open to the Congress to challenge their representative character. As Das himself believed that it was a mistake to boycott the legislatures, he did not join issue with Lord Ronaldshay on this point.

Das returned to the question of volunteers and informed Lord Ronaldshay that there were many instances in which the police had beaten up the volunteers and snatched away their money. In fact the custodians of law were committing flagrant violations of the law, but Lord Ronaldshay said that he had no information on the point.

Lord Ronaldshay again pressed Deshbandhu Das to stop the activities of the volunteers. Das replied that the volunteers were engaged in the discharge of their duties. It was for them almost a part of religion. He could not therefore ask the volunteers to desist.

Lord Ronaldshay replied that from the point of view of the Government the activities of the volunteer organisations were undesirable and he would have to take all steps necessary for the maintenance of law and order. Das replied that he was growing old, but he would, up to the last moment of his life, work to counteract the lawless law that was ruling the land.

Lord Ronaldshay expressed his regret for the arrest of Basanti Devi but made it clear that since there was no possibility of an amicable settlement, the Government would take all steps to curb the movement. Das came away from the interview with a clear conviction that he would soon be arrested and spent the next few days in making arrangements for the conduct of work during his absence.

At 4 p.m. on the 10th of December 1921, Das was having his afternoon tea with his daughters when a car-load of police officers arrived. One of his daughters exclaimed that the sergeants had come. Deshbandhu Das wrote out a brief message for his countrymen and handed it to his daughter.

Birendranath Sashmal was then sitting in the drawing room on the ground floor. A police officer entered the drawing room and asked him his name. When Sashmal gave his name he was told that he was under arrest. Two Deputy Commissioners of Police went up the first floor. Deshbandhu Das asked them: "Have you come to arrest me?" When they replied in the affirmative, he wanted to see the warrant of arrest. One of the officers said that the warrant had been left behind but the arrest was being effected under the Criminal Law Amendment Act. Das's only comment was, "Oh, it is the same stale act under which you are arresting my boys."

When he was being taken away, Deshbandhu Das told his daughters that they must not send any food from home for him. His daughters were worried, because Das had always been accustomed to good food. But he made it clear that he would now take the same food as was served to the other prisoners. He would not have for himself what his son and others, who had been arrested four days earlier, were not entitled to.

As he stepped into the police car, Deshbandhu Das said to the crowd which had gathered:

> "If our object be noble, don't worry about the consequences. The fire that has been kindled in the land is not likely to be extinguished. The result rests in the hand of God. Be strictly non-violent in your work and your object will be achieved.
>
> "Men and women of India, this is my message to you. Victory is in sight, if you are prepared to win it through suffering."

Conch-shells were blown and flowers showered on Das as the car moved.

Congress President

In 1921 Deshbandhu was elected president of the Congress at Allahabad session and in 1922 at the Gaya session he resigned from the post as he lost the motion on 'No Council Entry'. After that Deshbandhu founded the Swaraj Party with Motilal Nehru. Netaji Subhash Bose was a follower of Deshbandhu.

Gaya Congress Session

Deshbandhu's health had been affected during his imprisonment. After he was released he needed rest, but he had first to fulfil certain public engagements. He could not decline the series of receptions organised in his honour in different parts of Calcutta. At a meeting presided over by Sir P. C. Ray, Das referred to the hardship and sacrifice of students in the national cause. He declared that he was more than ever convinced that Indian freedom would be won through truth and non-violence, for without truth there was no other way.

The All-India Congress Committee had appointed an enquiry committee to study and report if the country was ready for civil disobedience. Its meetings were then being held at Patna. Deshbandhu Das wished to have a discussion with the committee and invited the members to Calcutta on the occasion of his daughter's marriage to Bhaskar Mukherjee, the grandson of Sir Surendra Nath Banerjea. During these talks, Pandit Motilal Nehru appealed to Das not to express any opinion on the issue till the report was published.

Deshbandhu Das left for Darjeeling towards the end of August but the change did him no good. He then decided to spend some time in Kashmir for recouping his health. There were many who read all kinds of meaning into this trip. Some bluntly asked whether he was going to Kashmir for health or for reasons of politics. When he reached the borders of Kashmir, the police wanted from him an assurance that he would not say anything on political questions. In fact he was told that unless he gave such "an assurance in writing he would not be permitted to enter the State.

Deshbandhu Das regarded this attitude as an affront and said to the police officer: "I know that you will not steal but if I ask you to give it in writing that you will not do so, are you prepared to give such an assurance?"

The officer said that he fully appreciated Deshbandhu Das's feelings but he was acting under the Maharaja's orders. Deshbandhu Das told the officer that the Maharaja could certainly have the pleasure of passing such orders but he in any case was not going to comply. He gave up the idea of going to Kashmir and went instead to Murree where he stayed for about a month.

The United Provinces Political Conference was held that year at Dehra Dun. Das, who was invited to preside, gave a detailed history of the political movement starting from the Satyagraha of the 6th of April 1919 and went on to declare: "I do not want a Swaraj which will satisfy only the middle classes. I want Swaraj for the masses, not for the classes."

This was perhaps the first time that a leader of the eminence of Deshbandhu Das declared from a political platform that the Swaraj which the Congress wanted was for all the people and not for the privileged few. Pandit Motilal Nehru and Sarojine Naidu who were present at the meeting congratulated Das on his bold declaration.

The Civil Disobedience Enquiry Committee, had by this time reported that the country was not prepared for mass civil disobedience. It, however, gave Provincial Congress Committees the freedom to undertake limited civil disobedience if they were satisfied that the necessary conditions were fulfilled in their Province. It suggested that such a programme might be limited to the breach of a particular law or order or the non-payment of a particular tax.

On the question of Council entry, the committee was divided. The chairman, Hakim Ajmal Khan, supported by Pandit Motilal Nehru and Vithalbhai Patel, was in favour of Council entry. Dr. Ansari, C. Rajagopalachari and Kasturi Ranga Iyengar were against it.

As mentioned earlier, Deshbandhu had promised Pandit Motilal Nehru that he would not speak on the question of Council entry till the Enquiry Committee had submitted its report. He was at Amaravati when the report was published. On the 7th of November he spoke in the following terms:

> "Reformed Councils are really a mask which the bureaucracy has put on. I conceive it our clear duty to tear those masks off its face. To end these Councils will be the most effective boycott. It is possible to achieve this if we get a majority. If we stand for elections in the beginning of 1923, the results will show that we have proceeded upon facts and not upon assumptions. I am sure of a majority for men of our views."

When he arrived in Calcutta on the 10th of November, Das was given a tremendous ovation at the Howrah station. He had not expected it, because his views on Council entry had not been unanimously shared. The Working Committee of the Provincial Congress Committee met on the 18th and 19th of November and passed a resolution recommending that Congressmen should contest elections on the issue of the Punjab and Khilafat wrongs and the immediate achievement of Swaraj. The All-India Congress Committee met on the 20th of November and was presided over by Deshbandhu Das.

Pandit Motilal Nehru, Hakim Ajmal Khan, Vithalbhai Patel, N. C. Kelkar, M. R. Jayakar, B. S. Moonje, Abhayankar, Dr. Alam Sherwani, Anugraha Narayan Sinha, S. Satyamurti. Rangaswami Iyengar, Lala Dunichand of Ambala, Shrimati Lajjabati Devi, J. M. Sen Gupta, B. N. Sashmal and many others spoke in favour of Council entry and Rajagopalachari, Rajendra Prasad, Vallabhbhai Patel, Shrimati Sarojini Naidu, Dr. Ansari, Moulvi Abbas Tayabji, T. Prakasam, Lala Duni Chand of Lahore, Jagadguru Sankaracharya, Gangadhar Deshpande and others spoke against.

The most enthusiastic amongst the opposing group was it was dishonest to enter Councils in any circumstances. He said that unity was good but honesty was better.

It will be remembered that Deshbandhu Das had been elected to preside over the Ahmedabad session of the Congress but could not do so because of his imprisonment. He was again elected the President of the Congress. The session was to be held at Gaya.

He devoted himself to organising public opinion in favour of Council entry before the session of the Congress. He had to face great difficulties in this task for he had little money and many of the old workers were against him.

In addition to his personal liabilities, the arrears of rent for the Congress office were also shifted on to his shoulders. His health was poor and almost all the newspapers were against the Council entry programme. Protest meetings were also organised and at times such meetings resorted to personal abuse. Friends turned into enemies. Some revolutionary groups even threatened to shoot him. It was suggested that he was keen on Council entry as he wanted to become a minister. Such people forgot that Deshbandhu Das had given up a princely fortune and voluntarily accepted poverty in the national cause. Threat and persuasion as well as abuse and insinuation, however, had no effect on Deshbandhu Das.

Deshbandhu Das's presidential address at Gaya was one of his most magnificent efforts but on the question of Council entry, the resolution supported by him was lost on the 31st of December 1922 by 1,748 votes to 890. He immediately resigned his office as President of the All-India Congress Committee and so did Pandit Motilal Nehru as General Secretary of the Congress. In his valedictory speech, Deshbandhu Das declared that although the majority had differed from him, he was confident that very soon the majority would support his views. On the 1st of January 1923, the day after their resignation, Deshbandhu Das and Motilal Nehru formed the Swarajya party.

Since this is one of Deshbandhu Das's major speeches, it is quoted in full as an Appendix. He discussed at length the principles of non-cooperation and explained the futility of boycotting the elections. His vision ranged over the problems not only of India but of the whole of Asia. He spoke in terms of a federation of Asian peoples which, in his view, was a condition for world peace. As this was perhaps the first time that this idea of an Asian federation was mooted from the Congress platform, it is appropriate it should be stated in his own words:

> "Even more important than this is the participation of India in the great Asiatic federation which I see in

the course of formation. I have hardly any doubt that the Pan-Islamic Movement which was started on a somewhat narrow basis, has given way or is about to give way to a great federation of all Asiatic peoples. It is the union of the oppressed nationalities of Asia. Is India to remain outside the union? I 'admit that our freedom must be won by ourselves but such bonds of friendship and love, of sympathy and cooperation between India and the rest of Asia, nay between India and all the liberty-loving people of the world is destined to bring about world peace. World peace to my mind means the freedom of every nationality and I go further and say that no nation on the face of the earth can be really free when other nations are in bondage. The policy which we have hitherto pursued was absolutely necessary for the consummation of the work which we took upon ourselves to perform and I agreed to that policy wholeheartedly. The hopes of attainment of Swaraj or a substantial basis of Swaraj in the course of the year made such concentration absolutely necessary. Today that very work demands broader sympathy and a wide outlook."

Swaraj Party

The new party which Deshbandhu Das and Pandit Motilal formed was at first given the name 'Congress Khilafat Swarajya Party but soon the words Congress and Khilafat were dropped and the party attained all-India status Deshbandhu Das and Pandit Nehru were realists and they felt that the Gaya Congress had been dogged by a lack of realism. Everybody knew that the programme of boycotting Councils, courts and educational institutions had failed. All these institutions were working as vigorously as before and yet the Gaya Congress repeated the old slogan of their boycott. Similarly, the Gaya Congress clung fondly to Satyagraha or civil disobedience even though the Enquiry Committee appointed by the Congress had itself reported that conditions in the country ruled out the possibility of any such movement. People went on shouting 'Mahatma Gandhi ki Jai' and protesting that Mahatma in jail was more powerful than Mahatma in liberty but few acted up to the principles which he had preached. The result was confusion and disillusionment in the public mind. The intellectual classes were growing cynical about Congress ideology and programme.

Fortunately for the Congress, Maulana Abul Kalam Azad was released soon after the Gaya Congress. He had a number of meetings with Deshbandhu Das for whom he had great admiration. Though unconnected with the Swarajya Party, Maulana Azad played an important part in bringing about its success. He requested Deshbandhu Das to wait till the 30th of April 1923 and assured him that if within that time the orthodox section of the Congress did not launch a mass Satyagraha, he would himself take the lead in calling for a special session of the Congress to approve the Council entry programme.

Deshbandhu Das agreed to this suggestion of Maulana Azad which was also accepted by the Congress Working Committee. A meeting of the All-India Congress Committee was held at Allahabad on the 27th of February 1923. This meeting was attended by Deshbandhu Das, Pandit Motilal Nehru and other Swarajists. Deshbandhu Das was unanimously elected the chairman of the meeting at which the following terms of compromise were settled between the Swarajya Party and the No-changers:

- Propaganda regarding Councils would be suspended on both sides till the 30th of April 1923.
- Both parties would be at liberty to work the remaining items of their respective programmes in the interval without interference with each other.
- The minority group would cooperate with the majority group in raising funds for constructive work.

Besides Maulana Azad, Pandit Jawaharlal Nehru also played a leading role in bringing about this compromise. Like all compromises, it did not satisfy either party fully but each felt that it had gained a useful point. The Swarajya Party was happy that the No-changers were prevented from carrying on propaganda against Council entry. The No-changers were happy because the

Swarajya Party could no longer carry on propaganda in favour of its stand and would thus lose valuable time when the elections were due.

A conference was held in Delhi on the 24th of April when leaders of the two sections of opinion met to find out a common programme. Deshbandhu Das, Pandit Motilal Nehru, Dr. Ansari Rajagopalachari, Hakim Ajmal Khan and Shrimati Sarojini Naidu held discussions for several days in an effort to place a united programme before the people. But the No-changers were not willing to yield on any point and Deshbandhu Das had to declare reluctantly that the last attempt to secure unity between the two wings of the Congress had failed. He was compelled to call on members of the Swarajya Party to launch intensive propaganda as the elections to Councils were drawing near.

Since the Swarajya Party was suggesting a change in the Congress programme, its leaders had naturally to explain their point of view. Das addressed a number of meetings in Calcutta and other parts of Bengal. The Bengal Provincial Congress Committee met at Barisal on the 13th of May where he was able to bring over the Committee to his point of view. He then undertook a countrywide tour to explain the view-point of the Swarajists. At a meeting of the All-India Congress Committee held in Bombay from the 25th to the 28th of May 1923, Deshbandhu Das was again elected chairman unanimously.

At this meeting Deshbandhu Das pointed out that there was little sign of Satyagraha or civil disobedience movement in any part of the country. In fact, the conditions for such a movement had become less favourable since the meeting of the All-India Congress Committee at Allahabad. Communal riots had broken out in various parts of the Punjab and United Provinces. It would be risky to talk in terms of Satyagraha or mass civil disobedience in a resolution moved by Purshottamdas Tandon and seconded by Pandit Jawaharlal Nehru was accepted. It said that all Congressmen "should close their ranks and present a united front. It (the Congress) therefore directs that no propaganda be carried amongst the voters in furtherance of the Gaya resolution."

This resolution marked a further advance for the Swarajya Party as it stopped propaganda against its standpoint. Voters were left free to vote in favour of candidates of their choice but the Swarajya Party was not fully satisfied as the resolution did not give Congressmen permission to seek election in the name of the Congress. Deshbandhu Das's attention was now directed towards carrying on propaganda throughout the country and convert the Congress to his point of view.

This session of the All-India Congress Committee in Bombay marked the close of a period in Congress history, Deshbandhu Das and Pandit Motilal Nehru had resigned during the session of the Gaya Congress but their resignation had not been accepted. In spite of some opposition from the middle-of-the-road Congressmen, Deshbandhu Das insisted that their resignation should be accepted and a homogeneous Working Committee set up. Accordingly, many of the old and prominent members left the Working Committee.

Deshbandhu Das continued his hurricane tour of India. He first went to Buldana to attend Maharashtra Provincial Conference. There he declared, for the first time in public, that it was a mistake not to have accepted the compromise proposal of the Viceroy in December 1921. He said that the situation had then been bungled and mismanaged and further bungling and mismanagement would follow unless the Congress adopted a new programme. He appealed to all Congressmen to support the Council entry programme so that the national demand could be pressed from within the legislatures.

Deshbandhu Das next went to Madras and addressed meetings at several towns and cities. His eloquence, earnestness and logic made a deep impression on the people. Within a month, the people of Madras had become the strongest supporters of his Council entry programme. He spoke everywhere of the need to keep the end in view and change tactics to suit changed circumstances. He pointed out the sense of depression and frustration which pervaded the country because of the failure to effect a compromise in December 1921. Those who did not wish to support the Council entry programme, he said, had not offered any alternative either. The civil disobedience movement had been called off and there was no likelihood of a new struggle being launched. In these circumstances the best policy would be to maintain the principle of non-violent non-cooperation but enter the legislatures in large numbers and press the national demand from the legislative platform. If the Government conceded, the demand, a great victory would have been won. If the Government refused, as was probable, it would raise the spirit of the people and create new enthusiasm both inside the legislatures and outside.

Deshbandhu Das argued that a mass civil disobedience movement would become feasible only if his advice was accepted. He made it clear that he had resigned from the Presidentship of the Congress on a question of principle. He would not therefore use the name of the Congress in his election campaign unless the Congress came round to his point of view. Everywhere his listeners found his logic irrefutable and his dynamism irresistible.

A report in one of the leading papers of the day gives us an idea of how Madras was affected by his speeches:

> "Madras was looking forward to Deshbandhu Das's first visit and its expectations were more than fulfilled by Deshbandhu's first speech. Misapprehensions and misunderstandings about his policy and programme were often found in various places, thanks largely to a hostile press. But Mr. Das takes the bull by the horns. He is not apologetic in tone or halting in manner or doubtful in his lead. He has sacrificed his all for the country as no one else has. He knows his programme is the only practical programme before the country. He knows the majority in the Congress is merely repeating meaningless 'mantras'. Above all he knows that, thanks to the ineffectiveness of the Congress, the bureaucracy is gaining in strength, while the people are losing. He is determined that this nation-killing process shall cease. And, to the extent to which it may be given to him, he will rouse the people and lead them on to the royal road of Swaraj from the quagmire of metaphysical disquisition and impotent hero-worship. This is the clarion call which is sounded in these speeches. He disclaims that he is either a rebel against the Congress or a prodigal son. But he

> does not mind even being called such names; for his justification is, 'Not that he loves the Congress less but that he loves the country more.' He elaborately defends his programme of Council entry and gives convincing arguments therefore. He explains how civil disobedience is impracticable in the present state of the country and how the majority party is postponing it from day to day.
>
> "Is Council entry against non-cooperation? No, it is only another form of the same activity. Is Council boycott a sacred thing not to be touched? Mr. Das answer, 'I assure you there is another thing which is more sacred than the Congress: that is the liberty of the Indian people'.

'The speech had a most telling effect on the audience and even the few who came to scoff remained to pray." In a lecture in the Deccan during this campaign Deshbandhu Das said:

> "Am I rebel? I would rather rebel against the Congress and any institution in India if I felt that the realisation of the demand of Swaraj makes it necessary. I want Swaraj. I want my liberty. I am prepared to fight. I have not been a coward at any time in my life. I am prepared to lay down my life. Begin today, test me and I shall prove if I cannot come to your standard."

Delhi Congress Session

After his Madras tour, during which many Congressmen were converted to the viewpoint of the Swarajya Party, Deshbandhu Das went to Nagpur to attend a meeting of the All-India Congress Committee. The new Working Committee of the Congress, which had been constituted in Bombay with Dr. Ansari as the chairman, offered its resignation at the Nagpur meeting. It was forced to do so because two Provincial Committees had disregarded the decision of the All-India Congress Committee and the Working Committee could do nothing about it. Pandit Jawaharlal Nehru has described this incident in his *Autobiography* thus:

> "Our resignation, was brought about by the failure of our attempt to censure Gujarat for its indiscipline. Even a short experience of party manoeuvres had been too much for me and I was quite shocked at the way some prominent Congressmen could intrigue." A new Working Committee with Konda Venkatappayya as president was elected and the meeting decided that the special session of the Congress should be held in Bombay under the presidentship of Maulana Abul Kalam Azad to review the situation and resolve the difficulties that had arisen."

The special session, however, was held not in Bombay but in, Delhi in September 1923. Dr. Ansari, who was the chairman of the reception committee, appealed for a united front. Maulana Azad reviewed the whole position and gave his decided opinion as follows:

> "After considering all aspects of the question I have come to the conclusion that it is useless for us to boycott the Councils and remain aloof. Even as a boycott of Councils was necessary for us in the last election, so, under the present circumstances, it is to our advantage to occupy as many seats as possible." The Maulana also expressed the view that conflict between Hindus and Muslims could have been avoided if the people had before them a programme of united work. He explained that non-violent, non-cooperation was based upon the universal faith that we should not cooperate with evil. But obviously such non-cooperation must not be identified with inactivity. Further, there was scope and even need for change in tactics according to changes in circumstances.

The resolution which permitted Congressmen to enter legislatures was moved by Maulana Mohammad Ali and supported by Dr. Kitchlew, Abbas Tayabji, Mrs. Sarojni Naidu and many others. Maulana Mohammad Ali declared that "by a process of soul force and by some mysterious wireless, I have been commanded by Mahatma Gandhi not to hesitate to modify the boycott programme if the interest of the country so demanded." In supporting his programme Deshbandhu Das said:

> "What are these Councils and what are these legislatures? Things of falsehood. Must we not remove them? Mahatma Gandhi intends to wreck the Reforms and I do the same thing by working from within, and the only way to do it is to make Government through Councils impossible. I will have nothing to do with those who go there for the sake of posts, who go there to get the little things they call good, crumbs from the legislative table. I abhor that I abominate that, I say that either I stand to wreck the Reforms— to wreck the monster that is drinking our lifeblood, or do not want to go there at all. I rejoice that this compromise resolution insists or principles of non-violent non-cooperation.
>
> If in a minority, I will keep these seats vacant like so many lamps of non-cooperation burning.
>
> Even if I could achieve complete victory by moving the Swarajya Party resolution making Council entry a part of the ordinary work of the Congress, I would not do it. It would be useless because a united Congress was much better than the victory I could secure."

The resolution was passed practically unanimously and when this fact was announced by Pandit Madan Mohan Malaviya, there were signs of enthusiasm and jubilation.

Now that it was agreed that Congressmen could seek election to the legislature, Deshbandhu Das and Pandit Motilal Nehru visited some of the important cities of the United Provinces. Deshbandhu Das then returned to Calcutta and made a rapid tour of the Province. He spoke everywhere in favour of his nominees and received warm response. He worked from morning till late at night and had hardly time for food or sleep.

The result of the elections in Bengal is now a matter of history. Veterans of public life were defeated by unknown men set up by Deshbandhu Das. Surendranath Banerjea, one of the pioneers of the Indian National Congress and a doyen of Indian politics, was defeated by Dr. Bidhan Chandra Roy, till then completely unknown in politics. Deshbandhu Das's own cousin S. R. Das, then Advocate-General of Bengal, was defeated by a comparatively unknown man like Satkaripati Roy. The eminent physician, Sir Nilratan Sarkar, was humbled by Bijoy Krishna Bose.

Deshbandhu Das had achieved almost the impossible. "Within barely one year he had converted the Congress to his own point of view. In the Bengal elections he had captured seats reserved for Muslims as well as general seats from some of the best known leaders of the day. He had achieved signal success but he had greatly taxed his health in the process. In addition, there was a new worry which troubled him. Some of his most ardent and loyal followers were being threatened under Regulation III of 1818.

Lord Lytton, then Governor of Bengal, invited Deshbandhu Das to form the new Ministry in Bengal. After consulting his colleagues Deshbandhu Das replied in the following terms:

"Your Excellency,

I placed before our party the position as explained by your Excellency and they have just declined to accept your Excellency's kind offer. The members of this party are pledge-bound to do everything in their power by using the legal right granted under the Reforms Act to put an end to the system of Dyarchy. This duty they cannot discharge if they accept office. The party is aware that it is possible to offer obstruction from within by accepting office, but they do not consider it honest to accept office which is under the existing system in your Excellency's gift and then turn it into an instrument of obstruction.

The awakened consciousness of the people of this country demands a change in the present system of Government and until that is done or unless there is some change in the general administration indicating a change of heart, the people of the country cannot offer willing cooperation. Under the circumstances, I regret I cannot undertake responsibility regarding the transferred departments. My party, however, wishes to place on record its appreciation of the spirit of constitutionalism which actuated you in making the offer which we feel bound not to accept.

Yours faithfully,

C. R. Das,"

The Swarajya Party thus came to be a powerful Opposition in the Bengal Legislative Council and inflicted repeated defeats upon the Government. Resolution for the release of the *detenus* and political prisoners was carried by an overwhelming majority. Three Ministries which were formed in succession were defeated and bureaucracy, in its earlier form, met its doom in Bengal.

4

At the Helm in Calcutta

Mayor of Calcutta Corporation

The Calcutta Municipal Act of 1923 was one of the major contributions of Sir Surendra Nath Banerjea to the development of local self-government in India. It widened the franchise and made the Calcutta Corporation a democratic body. Under the Act, the Calcutta Corporation was to have eighty members and five Eldermen. The Act abolished the post of the Chairman and provided instead a Mayor elected by the Councillors and Eldermen to preside over the general and special meetings of the Corporation. The executive functions of the Chairman were delegated to a Chief Executive Officer who would work under the general supervision of the Mayor.

Deshbandhu Das decided to contest the elections to the Corporation in the name of the Bengal Provincial Congress Committee. The Congress won most of the seats without contest. Where there were rival candidates Congressmen won both the general seats and the Muslim seats. It was the unanimous wish of the entire city that Deshbandhu Das should be the first Mayor of Calcutta and after some initial reluctance he agreed.

The inaugural speech of Deshbandhu Das as Mayor expressed in vivid terms his conception of civic administration. It was clear that his approach to civic life was different from his approach to Council entry. Here he was out to build and not to destroy. He laid down the following programme of work for the Corporation: free primary education, free medical relief to the poor, purer and cheaper food and milk supply, better supply of filtered water and unfiltered water, better sanitation in business and congested areas, housing for the poor, development of suburban areas, improved transport facilities and greater efficiency in administration at a cheaper cost.

In the course of his inaugural speech Deshbandhu Das also said:

> "It is the great ideal of the Indian people that they regard the poor as *Daridra Narayan*. To them God comes in the shape of the poor. The service of the poor is the service of God to the Indian mind. I shall, therefore, try to direct your activities to the service of the poor. You will have seen that in the programme which I have drawn up, most of the items deal with the poor. If the Corporation succeeds even to a very limited extent in this work it will have justified itself."

In order to ensure success in administration Deshbandhu Das chose Subhas Chandra Bose to be the Chief Executive Officer. Soon after Deshbandhu Das became Mayor there was a strike by the sweepers of the Calcutta Corporation. He called them and said that if they did not return to their work immediately he would himself, with the help of volunteers, undertake the work of scavenging. If on the other hand they come back to work unconditionally, he would take it as his own responsibility to improve their wages and redress their genuine grievances. His appeal had an immediate response and the strike was called off.

Mention may be made here of Deshbandhu Das's attempt to educate public opinion through journals expressing his point of view. In a sense, journalism was in his veins from the very outset. He was closely connected, with *New India* from 1901. *Narayan* in Bengali was a new type of literary and cultural journal. In 1922 he started a Bengali weekly to defend his point of view on Council entry.

In 1923 he promoted the Forward Publishing Company in which he had as fellow directors Pandit Motilal Nehru, Sarat Chandra Bose, Tulsi Goswami and P. D. Himatsingka. A daily paper under the name *Forward* came out on October 23, 1923. It established new standards in Indian journalism and had great influence on public opinion. Leading articles were written mostly under Das's personal direction. They were forceful but never extreme in tone or language. The journal's fair and free criticism attracted the attention of Government and people alike.

Subhas Chandra Bose was for some time in charge of the paper but when he became the Chief Executive Officer of the Calcutta Corporation, he had to give up this work. From the beginning Deshbandhu Das had laid it down that the paper must not only give political news but also have special pages devoted to art, literature, science, architecture, painting, sport, the stage and the screen. Its wide range of interests and its bold fair criticism soon made the *Forward* a power in the land.

Bengal Pact

Deshbandhu Das realised quite early in his political life that friendship and understanding between the Hindus and the Muslims were an essential condition for the attainment of India's independence. While relations between them were generally good in normal times, he noted with distress that the slightest cause often led to bitterness and conflict. He was particularly disturbed by the communal riots which occurred from time to time in the U.P., Bihar and the Punjab.

Bengal had on the whole been more fortunate but the Tala riots of 1891 and 1895 and the riots of 1912 had shown how precarious these good relations were. Deshbandhu Das remembered that in 1905 the British bureaucrats had tried to strengthen their position by playing the communities against one another. In fact Sir Bomfylde Fuller, then Lieutenant-Governor of the newly created Province of East Bengal and Assam, was reported to have openly said: "If the Hindu wife ill-treated him he would surely turn his affection to his Muslim wife." It was in the wake of such an attitude that separate electorates were for the first time introduced in the India Councils Act of 1909.

The Congress had for many years been aware of this problem . The Congress-League Pact of 1916 was intended to settle the outstanding issues between the two communities. The Congress also agreed to earmark fifty-one per cent of the seats in the Punjab Provincial Legislative Council for Muslims. The Calcutta Municipal Act of 1923 had also provided for special treatment of the Muslims for some years. It was against this background that Deshbandhu Das formulated his famous Hindu-Muslim Pact to promote permanent peace between the communities and provide a basis for joint demand and joint action.

The Pact provided that representation in the Bengal Legislative Council would be through joint electorates on the basis of population. It is also provided that special weightage would be given to Muslims if they made up their deficiency in the services and attained a proportion commensurate with their numbers. There were other provisions which dealt with matters like music before mosques and cow killing in which each community was required to refrain from any act which would hurt the feelings of the other community.

The Pact was conceived in the best of spirits but it became the nucleus of political controversy. Communal sections among the Hindus vilified Deshbandhu Das and said that he had surrendered the rights of the Hindus. Even the more moderate opinion among the Hindus held that Deshbandhu Das had gone too far in trying to win the confidence of the Muslims. The communal sections among Muslims said that the whole Pact was merely a camouflage and Deshbandhu Das was working to undermine the hold of Muslim leaders on their own community. The majority of Muslims, however, hailed this pact as a charter of their rights and almost overnight Deshbandhu Das became their unchallenged leader.

Deshbandhu Das had to fight hard in order to persuade doubters in both the communities. He pointed out that the Pact provided a basis for joint demand and joint action. Once the country became free; there would be no party to foment distrust and suspicion between the communities. They would learn to trust one another and cooperative action would become possible. Swarajya, he explained could not be attained without non-violent non-cooperation and a programme of non-violent non-cooperation could be effective only on the basis of unity action between Hindus and Muslims.

Deshbandhu Das realised that he must win the support of the Congress for his point of view. His impassioned appeal for national unity and independence enabled him to sway the Bengal Provincial Congress Committee which accepted the Pact. His next move was to secure the support of the All-India Congress Committee. The matter was discussed in the Congress where there was a move to shelve the Bengal Pact on the ground that an all-India pact was under the Committee's consideration in accordance with a resolution of the special session in Delhi. During the discussions at Cocanada some of the opponents of Deshbandhu Das went to the extent of demanding that the Bengal Pact should be set aside.

Deshbandhu Das expected some opposition but its extent surprised him. He was particularly offended by the attitude of some who wished to ignore completely whatever had been done in Bengal. In an indignant speech, he declared:

> "You may delete the Bengal Pact from the resolution but you cannot delete Bengal from the Indian National Congress. Bengal demands her rights of having her suggestion considered by the National Assembly. What right has anybody to say that Bengal has to be deprived of her right? Bengal will not be deleted in this unceremonious fashion. I cannot understand tine argument of those who cry 'delete the Bengal Pact".
>
> "Is Bengal untouchable? Will you deny Bengal the right of suggestion on such a vital question? If you do, Bengal can take care of itself. You can't refuse Bengal the right to make a suggestion."

The Cocanada Congress decided that the All-India Pact Committee would come to a decision only after the Provincial Congress Committees expressed their opinion on the proposals. This satisfied Deshbandhu Das, as the Bengal Provincial Congress Committee had already adopted the Bengal Pact and this would mean that the Bengal Pact would be considered by the All-India

Pact Committee. Another important resolution of the Cocanada Congress confirmed the position of the Swarajaya Party and accorded recognition to congressmen elected to the legislatures on the Swarajya ticket.

In May 1924, a session of the Bengal Provincial Congress was held at Serajgunge. The Pact was again the subject of debate, but after Deshbandhu Das replied to the critics in a speech which lasted for almost four hours, it was accepted with acclamation. The Pact continued to be the accepted programme of the Bengal Congress during Deshbandhu Das's lifetime.

There was controversy on another resolution which was passed by the Serajgunge conference. Gopinath Saha, a young revolutionary from Bengal, shot dead a British merchant named Ernest Day under the impression that he was Sir Charles Tegart, the Commissioner of Police, Calcutta. Saha was arrested and the case against him ended with his death by hanging. The Serajgunge conference passed a resolution on the incident in the following terms:

> "The Conference, while denouncing and disassociating itself from violence and adhering to the principle of non-violence, appreciates Gopinath Saha's ideal of self-sacrifice, misguided though it is in respect of the country's best interests, and expresses its respect for his great self-sacrifice."

This resolution, particularly because of the way in which the newspapers reported it, led to a good deal of misunderstanding and some people condemned Deshbandhu Das for his support of a resolution which implied condonation of violence. The resolution was moved also at the A.I.C.C. meeting at Ahmedabad, but it was defeated in spite of Deshbandhu Das's support. Deshbandhu Das declared on the occasion that although his resolution was lost, he had gained his point in having secured Mahatma Gandhi's open admission of admiration for Gopinath Saha's self-sacrifice. After Deshbandhu Das's death, Mahatma Gandhi himself said that the difference between them over this question was really a lovers' quarrel. It is of interest that, at the Karachi session of the Congress in 1931, over which Sardar Vallabhbhai Patel presided, a much stronger resolution was passed in the presence of Mahatma Gandhi himself regarding the action of Bhagat Singh, Sukhdeo and Rajguru. Subhas Chandra Bose, a frequent critic of Mahatma Gandhi, has this to say about the Karachi resolution:

> "The circumstances at Karachi were such that the resolution had to be swallowed by people who under ordinary circumstances would not come within miles of it. So far as the Mahatma was concerned, he had to make his conscience over the action somewhat elastic."

It is to be regretted that after Deshbandhu Das's death, the Bengal Pact was repudiated by some of his own followers. In Maulana Azad's opinion, the repudiation of this Pact was one of the factors which led to increasing discord between Hindus and Muslims culminating in the partition of the country. It is futile to speculate on the 'might-have-beens' of history, but it can be said with confidence that if Deshbandhu Das had lived, united India would in all likelihood have attained freedom long before 1947.

Tarakeswar Satyagraha

Before resuming the story of political events, it might be appropriate here to refer to what came to be known as the Tarakeswar affair. Tarakeswar was and still is a famous place of pilgrimage in Bengal. The earlier 'mahants' were men of piety but some of the latter 'mahants' did not enjoy a good reputation with the public. About a hundred years ago, Madhab Giri, who was the 'mahant in 1872, became involved in a murder case. A young girl called Elokeshi suffered death at the hands of her husband, Nabin; but many people believed that Madhab Giri was the real culprit. Abuse of privilege by 'mahants' continued and Swami Satyananda and Swami Viswananda of the Mahavir Dal started a movement to stop these practices.

Satis Giri, who was the 'mahant' in the early twenties, was too powerful for these reformists who turned to Deshbandhu Das for help.

Deshbandhu Das had himself been disturbed by some of the things he had heard about Tarakeswar. He therefore declared that he would take charge of the movement to save the honour of Bengal. At his bidding, hundreds of young men came forward to face the hardship of a struggle and suffered imprisonment. Deshbandhu Das's own son was one of the first volunteers to be arrested. The movement continued unabated. Lord Lytton, the Governor, referred to the Tarakeswar movement as a colossal hoax in a speech in Serampur. Deshbandhu Das, however, persisted in the course of action and soon proved that the movement was not a hoax but genuine.

Deshbundhu Das prepared himself for all eventualities. Even tarakeswar satyagraha when the police opened fire on the volunteers, he did not call off the movement. In fact the support given by the police to the 'mahant' made the volunteers more determined than ever, and young men came forward in their hundreds to make the movement a success. At last the 'mahant' realised that he could not continue, and he resigned. One of his disciples, Prabhat Giri became 'mahant' and he agreed to abide by the Congress decision. It was settled that the whole income of the endowments belonging to Tarakeswar as well as the contributions collected from the pilgrims would be spent in the service of the pilgrims. Any remainder would be spent in various nation-building activities.

At this stage the Brahmin Sabha of Bengal intervened to prevent the fulfilment of the agreement. A civil suit was filed at the Hooghly court, with the result that the *status quo* was maintained. The judgement was passed long after Deshbandhu Das's death, but the Bengal Provincial Congress Committee adopted a resolution condemning the intervention of the Brahmin Sabha.

Belgaum Congress

Deshbandhu Das had won his first point in securing sanction for his programme of contesting elections. The result was the formation of the Swarajya Party which virtually put an end to Dyarchy in Bengal. Deshbandhu Das did not at first stand for election himself, but one of his principal lieutenants, B. N. Sashmal, was returned from two places, Diamond Harbour and Midnapore. Sashmal resigned one of his seats and Deshbandhu Das was persuaded to stand. He thus became the first leader of the Swarajya Party in the Bengal Legislative Council.

The Party also achieved great success in the Central Legislative Assembly under the leadership of Pandit Motilal Nehru. One of its first triumphs was to elect Vithalbhai Patel as the President of the Assembly. Other successes followed. Unpopular measures were defeated and resolutions supporting nation-building activities carried by a clear majority.

The Swarajya Party met at Lucknow on the 9th of January 1924 under the presidentship of Deshbandhu Das and formulated the national demands to be presented in the Indian Legislative Assembly by the Leader of the Party. The demands were:

- All political prisoners and *detenus* must be released;
- All repressive laws must be repealed; and
- A national convention must be summoned to decide the principles for the future Constitution of India. In moving these demands, Pandit Motilal Nehru declared in the Assembly:

> "Our party cannot be dismissed as wreckers. We have come here to offer our cooperation. If the Government would revive this cooperation, they would find that the Swarajists were their men. If not, the Swarajists would stand on their rights and continue to non-cooperate, they would oppose the Budget and adopt the policy of wholesale obstruction."

Sir Malcolm Hailey, who was then Home Member, countered this move by saying that the Government was prepared to consider these demands in successive stages. He pointed out that the demands could not be accepted in the existing situation as they were not consistent with the special privileges reserved to the Viceroy under the Government of India Act of 1919. The Swarajya Party did not accept his contention and in this it had the support of the Nationalists and the independents in the Assembly. A pact was drawn up between the Swarajists and other members of the Assembly who accepted in full the three demands formulated by the Swarajya Party.

While feeling gratified at the capture of the legislature by the Swarajya Party, Deshbandhu Das felt that the Council entry programme ought to be accepted as the principal programme of the Congress as a whole. Mahatma Gandhi had been released in the meantime after an operation for appendicitis. He resumed editorship of his journal *Young India* and it soon became clear that he was as definitely in favour of boycott of legislatures as before.

Deshbandhu Das and Pandit Motilal Nehru met him at Juhu on the 18th of May 1924 to discuss the future programme of work. The two Swarajist leaders did not feel very happy after the discussions because Mahatma Gandhi had maintained his disapproval of the resolution on Council entry passed at the Delhi and the Cocanada sessions of the Congress.

Mahatma Gandhi later issued a statement which showed that the differences between the two attitudes were fundamental. The Mahatma believed that Council entry destroyed non-cooperation. He conceded, however, that Congressmen need not obstruct the Swarajists. The right programme for Congressmen was constructive work in the field of Khadi, boycott of foreign cloth, prohibition and economy in expenditure.

Deshbandhu Das and Pandit Motilal Nehru also issued a joint statement which put forth their reasons for not accepting Mahatma Gandhi's viewpoint on Council boycott. They maintained Council entry was another form of non-cooperation, because Swarajists were entering Councils only to create a constitutional deadlock.

The two leaders gave their full endorsement to the constructive programme of Mahatma Gandhi and to the concept of civil disobedience as enunciated by the Mahatma.

Their statement went on to say:

> "The moment we find that it is impossible to meet the selfish obstinacy of the bureaucracy without civil disobedience, we shall retire from the legislative bodies and take time to prepare the country for civil disobedience. If by that time the country has not already become prepared for civil disobedience, we will then unreservedly place ourselves under the

guidance of Mahatma Gandhi and work through the Congress organisation under his banner in order that we may unitedly work out a substantial programme of civil disobedience."

While he was at Juhu, Deshbandhu Das heard about the sudden death of Sir Ashutosh Mookerjee. He was deeply grieved and on his return to Calcutta he delivered a valedictory address from the Mayoral chair paying a great tribute to Sir Ashutosh for his services.

The next meeting of the All-India Congress Committee was held at Ahmedabad on the 27th of June 1924.

Mahatma Gandhi insisted on his programme of the five-fold boycott of titles, legislature, Schools and colleges, law courts and foreign cloth. He declared emphatically that those who did not accept the five-fold boycott and had any doubts about the principles of truth and non-violence should not remain on the Congress executive.

A resolution was also moved that elected members of all Congress organisations must spin on the Charkha every day and send every month at least 2,000 yards of yarn spun by them to the All-India Khadi Board. The resolution had a penalty clause which stated that a member who failed to carry either of these conditions would be deemed to have resigned from his office.

Pandit Motilal Nehru challenged the resolution on a point of order. He argued that members who had enlisted themselves after signing the Congress creed could not lose their seats by a condition newly introduced. He also challenged the provision which took away from ex-Presidents of the Congress their right to be *ex-officio members* of the All-India Congress Committee.

Maulana Mohammad Ali who was then President did not give a ruling on the point of order but put it to the vote. Pandit Motilal Nehru's contention was defeated by 83 to 67. He announced that Swarajists would leave in a body but would soon return in larger numbers and reverse the decision.

After the Swarajist members had left, the substantive resolution was put to vote. The penalty clause was accepted but only by

67 to 37. Mahatma Gandhi felt that it was in reality a defeat, for if these 37 votes were added to those of the 67 Swarajists who had walked out, the clause would have been rejected. He therefore himself pressed that the penalty clause be deleted.

There was a conference in the afternoon in which Mahatma Gandhi met Deshbandhu Das and Pandit Motilal Nehru. After these discussions it was agreed that the five-fold boycott programme would be placed before the open session, but after amending the reference to Council boycott to bring it in line with the resolutions passed at the Delhi and Cocanada sessions of the Congress. This compromise resolution was placed at the open meeting and the Swarajya Party was able to maintain its point of view.

A conference of the All-India Swarajya Party was held on the 16th of August 1924 in Calcutta. All the important leaders of the Party attended it. Addressing the conference Deshbandhu Das said:

> "Whatever name you may give to it—non-cooperation, responsive non-cooperation, responsive cooperation—I want to have my programme put absolutely clearly. We will not shrink from destroying any system which stands against our system. We will not shrink from telling the Government, 'Until and unless you recognise our legitimate rights we will try to destroy your system of Government. We cannot build our system without destroying your system.' Not that there is a particular in destruction, but we cannot build unless we remove, something which stands in our way."

He concluded with an appeal for the support of the Party: "I appeal to you—I make no appeal to the bureaucracy or to the Secretary of State—I appeal to you: stand fast by the principle which the Swarajists have put forward before the country. We will act, but give us breathing time. Do not overwhelm us with criticism and questions. I have thought and thought about it for the last twenty years of my life and now I have devoted the rest of my life to the cause of my country. Believe in me and I tell you, God willing, I shall not die before I have accomplished my object."

After the Ahmedabad meeting of the All-India Congress Committee, Mahatma Gandhi began to study anew the situation in the country. He was surprised and shocked when there were communal riots in various towns like Delhi. Shahjahanpur, Lucknow, Allahabad, Jabalpur and Nagpur. The worst disturbances were in the Mopla districts of Malabar where some four thousand people had to abandon their homes.

A committee was formed with Mahatma Gandhi and Maulana Shaukat Ali as members to investigate the causes of the disturbances. They could not agree, however, in their findings about the causes and the share of responsibility of different communities. Shaukat Ali had been one of the closest adherents of Mahatma Gandhi since 1919. He now repudiated Mahatma Gandhi's leadership as Mahatma Gandhi could not accept his views.

Mahatma Gandhi was so disturbed by the atrocious way in which many Indians had behaved that he resolved to undertake a fast for twenty-one days. This led to a conference of the leading men of India. The Anglican Metropolitan of India and some representative Britons also attended this conference which met in Delhi and came to be known as the Unity Conference. Deshbandhu Das took a leading part in the deliberations. Some of the decisions reached at the conference were: that (i) everyone should have full liberty of worship, (ii) that the Hindus must not expect that cow-slaughter could be stopped by force or legislation but only by mutual trust and consent, and (iii) that likewise the Muslims must not expect to stop the Hindu music near mosques by legislative force or order of court but by mutual consent or trust.

The conference also recommended the Constitution of Panchayats at the national as well as local levels. The Central National Panchayat had Mahatma Gandhi as its chairman and included Hakim Ajmal Khan, Lala Lajpat Rai and three other members. The Central Committee proposed measures for promoting communal unity and laid down a procedure for intervention whenever and wherever communal trouble broke out.

After the conference Deshbandhu Das left for Simla. His health was causing anxiety and he needed a change. This, however, was not to be. While in Simla he heard of the arrest of Subhas Chandra Bose and many of his other... lieutenants. He immediately returned to Calcutta. At a meeting of the Corporation, he said:

> "Every honest man in the country is bound to say I. love my country—I love my freedom, I will have the right to manage my own affairs."
>
> "If that is a crime. I plead guilty to that charge. If that is a crime. I am willing to he hanged for that rather than shirk my duty which I feel to be the only duty of every Indian of the present day.
>
> "All that I want to say is that Subhas is no more a revolutionary than I am. Why have they not arrested me? I should like to know why? If love of country is a crime, I am a criminal. If Subhas is a criminal, I am a criminal. Not only the Chief Executive Officer of this Corporation but the Mayor of the Corporation is equally guilty,
>
> "I can only say that these Ordinances are directed against us only to put down lawful organisations.
>
> "Subhas Bose's arrest under Regulation III is sheer brute force on the part of the bureaucracy. One fine morning he went out to do his work as the Chief Executive Officer of the Corporation. He returned home and found the Police force in his house. Not one charge has been made against him. No explanation was asked from him. Not one reason was urged before him but he was simply told, 'We have got the brute force 'and we shall drag you to imprisonment.' Is this law? Is this justice?"

As soon as he reached Calcutta, Deshbandhu Das wired to Mahatma Gandhi, Pandit Motilal Nehru, Mrs. Sarojini Naidu and other leaders about this new attack by the bureaucracy. Nearly all the prominent leaders of India came to Calcutta and there was widespread condemnation of the repressive measures throughout India. Bengal reacted strongly and over a hundred and fifty thousand people attended a meeting which was held on the 31st of October, to protest against Government's action. Mahatma Gandhi, Pandit Motilal Nehru and others came in the first week of November and joined Deshbandhu Das. Mahatma Gandhi was now convinced that it was the Swarajya Party's success in the Bengal Legislative Council and the Calcutta Corporation which made the bureaucracy resort to such violent measures. The Government was anxious to defeat the Swarajya Party's programme by imprisoning its best workers.

The country's leaders realised that they must resolve their differences and prepare an agreed programme of struggle. Mahatma Gandhi, Deshbandhu Das and Pandit Motilal Nehru issued a joint statement in which they pointed to the success of the Swarajists in the legislatures, specially in. Bengal and in the Centre, and demanded that the programme of the Swarajya Party should now become the main programme of the Congress. Among other things they declared that (1) the programme of non-cooperation should be suspended as the national programme except in respect of refusal to use foreign cloth; (2) the constructive programme should be prosecuted by all sections; (3) the Swarajya Party should, *cm* behalf of the Congress, carry on their work in the Councils, and (4) Congress members would have to send 2,000 yards of handspun yarn instead of 4,000 as annual subscription.

It is evidence of Mahatma Gandhi's open mind and political sagacity that he was now willing to abandon his own programme of boycott *of* legislatures and accept Council entry as the main political programme of the Congress. The All-India Congress Committee which met on the 23rd of November 1924 in Bombay gave its full support to the joint statement issued by the three leaders.

Deshbandhu Das now turned his whole energies to constructive work in the villages and issued the following appeal:

> "The Executive Council of the Swarajya Party of Bengal has decided to devote the first week of December exclusively to work for Swaraj in Calcutta and Howrah. There will be meetings explaining the present situation, the repressive policy of the bureaucracy culminating in the recent arrests, the revival of

Regulation III and the promulgation of the new Ordinance, the results achieved at the All-Party Conference now holding its sessions in Bombay, the future programme of the Swarajya Party in the Council and outside it and collection of funds. It is needless for me to impress on my countrymen the supreme necessity of presenting a united front to the Government at the present moment and in that view of mobilising our resources in men and money. I appeal to all to help us with whatever resources they can spare for the country's work. Our volunteers with sealed boxes will make house-to-house collection. I expect that every citizen of Calcutta and Howrah will pay at least one rupee. A Swarajya Week will be held also for the 'Mofussil the date of which will be announced shortly. I appeal to you to work in the villages where, as I have always believed, lies our salvation."

As already mentioned, Deshbandhu Das had not been feeling well when the arrest of his chief lieutenants compelled him to cut short his holiday at Simla and return to Calcutta. The incessant toil which he undertook during the three succeeding weeks in organising the country and raising a hundred thousand rupees for the Swarajya Fund told heavily on his health and he fell seriously ill. He nevertheless could not remain absent from the next session of the Congress due to be held at Belgaum under Mahatma Gandhi's presidentship, as the programme of Council entry would come up before it.

There was also a complete reconciliation between Mahatma Gandhi and Deshbandhu Das at Belgaum. Deshbandhu Das said:

"I knew that lasting unity would be achieved when Mahatma Gandhi would be released and I was right. The bureaucracy challenged India in Bengal, and what was the reply to the challenge? Boycott of foreign cloth. The bureaucracy expected a feast of quarrels at Belgaum, but Mahatma has disappointed it. I fully believe in constructive programme, but I also believe in giving the enemy no quarter in uprooting its

> foundation wherever possible. Councils, I know, will not bring Swaraj, but they impede our progress and must be destroyed. Local bodies should be captured to build up our lives. Council work is not the permanent point of activity with the Swarajists. We should come out after destroying them."

The Belgaum Congress was a personal triumph for Deshbandhu Das and Pandit Motilal Nehru as it accepted their programme of capturing the legislatures as the main political programme of the Congress. Only the boycott of foreign cloth remained but other, boycotts were withdrawn. Thus, before the end of the year, the Swarajya Party had again become the strongest force within the Congress organisation. This was the last session of the Congress which Deshbandhu Das attended.

Last Leg of the Political Journey

After he gave up his practice, Deshbandhu Das changed overnight from one of the richest men of Calcutta to one of the poorest. His responsibilities, however, remained, for he had to support a large number of workers who looked up to him. The only asset he now had was his palatial house at Bhowanipore. Even this had been pledged in order to meet the many demands of his workers. Some of his friends tried to save the house for the family but Deshbandhu Das decided that even this should be given as a gift to the nation. The property was evaluated at Rs. 326,000 but there were liabilities which amounted to over a hundred thousand rupees. Deshbandhu Das decided that after the liabilities had been cleared, the balance should be used to create a trust devoted to the following purposes:

- Education,
- Building a temple and installing a deity and arrangements for its daily worship,
- Religious education of Hindu boys,
- Establishment of Matrimandir (orphanage for destitute children, including a home for helpless girls of all communities), and
- Helping the poor and the distressed.

As trustees, Deshbandhu Das selected Tulsi Chandra Goswami, Nirmal Chandra Chander, Nalini R. Sarkar, Satya Mohan Ghosal and Dr. Bidhan Chandra Roy. After Deshbandhu's death, two more trustees were added, Sir Nilratan Sarkar and S. R. Das. Mahatma Gandhi also intervened and in consultation with the trustees created a Deshbandhu Memorial Fund which amounted to over Rs. 800,000. Many of the creditors willingly gave up their claims and the house of Deshbandhu Das was used by the trustees for starting a hospital for women known as Chittaranjan Seva Sadan. It is today a magnificent institution where hundreds of women are treated free or at concessional rates. A good deal of the credit for its success belongs to Dr. B. C. Roy, the late Chief Minister of West Bengal.

Deshbandhu Das returned from Belgaum with fever. He was suffering from bilious colic, but he decided, nevertheless, to attend the session of the Council which was going to discuss the Bengal Ordinance. On the morning of the 7th of January 1925, Deshbandhu Das declared from his sick bed: "The Black Bill is coming up for discussion. I must attend at any cost and oppose it." He was carried to the Council Chamber in a stretcher and had Dr. B. C. Roy and Dr. J. M. Das Gupta, also members of the Council, by his side as medical attendants. The Bill was defeated and Deshbandhu Das recovered in spirit and also partly in health. The doctors advised him complete rest for at least three months and he left Calcutta for Patna on the 27th of January.

From Patna, Deshbandhu Das went to Rajgir but he continued to suffer from insomnia and weakness. A homoeopathic physician of Patna started treating him at this stage and he obtained some relief. He had, however, to return to Calcutta to attend the March session of the Legislative Council when the question of a Ministry for the Province was again discussed. It was during this session that he delivered his last speech in the Bengal Legislative Council.

After meeting the arguments in favour of the Ministry in his characteristic way, Deshbandhu Das said:

> "We want a living Constitution, a free Constitution, a Constitution in which honourable men can work with honourable friends, and we say that the whole field is at present covered with a sham Constitution.

'The effect of killing Dyarchy will enable us to build the beautiful mansion to which I have referred.

"It is not very difficult to understand that if you feel that a Government must mean a government by the people, for the people and for the good of the people, the Ministers under the present system will serve no purpose.

"I now venture to think that no Government in the world— Conservative or Labour or Liberal—no Government in the world can ever dispute the will of a great country like India." For the third time, the Bengal Ministers were refused their salaries on Monday the 23rd of March 1925. Thus ended Dyarchy in Bengal and it was not revived during Deshbandhu Das's lifetime. *The Statesman* of Calcutta referred to him as "India's genius, servant of chaos, whose spiritual house was Moscow, the general headquarters of the forces of hate".

His success in bringing Dyarchy to an end in Bengal seemed to give Deshbandhu Das a new vigour and energy. His thoughts now turned towards removing the economic bondage in which the country was held by British interests. In a speech he delivered about this time he favoured the establishment of a National Bank with three hundred million of rupees with which the condition of the cultivators could be improved. Deshbandhu Das was interested in business from the beginning. While at the Bar, he contributed a large sum towards the Indian Navigation Company. He also took great interest in the Jessore Jhinaidah Light Railway Company. He used to say: 'The political programme would better be looked to by Subhas, Tulsi and others and I shall devote myself to remove the economic slavery of the people."

Another development which seemed encouraging to Deshbandhu Das was an attempt by some British citizens of Calcutta to bring about a settlement between the Government and the people. Mr. Thorn and an English lady who was an admirer of Ramakrishna and Vivekananda brought about a meeting between Deshbandhu Das and Lord Lytton. The Ministers' salaries had been refused and Dyarchy could no longer function. On the other hand, there were sporadic outbursts of violence. Terrorist activities flourished against a background of imprisonment, internment and oppression by the police. Deshbandhu Das was anxious for an early settlement of the Indian political problem as he wanted to utilise the machinery of Government in the service of the people. Besides, he believed that "nonviolence may, but violence will never bring about Swaraj."

The Government was also anxious to bring about an improvement of the situation. In view of all these considerations, Deshbandhu Das readily agreed to Lord Lytton's request that he should make a public statement condemning violence as an instrument of political action.

On the 29th of March 1925 Deshbandhu Das issued the following manifesto:

> "I have made *it* clear and I do it once again that I am opposed to the principle of political assassination and violence in any shape or form. It is absolutely abhorrent to me and to my Party. I consider it an obstacle to our political progress. It is also opposed to our religious teachings. As a question of practical politics, I feel certain that if violence is to take root in the political life of our country it will be the end of our *Swaraj* for all time to come. I am therefore eager that this evil should not grow any further and that this method should cease as a political weapon in my country.
>
> "I have also made it clear and I again make it clear that I am equally opposed to and equally abhor any form of repression by the Government. Repression will never stop political 'assassination and will only encourage it and give life to it.
>
> "We are determined to secure *Swaraj* and political emancipation of India on terms of equality and honourable partnership in the Empire.
>
> "The fight may be long, the struggle for it may be arduous, but we are determined to fight to the last.

'To the young sons of Bengal I say, fight for your battle for *Swaraj* but fight it clean. Let there be no stain upon the justness of our cause. Fight hard and incessantly. Press onward and disarm all obstruction and win Swaraj.

'To the Europeans I say, don't misunderstand us. Lay aside your unjust suspicion. Do not support the Government in its repression and thus help unconsciously though necessarily to instal the method of violence as a permanent fixture in our political life."

Lord Birkenhead, who was then Secretary of State for India, responded to this gesture immediately. In the course of a debate on the Bengal Ordinance in the House of Lords, he declared that he was willing to lay aside all suspicions from his mind. He appealed to Indian citizens to move forward on the lines of Deshbandhu's appeal and cooperate with the Government in bringing to an end violence and terror in political life.

The Last Testament

Deshbandhu Das replied thus in his speech at Patna on April 3:

"Lord Birkenhead's position is frank 'and courageous. I am glad his Lordship is prepared to lay aside undue suspicion and watch events.

"This itself is a declaration of no mean significance. "I have made my position quite clear in my Gaya speech in 1922. I am not only very willing but anxious to carry on an active programme against evil which is a standing menace to the establishment of *Swaraj*, but all my efforts are bound to be ineffective unless a favourable atmosphere is created by the Government.

'The Bengal Ordinance has empowered persons in authority to usurp the functions of Courts of Law and exercise wide and arbitrary powers of constraint.

"Bacon, once Lord Chancellor of England, said "the surest way to prevent sedition is to take away the matter of them, for if there be fuel prepared, it is hard to tell whence the spark will set it on fire. The matter of sedition is of two kinds much poverty and much discontentment. I firmly believe that India's freedom can only be attained by non-violence.

"I invite Lord Birkenhead to cause a searching enquiry to be made into the causes which have brought about the revolutionary movement in India and then set about applying the proper remedy so that there may be a radical and permanent cure of the disease. It is no use treating merely the outward symptoms. The moment they find that the foundation of freedom is laid by Government, I venture to assert that the revolutionary movement will be a thing of the past. Although I think a favourable atmosphere has been created for further discussion, I am unable to cooperate with the Government in its present policy of repression.

"I have condemned both the violence of the revolutionary party and the repression of the Government, which is another form of violence. I have stated the terms on which a self-respecting people can cooperate.

"It now rests with Europeans and the Government to take the next step."

British papers like *The Times* and *The Daily Herald* welcomed this declaration and the Under Secretary of State for India stated in the House of Commons that the Government welcomed Deshbandhu Das's declaration on violence.

Soon after this, a session of the Bengal Provincial Conference was held at Faridpur on the 2nd of May 1925. The date was fixed by Deshbandhu Das after consulting Mahatma Gandhi. Whether he had a premonition or not of his approaching end, Deshbandhu Das took special care to prepare the speech he was to make at this conference. He consulted his colleagues and was glad to find that they all supported his analysis and approach. Mahatma Gandhi reached Calcutta on the 1st of May and was moved with deep emotion when he was taken to Deshbandhu's house. He knew that Deshbandhu Das had made a gift of his house to the nation and in a speech that afternoon at the Mirzapur Park Mahatma Gandhi expressed his feelings in the following words:

> "I was overwhelmed with grief when I came to the house today. That house — a beautiful mansion — no longer belongs to Deshbandhu. He has placed it in the hands of the trustees in order to divest himself of the last vestige of wealth that he possessed in this world. I could not help shedding tears when I thought of him. He has not yet been able to repair his health. With his broken-down Constitution, he has gone to Faridpur in advance. I cannot easily conceive of such stupendous sacrifice of everything one may call one's own.
>
> "Indeed the climax was reached when he made the trust for the remnant of earthly gains, but that too was not the last." Deshbandhu Das, accompanied by Basanti Devi, reached Faridpur on the 1st of May 1925. Mahatma Gandhi reached there the next morning. Both the leaders were given a tumultuous reception.

Before reading the text of his prepared speech, Deshbandhu Das addressed Mahatma Gandhi in the following words:

> "Mahatmaji, it is my proud privilege to welcome you as President of the Bengal Provincial Conference. I have been your follower from the beginning of the non-cooperation movement 'and I am still your follower and co-worker. It is not for me to sing your praise here. It is for the world and I feel sure that the world will listen to you as India is listening today. We want your inspiration and guidance. If your inspiration and message was necessary at the beginning of the non-cooperation movement, it is still more necessary today, because I do not for a moment believe that the movement has been a failure. On the contrary, I feel that we are nearer to *Swaraj* and for the work of consolidation without which Swaraj is impossible. It is impossible for India to do without your guidance today and at any time. May God guide us and inspire

us till *Swaraj* is attained and we pray for that and for your long life." The Faridpur speech was Deshbandhu's last testament to the nation and will always remain a landmark in the history of India's constitutional development. An English version of the speech is quoted in full in an Appendix but the main points may be briefly mentioned here. Deshbandhu Das declared that if the British Empire wished to dominate over India, he would resist it with his last breath and work for taking India out of the Empire. If, on the other hand, the British people recognised the right of India to lead her own life, he would gladly remain within the Commonwealth. In fact he would prefer membership of the Commonwealth as it would, in his view, be helpful for maintenance of world peace. In order to achieve such a consummation, he was willing to work for a compromise with the British Government on honourable terms. If the British Government declined this friendly offer, the country must be prepared for mass civil disobedience. As a preliminary step, emphasis must be placed on the constructive programme which had been sketched out by Mahatma Gandhi.

Deshbundhu Das also pointed out that free alliance within the Commonwealth carried with it the right of separation. No nation could live in isolation in the modern age and the idea of Commonwealth had for him a spiritual connotation. In his own words:

> "The idea of Commonwealth has a deep significance for me. I believe in world peace, in the ultimate federation of the world and I think that the great Commonwealth of the Nations of the world — a federation of diverse races, each with its distinct life, distinct civilization, its distinct moral outlook—if properly led by statesmen at the helm — is bound to make a lasting contribution to the great problem, the problem of knitting the world into the greatest

federation the mind can conceive, the federation of the human race. It must be properly led by statesmen at the helm, for the development of the idea involves apparent sacrifice on the part of the constituent nations, involves the giving up for good the Empire idea with its ugly attribute of domination. I think it is for the good of India, for the good of the Commonwealth, for the good of the world that India should strive with the Commonwealth for the freedom of all people of all countries and thus serve the cause of humanity."

About repression Deshbandhu said:

"It is a process in the consolidation of arbitrary powers. I condemn violence of the Government — for repression is the most violent form of violence — just as strongly as I condemn violence as a method of winning political liberty."

About Reforms he said:

"Nothing has been given by the Government of India Act of 1919 and I have shown it fully in my Ahmedabad speech in 1921. Evidence by persons of moderation before the Muddiman Committee also proved the uselessness of Reforms. Yet if *Swaraj* in the fullest sense is guaranteed to us at once, to come automatically in near future, and some real responsibility is transferred to the people and there is really a change of heart of the Rulers, there is no reason why we should not cooperate with the Government. I have always maintained that we should make large sacrifices in order to have the opportunity to begin our constructive work at once.

"if our offer of settlement should not meet with any response, we must go on with our national work on the lines we have pursued for the last two years so that it may be impossible for the Government to carry on the administration of the country except by the exercise of its exceptional powers."

About the weapon with which the battle of freedom is to be fought, Deshbandhu Das said:

> "I want to create the atmosphere of national civil disobedience which must be the last weapon in the hand of the people striving for freedom.. . . But civil disobedience requires a high stage of organisation, an infinite capacity for sacrifice and a real desire to subordinate personal and communal interest to the common interest of the nation. I can see little hope of India ever being ready for civil disobedience until she is prepared to work Mahatma Gandhi's constructive programme to the fullest extent.
>
> "But I see signs of reconciliation everywhere. India has a message to deliver and she is anxious to deliver it in the Council Chamber of that great Commonwealth of Nations of which I have spoken. Will British statesmen rise to the occasion? They can have peace today on terms that are honourable both to them and us.
>
> "To the people of the country I say:—You have made great sacrifices for daring to win political freedom and on you has fallen the brunt of official wrath. But the time is not yet for putting aside your political weapons. Fight hard but fight clean and when the time for settlement comes, as it is bound to come, enter the peace conference not in the spirit of arrogance but with becoming humility so that it may be said of you that you were greater in your achievement than in adversity and when you discuss the terms of settlement do not forget the larger claims of humanity in your pride of nationalism which is but a process in self-realisation, self-development and self-fulfilment and is not an end in itself.

> "I have a clear vision as to what I seek. I seek a federation of the states of India, each free to follow, as it must follow, the culture and tradition of its own people, each bound to each in the common service of all....a great federation within a great federation of free nations whose freedom is the freedom of the people, whose service is to man and whose unity is the hope of peace among the people of the earth."

[Courtesy: Mr. Hemendranath Das Gupta]

5

Significant Speeches

Meaning of Freedom

[Excerpts from the Presidential speech at the Ahmedabad session of the Congress, 1921]

I come from a city which has felt the full force of the wrath of the Government. Measures for stifling political life have been taken, as I believe, in order to coerce the people to receive his Royal Highness the Prince of Wales; but it is the imprisoned soul of Calcutta that will greet His Royal Highness on the 24th of December. I come from the struggle which has just begun in Calcutta chastened and purified and, if I have no wordily wisdom to give, I at least bring before you unbounded enthusiasm, and a resolute determination to see this struggle through.

Freedom, in the first place, does not imply absence of all restraint... In the second place, freedom does not necessarily imply absence of the idea of dependence. But though there is no necessary opposition between freedom and restraints and freedom and dependence, it must be remembered that restraint that does not deny freedom can only be little restraint. [Deshbandhu Das, who was elected President of the Ahmedabad session of the Congress, could not attend it because he was arrested a few days earlier. His address was read out by Shrimati Sarojini Naidu. Mahatma Gandhi, in an introductory speech said:]

> "Deshbandhu's intention was to give a review of the year's work and his considered opinion in detail of Non-cooperation. But sufficient appears in the printed text to enable us to know his opinion. We know it too from his emphatic and stirring messages to the country just before he was silenced. In appreciating the address the reader will be helped to know that it was prepared just before his arrest. The reader will not fail to note the marked self-restraint with which the address is prepared and also the fact that Deshbandhu believes in non-violence as his final creed. That the only use the Government has for such a man is to put him in prison is about the greatest condemnation it can pronounce upon itself."

Sanction of the people behind it; and dependence consistent with freedom can only be such dependence as is willingly suffered by the people for its own protection.

What is then freedom? It is impossible to define the term; but one may describe it as that state, that condition, which makes it possible for a nation to realise its own individuality and to evolve its own destiny. The history of mankind is full of stirring stories as to how nations have struck for freedom in order to keep their nationalism and their individuality inviolate and untarnished. To take only modern instances, one may refer to Finland and Poland, Ireland, Egypt and India. Each of these nations has offered a determined resistance to the imposition of a foreign culture upon it.

We stand then for freedom, because we claim the right to develop our own individuality and evolve our own destiny along our own lines, unembarrassed by what Western Civilization has to teach us and unhampered by the institutions which the West has imposed on us. But here a voice interrupts me, the voice of Rabindranath, the poet of India. He says, "The Western culture is standing at our door; must we be so inhospitable as to turn it away or ought we not to acknowledge that in the union of the cultures of the East and the West is the salvation of the world?" I admit that if Indian nationalism has to live, it cannot afford to isolate itself from other nations, but I have two observations to make on the criticism of Rabindranath: first, we must have a house of our own before we can receive a guest; and, secondly, Indian culture must discover itself before it can be ready to assimilate Western culture. In my opinion, there can be no true assimilation before freedom comes, although there may be, as there has been, a slavish imitation. The cultural conquest of India is all but complete; it was the inevitable result of her political conquest. India must resist it. She must vibrate with national life and then we may talk of the union of the two civilizations.

I must dispose of another objection, this time, of my Moderate friends. "You concede," I hear them say, "that freedom is not an end in itself but a means to an end, the end being control; why not work out your destiny within the British Empire? My answer is that so long as India occupies the position of a dependency in the British Empire, the task cannot be undertaken. Go into the villages, the heart of India, and see the life that is lived by the average Indian. They are sturdy men and fearless men, they are men of whom any country could be proud; but the degradation that must inevitably follow subjection is writ large on their brow and their lot is made up of caste troubles petty squabbles, and endless pursuit of litigation for litigation's sake. Where are now the institutions that made them self-dependent and self-contained? Where is the life that enabled them to earn their livelihood and yet left them free to worship the God of their fathers?. ..I think that we should solemnly declare, in open Congress, that Freedom is inherent in every nation and that India has and possesses the right to develop her own individuality and to evolve her own destiny unhampered by what the British Parliament has decided or may decide for us. I think that we should recognise that any power that in any way hampers or embarrasses the self-realisation and self-fulfilment of the Indian nation is an enemy of India and must, as such, be resisted. I am willing to cooperate with England but on one condition only, that she recognises this inherent right of India. That recognition you will not find anywhere in the Government of India Act, and I, for one, will not be a party to the perpetuation of British domination in India. But my Moderate friends tell me that though the freedom of the Indian people, in the sense in which I understand the term, has not been recognised in the Act of Parliament, still, if we work the Reforms, it will not be in the power of Parliament to deny us freedom. I do not doubt the wisdom of my friends nor deny their patriotism; but the question, in my opinion is entirely irrelevant. My position is this, that however willing I may be to enter into a compromise with the English Government in matters of detail, and I am willing to make great sacrifices, I will not enter into any compromise on the question which I hold to be fundamental. Freedom is my birthright, and I demand a recognition of that right, not by instalments nor in compartments, but whole and entire. I do not doubt that victory will be on our side, but supposing we fail; we would at least have preserved inviolate our national self-respect and dignity. We would at any rate have repudiated the insult on which the Government of India Act is based. The difference between the Indian National Congress and the Ministers who are working the Reform Act seems to me to be fundamental, in that it has its eye fixed on the ultimate and would reject as essentially false anything that does not recognise the freedom of the Indian people, whereas the Ministers have their eyes fixed on the departments of which they are in charge, and hope to attain freedom through the successful working of those departments.

This then, is the scheme which is being worked by the Ministers, and we have been solemnly assured by the Moderates that the beginning of Swaraj is to be found in the scheme. Much as I would like to end all unnecessary conflict, I cannot recommend to you the acceptance of the Act as a basis for cooperation with the Government. I will not purchase peace with dishonour, and so long as the Preamble to the Government of India Act stands and our right, our inherent right, to regulate our own affairs, develop our own individuality and evolve our own destiny is not recognised, I decline to consider any terms of peace.

The only other method of warfare open to us is Non-cooperation; and that is the programme which we adopted at two successive Congresses. We are devoted to the doctrine of Non-cooperation, and you will not require me to discuss with you its ethics.

This is the essence of the doctrine of nationalism tor which men have been ready to lay down their lives. Nationalism is not an aggressive assertion of its individuality, distinct and separate from the other nations, but it is a yearning for self-fulfilment and self-determination and self-realisation as a part of the scheme of the universal humanity by which alone humanity can fulfil itself, determine itself and realise itself. Non-cooperation, therefore, though it does not refuse cooperation with the English because they are English, will refuse to cooperate with any power or institution which embarrasses in any way the growth of the individuality of the Indian nation or hampers its self-fulfilment. Non-cooperation again does not reject Western culture because it is Western culture. But it recognises that there must be rejection in order that there may be whole-hearted acceptance.

What then is non-cooperation? I cannot do better than quote the eloquent words of Mr. Stokes: "It is the refusal to be a party to preventable evil; it is the refusal to accept or have any part in injustice; it is the refusal to acquiesce in wrongs that can be righted, or to submit to a state of affairs which is manifestly inconsistent with the dictates of righteousness. And as a consequence it is the refusal to work with those who on grounds of interest or expediency insist upon committing or perpetuating wrong."

But it is argued that the whole doctrine is a doctrine of negation, a doctrine of despair. I agree that in form the doctrine is one of negation, but I maintain that in substance it is one of affirmation. We break in order to build; we destroy in order to construct; we reject in order to accept. This is the whole history of human endeavours. If subjection be an evil, then we are bound to non-cooperate with every agency that seeks to perpetuate our subjection. That is a negation; but it affirms our determination to be free, to win our liberty at any cost nor do I agree that the, doctrine is one of despair. It is a doctrine of hope and of confidence and of unbounded faith in its efficacy.

One has only to look at the faces of the sufferers as they are led to prison to realise that victory is already ours. It is not for nothing that Mohammed Ali and Shaukat Ali, courageous and resourceful, have lived and suffered; it is not for nothing that Lajpat Rai, one of the bravest of spirits that ever faced the sun, flung the order of the bureaucracy in its face, and marched boldly into the prison that awaited him.

This, then, is the philosophy on which the non-cooperation movement is based: to defy with absolute constancy the hostile powers that would hamper in any way our growth and self-fulfilment as a nation, to keep its evil always in view, not hating it, but recognising the evil as an evil and refusing no pain that power can invent.

The fact that disturbances have taken place is no argument against the essential truth of our movement. We must meet the situation with courage and devise means to prevent the recurrence of those disturbances; but I cannot and I will not advise you to stay your hand from the non-cooperation movement. The fact that India has remained calm in spite of the recent arrests shows that the Bombay lesson has gone home. The recent manifestation of courage, endurance and remarkable self-control has in my opinion demonstrated the efficacy and the necessity of non-violent non-cooperation and nothing can stop our onward march if the same spirit is still further developed and retained to the end.

Lord Reading is obviously in error in suggesting, as he has done, that the arrests now being made in Calcutta and in other parts of India are under the ordinary criminal law of the land. Rightly or wrongly, the Congress has adopted the policy of non-cooperation as the only legitimate political weapon available for its use. That is not breaking the law. Rightly or wrongly, the Congress has decided to boycott foreign goods and especially foreign cloth. That is not breaking the law. Rightly or wrongly, the Congress has decided to boycott the visit of His Royal Highness the Prince of Wales. That is not breaking the law. Now, in what way is the Congress to carry on its work except through the voluntary organisations which you have proclaimed unlawful under the Indian Criminal Law Amendment Act? In striking at these voluntary organisations, you strike at the Congress propaganda which, you are bound to admit, is not unlawful. Why should it puzzle Your Excellency, assuming you credit us with the same amount of patriotism which you have, that we have solemnly resolved to disobey your orders and court imprisonment? I assert that it is you who have broken the law and not we. You have transgressed the law which secures to every subject freedom of speech and action, so long as the speech and the action do not offend against the ordinary criminal law of the land. You have transgressed the law which secures to the subject the unrestricted right to hold meetings, so long as these meetings do not degenerate into unlawful assemblies. These are the common law rights of the subject which you have transgressed, and I would remind Your Excellency that it is on the due observance of these elementary rights that the allegiance of the subject depends.

But then, it is said that these associations interfere with the administration of the law and order. If they do, then the ordinary criminal law is there, and it ought to be sufficient. I have heard of no instance of violence in Calcutta; certainly none was reported to the police. Charges of violence can be investigated, and therefore, they were not made.

But charges of threat and intimidation are easy to make because they cannot be investigated. I would ask the authorities one question: "Was any case of threat or intimidation reported to the police? Has the local Government found, on enquiry, that quite apart from general allegations which can easily be made, there were specific cases of threat or intimidation practised by the non-cooperators on the loyalists' of Calcutta. An English journalist, signing himself as "Nominis Umbra", gave as his opinion to an English paper in Calcutta (Now, Kolkata) that the 'hartal' was willingly acquiesced in by the people. We read in "A Ditcher's Diary" in *Capital* of the 24th November last: "The people surrendered at discretion, but it was impossible for a careful observer not to see that not only were they, for the most part, willing victims of new zoolum, but also that they exulted in the discomfiture of the Sarkar." If that be so, then what case is there for the declaration under Section 16 of the Indian Criminal Law Amendment Act? Was the position in Calcutta on the 17th of November last worse than the position in England when a big strike is in progress? And is it suggested that there resides any power in the Cabinet of England to put down a strike and prevent picketing? No gentlemen, the real object of the application of the Indian Criminal Law Amendment Act is not to protect society against the threats and intimidation of the non-cooperators, but to crush the Congress and the non-cooperation movement. It is to such threat that you have to return an answer.

There is another object which the Government has in view; it is to make by threat, intimidation and coercion, the visit of His Royal Highness the Prince of Wales to Calcutta a success. On your behalf I would respectfully lay before His Royal Highness our wishes of goodwill to him personally. There is no quarrel between us and the Royal House of England; but he comes here as the ambassador of a Power with which we have decided not to cooperate; as such we cannot receive him. Also, we are in no mood to take part in any rejoicing. We are fighting for our national existence, for the recognition of our elementary rights freely to live our own life and evolve our own destiny according to our rights. It would be sheer hypocrisy on our part to extend a national welcome to the ambassador of the Power that would deny us our elementary rights. There is in the refusal to extend a national welcome to His Royal Highness, no disrespect either to him or to the Royal House of England. There is only a determination not to cooperate with the bureaucracy.

Swaraj and Dominion Status

[English Version of the Presidential Address at the Bengal Provincial Conference, Faridpur, May 1925]

Again and again has India asked: "Which way lies salvation?" In the dim past it was the obstinate questioning of the individual soul weary of shadows and seeking for Reality. In the living present it is the tortured cry of the soul of India: "Which way lies salvation?"

Let me put this question to you again so that we may obtain a clear vision as to what it is that we must accomplish.

As with the individual, so with the nation, the question is to find out the meaning of deliverance from bondage and, let me add, sin. It is a sin of those who forge the fetters of bondage; it is also a sin of those who allow the fetters to be forged.

Many ideas have been presented—Self-Government, Home Rule, Independence and Swaraj—but these are all names unless the full implications are vividly realised, and in the process of such realisation must come a consideration of the method of attaining the object in view.

There are those who declare in favour of peaceful and legitimate methods. There are others who claim that without the use of force or violence *Swaraj* is impossible of attainment.

I desire to offer only a few suggestions to help you in deciding these momentous questions. Let the Bengal Provincial Conference declare, in no uncertain voice, what the national ideal of freedom is, and what the method is that it calls upon the country to adopt for the fulfilment of that ideal.

Swaraj and Independence

Independence, to my mind, is a narrower ideal than Swaraj. It implies, it is true, the negative of dependence; but by itself it gives us no positive ideal. I do not for a moment suggest that independence is not consistent with Swaraj. But what is necessary is not mere independence, but the establishment of Swaraj. India may be independent tomorrow in the sense that the British people may leave us to our destiny but that will not necessarily give us what I understand by Swaraj. As I pointed out in my presidential address at Gaya, India presents an interesting but a complicated problem of consolidating the many apparently conflicting elements which go to make up the Indian people. This work of consolidation is a long process, may even be a weary process; but without this no *Swaraj* is possible. Herein lies the great wisdom of Mahatma Gandhi's constructive programme. It is unnecessary for me here to discuss that programme, as we are all privileged today to hear his message from his own lips. With that programme I entirely agree and I cannot but strongly urge upon my countrymen to give it not merely intellectual assent, but practical support, by working it out to the fullest extent.

Independence, in the second place, does not give you that idea of order which is the essence of Swaraj. The work of consolidation which I have mentioned means the establishment of that order. But let it be clearly understood that what is sought to be established must be consistent with the genius, the temperament and the traditions of the Indian people. To my mind, Swaraj implies, firstly, that we must have the freedom of working out the consolidation of the diverse elements of the

Indian people; secondly, we must proceed with this work on national lines—not going back two thousand years ago, but going forward in the light and in the spirit of our national genius and temperament. For instance, when I speak of order, I mean a thing which is totally different from the idea of discipline which obtains in Europe. In Europe the foundation of society and government is discipline; and the spirit of discipline upon which everything rests is entirely military; and discipline which has made England what she is today is also of the same military type. It is not for me to decry European civilization. That is their way, and they must fulfil themselves. But our way is not their way, and we must also fulfil ourselves.

Thirdly, in the work before us, we must not be obstructed by any foreign power.

What, then, we have to fix upon as our ideal is what I call Swaraj and not mere Independence which may be the negation of Swaraj. When we are asked what our national ideal of freedom is, the only answer which is possible to give is Swaraj. I do not like either Home Rule or Self-Government. Possibly they come within what I have described as Swaraj. But my culture, somehow or other, is antagonistic to the word 'rule'—be it 'home rule' or 'foreign rule'. My objection to the word Self-Government is exactly the same. If it is defined as government by self and for self, my objection may be met, but in that case Swaraj includes all those elements.

Then comes the question whether this ideal is to be realised within the Empire or outside it. The answer which the Congress has always given is "within the Empire if the Empire will recognise our rights, and outside the Empire if it does not." We must have opportunity to live our lite—opportunity for self-realisation, self-development and self-fulfilment. The question is of living our life. If the Empire furnishes sufficient scope for the growth and development of our national life, the Empire idea is to be preferred. If, on the contrary, the Empire, like the Car of Juggernaut, crushes our life in the sweep of its imperialistic march, there will be justification for the idea of the establishment of *Swaraj* outside the Empire.

Swaraj within the Empire

Indeed, the Empire idea gives us a vivid sense of many advantages. Dominion Status today is in no sense servitude.

It is essentially an alliance, by the consent of those who form part of the Empire, for material advantages in the real spirit of cooperation. Free alliance necessarily carries with it the right of separation. Before the War a separatist tendency was growing up in several parts of the Empire, but, after the War, it is generally believed that it is only as a great Confederation that the Empire or its component parts can live. It is realised that under modern conditions no nation can live in isolation, and the Dominion Status, while it affords complete protection to each constituent composing the great Commonwealth of Nations called the British Empire, secures to each the right to realise itself, develop itself and fulfil itself, and therefore it expresses and implies all the elements of *Swaraj* which I have mentioned. To me the idea is specially attractive because of its deep spiritual significance. I believe in world peace, in the ultimate Federation of the World; and I think that the great Commonwealth of Nations called the British Empire—a federation of diverse races, each with its distinct life, distinct civilization, distinct mental outlook—if properly led by the statesmen at the helm—is bound to make lasting contribution to the great problem that awaits the statesmen, the problem of knitting the world into the greatest federation the mind can conceive—the Federation of the Human Race; but only if properly led by the statesmen at the helm—for, the development of the idea involves apparent sacrifice on the part of the constituent nations, and it certainly involves the giving up for good the Empire idea, with its ugly attribute of domination. I think it is for the good of India, for the good of the Commonwealth, for the good of the world that India should strive for freedom within the Commonwealth and so serve the cause of humanity.

Method of Violence Opposed to Indian Tradition and Culture

I now come to the question of method. In my judgement the method is always a part of the ideal. So that when we are considering the question of method, we cannot forget the larger aspect of the object, we have in view.

Viewed in this light, the method of violence is hardly in keeping with our life and culture. I am not suggesting for a moment that the history of India shows no wars nor the application of violence. Every superficial student of our history knows that it is not so. But sometimes things are forced upon our life which a critical student of our history must know how to separate from the real bent of our genius. Violence is not a part of our being as it is of Europe. That violence in Europe is checked by a system of law which, in the ultimate resort, is also based on physical force. The Indian people have always been in the habit of following traditions and customs, and so keeping themselves free from violent methods.

Our village organisations were a marvel of non-violent activities. Our institutions have always grown naturally like the unfolding of a flower. Strifes there have been of the intellect. Cravings there have been of the soul. Disputes and quarrels have always arisen, but only to be settled by peaceful arbitration. Any thing contrary, or antagonistic to this temperament is a method which is not only immoral from the highest standpoint, but is bound to fail. I have no hesitation in proclaiming my conviction that our freedom will never be won by revolutionary violence.

In the next place, apart from the special psychology of the Indian mind, how is it possible, by offering such violence, as it is possible for a subject race to offer, to contend against the highly organised governmental violence of the present day? It is no use quoting the incidents of the French and other Revolutions. Those were days when the people fought with spikes and often won. Is it conceivable that at the present moment we can overthrow any organised government of the modern type by such methods? I venture to think that any such armed revolution would be impossible today even in England.

In the next place, the application of violence cuts at the root of that consolidation without which, as I have said, the attainment of Swaraj is impossible. Violence is sure to be followed by more violence on the part of the Government, and repression may be so violent that its only effect on the Indian people would be to check their enthusiasm for Swaraj. I ask those young men who are addicted to revolutionary methods: Do they think that the people will side with them? When life and property is threatened, the inevitable result is that the people who suffer or who think they may suffer recoil from such activities. This method, therefore, is impracticable. Far be it for me to say one word against the honesty of purpose or the ardour of patriotism which these young men are capable of showing. But as I have said, the method is unsuited to our temperament: therefore the application of it is, to quote the words of Mahatma Gandhi, "waste of time and energy." I appeal to the young men of Bengal who may, even in their heart of hearts, think in favour of violent methods, to desist from such thought, and I appeal to the Bengal Provincial Conference to declare clearly and unequivocally that in its opinion freedom cannot be achieved by such methods.

Genesis of the Revolutionary Party

But if I am against the application of such methods, I feel bound to point out that it is the violence of the Government which has to a great extent helped the revolutionary movement in Bengal. I believe it is Professor Dicey who points out that for the last thirty years there has been a singular decline among modern Englishmen in their respect or reverence for law and order and he shows that this result is directly traceable to modem legislation which has had the effect of diminishing the authority of the law-courts and thereby imperilling the rule of law. In other words, violence always begets violence; and if the Government embarks on a career of lawlessness for the purpose of stifling legitimate activities, it cannot but bring into existence what Dicey calls "a zeal for lawlessness" in the subject. The history of India and particularly of Bengal supports the observation of Professor Dicey.

The revolutionary atmosphere in India has not been created all of a sudden. In this country, as elsewhere, it has passed through several stages. The first period was one of unrest brought about by the cumulative effect of a century of administration solely maintained in the interest of England and the English people. The period of unrest was further continued and strengthened when India came under the Crown in 1858. From 1858 to the end of the century covering the better part of the Victorian Era, an alien bureaucracy administered the affairs of this country in complete forgetfulness of the best interest of the Indian people. This period was principally noted for the carefully studied neglect of the real Indian interest and for the opinion of an articulate and educated people. I do not for a moment deny that the administration in the country in the later part of the Victorian Era was sometimes punctuated by acts of benevolent despotism—such as Lord Ripon's Repeal of the Vernacular Press Act, the inauguration of Local Self-Government, the Ilbert Bill and the Revision of the Indian Council Act, 1891, during Lord Lansdowne's viceroyalty. I call these acts of benevolent despotism because the underlying feature of most of them was the consolidation of the power of the bureaucracy. The only measure of real importance was local self-government, but if one carefully studies it one finds that it is not what it pretends to be. Real power was never parted with even when measures were adopted which superficially considered may be supposed to be for the good of the people. On the other side, measures like Lord Lytton's Vernacular Press Act, the contemptuous reference by Lord Dufferin to the growing *intelligentsia* of India as "a microscopic minority" and the niggardly grant for famine relief—now and again—prepared the soil upon which the revolutionary mentality of the later days was built up.

Lord Curzon, however, inaugurated the second stage, or the stage of revolutionary mentality, by the blazing indiscretions of his inglorious viceroyalty. He it was who for the first time set up the fetish of administrative "efficiency" and placed it above the requirements of the people. On the one hand, he set up this fetish; on the other, he began to flout Indian public opinion in a most persistent and obnoxious way. Circular after circular was issued to counteract and stifle national movements leading to the inauguration of the policy of repression and tyranny— repression and tyranny on the one side and the foundation of a real revolutionary mentality among a section of the Indian *intelligentsia* on the other.

After Lord Curzon the third stage was reached when the revolutionary mentality induced some youths to translate their feverish anxiety for retaliation and freedom into real revolutionary activities. During Lord Minto's viceroyalty the Government showed its mailed fist and, with the velvet gloves taken off, a reign of terror was started. A section of the young men of Bengal attempted to reply to this reign of terror by the free use of bombs and revolvers.

One notable feature of this new psychology ought not to be forgotten or lost sight of if the question has to be studied from a broader point of view. The foundation of Indian unrest and of a revolutionary mentality has no doubt been laid by the persistent flouting of the Indian people and by a policy of repression and tyranny. But one is bound to admit that the success of the Japanese over the Russians in the bloody war early in the present century and the consequent reawakening of Asia, the guerilla campaign of the Egyptian Nationalists and the activities of the Irish Republicans and the subsequent foundation of the Soviet Russia with its worldwide Bolshevik propaganda and, lastly, the success of the Angora Government in bringing the English and the Greeks down on their knees—have contributed not a little to the conviction that India's freedom must be won by whatever means possible.

It may be tedious but it will be profitable to give a chronology of leading events in India from 1905 to 1909 bearing on this question.

1905:

February 3—Lord Curzon introduced a Bill to officialese the Universities of India and got this Bill through the Council on February 10.

February 11—Lord Curzon's speech at the University Convocation, Calcutta, impugning Indian veracity.

July 19—Government of India's Resolution on the Partition of Bengal published.

August 7—Anti-Partition demonstration in Calcutta. Boycott agitation started in the Town Hall under the presidency of the Maharaja of Kasimbazar.

August 21—Lord Curzon's resignation of viceroyalty announced. (He left India on November 17).

September 1—Proclamation of the Partition of Bengal is issued from Simla.

September 2—A general mourning observed all over Bengal on account of the Partition Proclamation.

September 22—In connection with the Partition agitation and the Swadeshi movement a mass meeting was held at the Calcutta Town Hall under the presidency of Mr. Lal Mohan Ghose and attended by 4.000 people.

September 25—Anti-Partition demonstration in the Calcutta Maidan prohibited by the Police.

September 29—A meeting of the Supreme Legislative Council was held at Simla in which the Bengal Partition Bill was passed into law.

October 8—The leading Marwaris, owing to the boycott propaganda in connection with the Partition of Bengal, refuse to send forward contracts to Manchester for cotton goods.

October 10—Mr. Carlyle of the Government of Bengal issues an anti-Swadeshi circular prohibiting students from joining in picketing.

October 12—Papers relating to the Partition of Bengal are officially published.

October 16—The new Province of Eastern Bengal and Assam is formally inaugurated at Shillong by Sir Bomfylde Fuller, its first Lieutenant Governor. The foundation of Federation Hall and a day of general mourning all over Bengal and the "Rakhi" (Union) Day inaugurated under the presidency of the late Mr. A. M. Bose.

November 1—The People's Proclamation urging on the Unity of Bengal read throughout the Province.

November 8—Mr. P. C. Lyon, Chief Secretary of Sir B. Fuller, issues a circular against the shouting of "Bande Mataram" in open streets and parks.

1906:

January 12—In reply to a deputation from the Indian Association, Lord Minto declares the Partition of Bengal to be "an accomplished fact".

April 15—The Barisal Conference is dispersed under orders of the District Magistrate, Mr. Emerson.

October 27—Some gentlemen and students wantonly assaulted by the Police at Mymensingh.

1907:

January 1—Queen Victoria's statue on the Maidan is tarred and mutilated.

May 9—Lala Lajpat Rai is arrested and deported under Regulation III of 1818.

May 20—A detachment of Gurkhas arrives at Sirajganj where great 'panic prevails among the Hindu population.

June 17—The Amritsar District is proclaimed under the Meetings Ordinance. The Editor of the HINDUSTAN newspaper is arrested and handcuffed at Lahore.

July 11—The Faridpur District Conference, of which Mr. Prithwis Chandra Ray was elected President, is prohibited.

October 2—Police forcibly break a Swadeshi meeting at Beadon Square assaulting innocent men, and in the night "loot" many shops in the neighbourhood.

October 10—Meetings are proclaimed in all public squares of Calcutta with the exception of Greer Park under orders of the Presidency Magistrate, Mr. Swinhoe.

November 1—Seditious Meetings Bill passed into law.

December 26—The 23rd Indian National Congress broken up at Surat.

1908:

February 3—A proposed scheme for dividing Mymensingh into three district is announced.

April 30—A serious bomb outrage takes place at Muzaffarpore. The bomb was thrown at a carriage containing Mrs. and Miss Kennedy.

May 1—The Manicktola Bomb conspirators rounded up.

May 1—Khudiram Bose is arrested at Waini on suspicion as the murderer of Mrs. and Miss Kennedy.

May 2—Hemchandra Das is arrested at 38-4, Raja Naba Kissen Street. Babu Aurobindo Ghose and Sailendra Nath Bose and

Abinash Chandra Bhattacharya, manager and assistant manager respectively of the NAVASAKTI, are arrested at the NAVASAKTI office for their alleged complicity in the bomb conspiracy.

May 2—Barindra Kumar Ghose, Ullaskar Dutta, Indu-bhusan Ray and ten others are arrested with bombs, explosives and ammunition at a garden house at 32, Muraripukur Road.

May 3—Profulla Chandra Chaki, while being arrested at Mokamah on suspicion as one of the murderers of Mrs. and Miss Kennedy shot himself dead by a revolver.

May 5—Narendra Nath Goswami is arrested at Srirampore in connection with the Manicktola Bomb conspiracy.

May 6—Five Bengali Hindus are arrested at Kustea as implicated in the case of shooting Mr. Hickinbotharn, a Christian missionary.

May 15—A bomb explosion takes place on the tramway line in Grey Street in Calcutta, injuring four persons.

May 24—Two bombs were discovered in a third class railway carriage of a passenger train at Howrah.

June 2—An armed dacoity took place at Barha in Dacca in which forty armed men fought with nearly 300 villagers, killing four.

June 8—The Newspapers Act and the Explosives Act passed by the Governor-General-in-Council.

June 21—A bomb thrown into a second class railway compartment at Kakinarah, seriously injuring one European passenger.

June 22—Narendra Nath Goswami, one of the accused of the Manicktola Bomb Conspiracy case, turns a King's witness and makes sensational statements implicating Aurobindo Ghose and several well-known men in Bengal with dacoity and attempts at murder.

August 2—Of the six accused in the Harrison Road case under the Arms Act, Nagen and Dharani Gupta and Ullaskar Dutta are sentenced to seven years' rigorous imprisonment each, and the rest are acquitted.

August 11—Khudiram Bose hanged.

August 12—Two bombs are discovered near the Chandannagore railway station.

August 28—Raja Narendra Lal Khan of Narajole and eight other respectable persons are arrested at Midnapur for complicity in alleged conspiracy to kill all European officials at Midnapur. (Released on bail on September 18 and the case against them withdrawn by the hon'ble S. P. Sinha on December 9.)

August 31—Narendra Nath Goswami, the approver in the Manicktola Bomb Conspiracy case, is shot dead in the Alipore Jail.

September 8—Mr. Dadabhai Naoroji sends a message from Versova urging his countrymen to avoid all resort to violence.

September 20—Mr. Tilak's conviction for sedition with six years' transportation is reduced to six years' simple imprisonment by the Bombay Government.

October 14—The Bengal Government issues a resolution extending the order of the Chief Presidency Magistrate of Calcutta and the District Magistrate of 24-Parganas prohibiting the holding of any public meeting in any place under their jurisdiction to a further period of six months from October 22.

November 7—At a meeting in the Overtoun Hall in Calcutta a daring attempt is made on the life of Sir Andrew Fraser, the Lieutenant Governor of Bengal, by one Jitendra Nath Roy Chowdhury.

November 9—Nandalal Banerji of the Bengal C.I.D. who attempted to arrest Profulla Chaki is shot dead in a Calcutta lane.

November 10—Kanailal Dutt is hanged in the Alipore Central Jail and is given a public funeral by a large crowd of Indian men and women.

November 23—Satyendra Nath Bose, convicted of the murder of Narendra Nath Goswami, is hanged in the Alipur Jail.

November 30—Mr. Gokhale in an address before the New Reform Club in London states that the condition in India is getting serious and declares that nothing short of the reversal of the Partition of Bengal and a general amnesty to all political prisoners will ever pacify Bengal.

December 1—Mr. Rees in the House of Commons suggested the prohibition of seditious literature from France into India.

December 11—A special Crimes Act for the summary trial of political prisoners and proscribing certain associations and organisations is passed into law at one single meeting of the Indian Legislative Council.

December 11—Krishna Kumar Mitter arrested and deported under Regulation III of 1818.

December 13—Aswini Kumar Dutt, Subodh Chandra Mallik and five others arrested and deported under Regulation HI of 1818.

1909:

January 6—Several Samitees in Eastern Bengal proclaimed under the new Crimes Act.

February 10—Babu Ashutosh Biswas, Government Pleader and Public Prosecutor of the 24-Parganas, is shot dead in the precincts of the Alipore Magistrate's Court by one Charu Chandra Basu.

March 2—A question was put in the House of Commons by Mr. Lupton as to the difference in the Russian and Indian method of repression. The Under-Secretary made no reply.

April 15—The prohibition to hold public meetings in Calcutta squares within half an hour of sunset is extended for another year.

May 6—Judgement delivered in the Alipore Bomb Case "by Mr. Justice Beachcroft.

In summer a revision of the Indian Councils Act is passed in Parliament incorporating the Morley-Minto Reforms.

1910:

The Minto-Morley Reform Scheme is inaugurated, and drastic Press Act passed.

I have omitted to state in this chronology the principal events from 1910 to the present day as they may be fresh in your memory. The annulment of the Partition of Bengal in 1912, the throwing of a bomb on Lord Hardinge at Chandni Chowk in Delhi while passing in a State procession, internments under the Defence of India Act, the Rowlatt Act, the *Jalianwallabagh* tragedy and the incidents of the *Komagata Maru* may be remembered as the principal events of this period.

It is thus clear that repression was followed by revolutionary movement which again was followed by further repression and that even when the British Government allowed measures which may be described as benevolent, they were always attended by others of a repressive character.

Mahatma Gandhi and Nonviolence

With the *Jalianwallabagh* tragedy was started the new era in which Mahatma Gandhi initiated a propaganda of non-violent activity as a new way to fight for India's freedom. Let us hope that the whole of India has accepted it, and I would press both upon the Government and my revolutionary friends the utter futility of violence in any shape or form.

New Bengal Ordinance and the Internments

The new Ordinance Act is a misguided attempt to perpetrate violence upon the people. The whole of India has with one voice condemned it and I cannot trust myself to express my feeling about it in fitting terms as I desire to Speak with all restraint. I shall content myself by saying that I unhesitatingly condemn it and I have given the only answer which it is possible for any Indian to give to the recent speech of Lord Birkenhead inviting me to cooperate with the Government in its repressive policy.

You will remember that Lord Birkenhead said that the Ordinance has not hurt anybody but the criminals. May I point out that his Lordship here is begging the whole question? We deny that the men imprisoned under the Ordinance are criminals and the only way to decide whether they are criminals or not is to hold an open trial and proceed, not on secret information, but on actual evidence which might be tested in open court.

The insecurity to which eminent writers of constitutional history in England have referred is the insecurity to the public by the attempt of the Executive to arrogate to itself the position of a Court of Law.

I will not weary you by dealing with each particular case which has been brought forward by the Government as a justification for the policy of repression. Pandit Motilal Nehru in his speech in the Legislative Assembly on the Bengal Ordinance on the 25th of February last has dealt with it exhaustively and I ask everyone of you to read that speech if you have any doubt on the point that there has been put forward no instance upon which the Government can possibly substantiate its unjust claim. I must also point out that it is difficult to believe in the statement put forward in support of the repressive measures by the Government. I shall quote only one instance and I have done. Speaking of the arrest and detention of the nine Bengali gentlemen including Srijut Krishna Kumar Mitter and late Ashwini Kumar Dutt on the 11th of December 1908, Lord Morley, then Secretary of State, in his letter to Lord Minto stated as follows:

> "You have nine men locked up a year ago by *lettrc de cachet,* because you believed them to be criminally connected with criminal plots, and because you expected their arrests to check these plots."

But let us hear what Sir Hugh Stephenson has to say on the point. It is only the other day that he said from his place in the Bengal Council:

> "I should like to mention three cases which have been used in the Press to throw doubts on the efficiency, if not on the *bona fides* of our methods. The first two are those of Babu Ashwini Kumar Dutt and Babu Krishna Kumar Mitter. It has been said that no one will believe that they had anything to do with terrorist crime and that therefore the secret information of the police must have been false and Government may equally well be deceived by such false information now. I never knew Babu Ashwini Kumar Dutt, but I am glad to think that Babu Krishna Kumar Mitter is a personal friend and I entirely acquit him of sympathy with terrorist crime. But as far as I know none has ever accused him or Babu Ashwini Kumar Dutt of promoting crime, still less of taking part in it.

> The Bengal Government asked for the use of Regulation III in the case of Babu Ashwini Kumar Dutt because of his whirlwind campaign of anti-Government speeches."

It follows conclusively that the discretionary power which the Government in this country enjoys of promulgating illegal laws is capable of being abused. Indeed, it must be so from the very nature of things. The history of the world shows that bureaucratic governments have always tried to consolidate their power through the process of "law and order" which is an excellent phrase but which means, in countries where the rule of law does not prevail, the exercise by persons in authority of wide arbitrary or discretionary powers of constraint. Repression is a process in the consolidation of arbitrary powers, and I condemn the violence of the Government—for repression is the most violent form of violence— just as strongly as I condemn violence as a method of winning political liberty. I must warn the Government that the policy of repression is a short-sighted policy. It may strengthen its hands for the time being, but I am sure, Lord Birkenhead realises that, as an instrument of Government, it is bound to fail.

Reform Act and Cooperation

I have so far dealt with the question of method in order to show that violence is both immoral and inexpedient—immoral,, because it is not in keeping with our life and culture—inexpedient, because it is inconceivable that at the present day we can overthrow any organised Government by bombs and' revolvers. Then the question arises: What method should we pursue in order to win Swaraj? We have been gravely told that *Swaraj* is within our grasp if only we cooperate with the Government in working the present Reforms Act. With regard to that argument, my position is perfectly clear, and I should like to restate it, so that there may be no controversy about it.

If I were satisfied that the present Act has transferred any real responsibility to the people—that there is opportunity for self-realisation, self-development and self-fulfilment under the Act—I would unhesitatingly cooperate with the Government and begin the constructive work within the Council Chamber. But I am not willing to sacrifice the substance for the shadow. I will not detain you today with any arguments tending to show that the Reforms Act has not transferred any responsibility to the people. I have dealt with the question exhaustively in my address at the Ahmedabad Congress, and if further arguments are necessary, they will be found in the evidence given before the Muddiman Committee by men whose moderation cannot be questioned by the Government. The basis of the present Act is distrust of the Ministers; and there can be no talk of cooperation in any atmosphere of distrust. At the same time, I must make clear my position — and, I hope, of the Bengal Provincial Conference—that, provided some real responsibility is transferred to the people, there is no reason why we should not cooperate with the Government. But to make such cooperation real and effective two things are necessary—first, there should be a real change of heart in our rulers; secondly, *Swaraj* in the fullest sense must be guaranteed to us at once, to come automatically in the near future. I have always maintained that we should make large sacrifices in order to have the opportunity to begin our constructive work at once; and I think you will realise that a few years are nothing in the history of a nation, provided the foundation of *Swaraj* is laid at once and there is a real change of heart both in the ruler and in the subject.

You will tell me that "change of heart" is a fine phrase, and that some practical demonstration should be given of that change. I agree. But that demonstration must necessarily depend on the atmosphere created by any proposed settlement. An atmosphere of trust or distrust may be easily felt, and in any matter of peaceful settlement a great deal more depends on the spirit behind the terms than the actual terms themselves. It is impossible to lay down the exact terms of any such settlement at the present moment; but if a change of heart takes place and negotiations are carried on by both sides in the spirit of peace, harmony and mutual trust, such terms arc capable of precise definition.

Conditions, Precedent to Cooperation

A few suggestions may, however, be made having regard to what is nearest to the hearts of the people of Bengal.

In the first place, the Government should divest itself of its wide discretionary powers of constraint, and follow it up by proclaiming a general amnesty of all political prisoners. In the next place, the Government should guarantee to us the fullest recognition of our right to the establishment of Swaraj within the Commonwealth, in the near future and that in the meantime, till *Swaraj* comes, a sure and sufficient foundation of such. Swaraj should be laid at once. What is a sufficient foundation is, and must necessarily be, a matter of negotiation and settlement—settlement not only between the Government and the people as a whole, but also between the different communities, not excluding the European and Anglo-Indian communities, as I said in my Presidential Speech at Gaya.

I must also add that we on our part should be in a position to give some sort of undertaking that we shall not by word, deed, or gesture encourage the revolutionary propaganda and that we shall make every effort to put an end to such a movement. This undertaking is not needed, for the Bengal Provincial Conference has never identified itself with the revolutionary propaganda. I believe that with a change of heart on the part of the Government, there is bound to be produced a change in the mental outlook of the revolutionary, and with settlement such as I have described, the revolutionary movement will be a thing of the past, and the very power and energy which is now directed against the Government will be devoted to the real service of the people.

What to Do if Government Rejects Offer of Settlement?

If, however, our offer of a settlement should not meet with any response, we must go on with our national work on the lines which we have pursued for the last two years so that it may become impossible for the Government to carry on the administration of the country except by the exercise of its exceptional powers. There are some who shrink from this step, who point out with perfect logic that we have no right to refuse supplies unless we are prepared to go to the country and advise the subject not to pay the taxes. My answer is that I want to create the atmosphere for national civil disobedience, which must be the last weapon in the hand of the people striving for freedom. I have no use for historical precedent; but if reference is to be made to

English history in our present struggle, I may point out that refusal to pay taxes in England in the time of the: Stuarts came many years after the determination of the Parliament to refuse supplies. The atmosphere for civil disobedience is created by compelling the Government to raise money by the exercise of its exceptional powers; and when the time comes we shall not hesitate to advise our countrymen not to pay taxes which are sought to be raised by the exercise of the exceptional powers vested in the Government.

I hope that time will never come—indeed I see signs of a real change of heart everywhere—but let us face the fact that it may be necessary for us to have recourse to civil disobedience if all hopes of reconciliation fail. But let us also face the fact that civil disobedience requires a high stage of organisation, an infinite capacity for sacrifice, and a real desire to subordinate personal and communal interest to the common interest of the nation—and I can see little hope of India ever being ready for civil disobedience until she is prepared to work. Mahatma Gandhi's constructive programme to the fullest extent. The end, however, must be kept in view, for freedom must be won.

Final Message and Appeal

But, as I have said, I see signs of reconciliation everywhere. The world is tired of conflicts, and I think I see a real desire for construction, for consolidation. I believe that India has a great part to play in the history of the world. She has a message to deliver and she is anxious to deliver it in the Council Chamber of that great Commonwealth of Nations of which I have spoken. Will British statesmen rise to the occasion? To them I say: You can have peace today on terms that are honourable both to you and to us. To the British Community in India, I say: You have come with traditions of freedom, and you cannot refuse to cooperate with us in our national struggle, provided we recognise your right to be heart in the final settlement. To the people of Bengal I say: You have made great sacrifices for daring to win political freedom, and on you has fallen the brunt of official wrath. The time is not yet for putting aside your political weapons. *Fight hard, but fight clean;* and when the time for settlement comes, as it is bound to come, enter the Peace Conference, not in a spirit of arrogance, but with becoming humility, so that it may be said of you that you were greater in your achievement than in adversity. Nationalism is merely a process in self-realisation, self-development and self-fulfilment. It is not an end in itself. The growth and development of nationalism is necessary so that humanity may realise itself, develop itself, and fulfil itself; and I beseech you, when you discuss the terms of settlement, do not forget the larger claim of humanity in your pride of nationalism. For myself, I have a clear vision as to what I seek. I seek a Federation of the States of India: each free to follow—as it must follow—the culture and the tradition of its own people: each bound to each in the common service of all: a great federation within a great federation—the Federation of Free Nations —whose freedom is the measure of their service to Man, and whose unity the hope of peace among the people of the earth.

Bande Mataram

Noncooperation and Council Entry

[Presidential address delivered at the session of the Congress held at Gaya in December, 1922]

Sisters and Brothers,

As I stand before you today a sense of overwhelming loss overtakes me, and I can scarcely give expression to what is uppermost in the minds of all and everyone of us. After a memorable battle which he gave to the bureaucracy, Mahatma Gandhi has been seized and cast into prison; and we shall not have his guidance in the proceedings of the Congress this year. But there is inspiration for all of us in the last stand which he made in the citadel of the enemy, in the last defiance which he hurled at the agents of the bureaucracy. To read a story equal in pathos, in dignity, and in sublimity, you have to go back over two thousand years, when Jesus of Nazareth, "as one that perverted the people,' stood to take, his trial before a foreign tribunal.

> "And Jesus stood before the Governor: and the Governor asked him, saying, Art thou the King of the Jews? And Jesus said unto him. Thou sayest.

"And when he was accused of the chief priests and elders, he answered nothing.

"Then said Pilate unto him, Hearest thou not how many things they witness against thee?

"And he answered him to never a word; in so much that the Governor marvelled greatly."

Mahatma Gandhi took a different course. He admitted that he was guilty, and he pointed out to the Public Prosecutor that his guilt was greater than he, the Prosecutor, had alleged, but he maintained that if he had offended against the law of bureaucracy, in so offending he had obeyed the law of God. If I may hazard a guess, the judge who tried him and who passed a sentence of imprisonment on him was filled with the same feeling of marvel as Pontius Pilate had been.

Great in taking decisions, great in executing them, Mahatma Gandhi was incomparably great in the last stand which he made on behalf of his country. He is undoubtedly one of the greatest man that the world has ever seen. The world has need of him, and if he is mocked and jeered at by "the people of importance." "the people with a stake in the country" — Scribes and Pharisees of the days of Christ — he will be gratefully remembered, now and always, by a nation which he Jed from victory to victory.

Law and Order

Gentlemen, the time is a critical one and it is important to seize upon the real issue which divides the people from the bureaucracy and its Indian allies. During the period of repression which began about this time last year it was this issue which pressed itself on our attention. This policy of repression was supported and in some cases instigated by the Moderate leaders who are in the Executive Government. I do not charge those who supported Government with dishonesty or want of patriotism. I say they were led away by the battle-cry of Law and Order. And it is because I believe that there is a fundamental confusion of thought behind this attitude of mind that I propose to discuss this plea of Law and Order. 'Taw and Order" has indeed been the last refuge of bureaucracies all over the world.

It has been gravely asserted not only by the bureaucracy but also by its apologists, the Moderate Party, that a settled government is the first necessity of any people and that the subject has no right to present his grievances except in a constitutional way, by which I understand in some way recognised by the Constitution. "If you cannot actively cooperate in the maintenance of the law of the land," they say, "it is your duty as a responsible citizen to obey it passively. Non-resistance is the least that the Government is entitled to expect from you. This is the whole political philosophy of the bureaucracy—the maintenance of law and order on the part of the Government, and an attitude of passive obedience and non-resistance on the part of the subject. But was not that the political philosophy of every English King from William the Conqueror to James II? And was not that the political philosophy of the Romanoffs, the Hohenzollerns and of the Bourbons? And yet freedom has come, where it has come, by disobedience of the very laws which were proclaimed in the name of law and order. Where the Government is arbitrary and despotic and the fundamental rights of the people are not recognised, it is idle to talk of law and order.

The doctrine has apparently made its way to this country from England. I shall, therefore, refer to English history to find out the truth about this doctrine. That history has recorded that most of the despots in England who exercised arbitrary sway over the people proposed to act for the good of the people and for the maintenance of law and order, English absolutism from the Normans down to the Stuarts tried to put itself on a constitutional basis through the process of this very law and order. The pathetic speech delivered by Charles I just before his execution puts the whole doctrine in a nutshell. "For the people," he said, "truly I desire their liberty and freedom as much as anybody whatsoever, but I must tell you that their liberty and freedom consist in leaving to Government those laws by which their lives and their goods may be their own. It is not their having a share in the Government; that is nothing appertaining to them. A subject and a sovereign are clear different things." The doctrine of law and order could not be stated with more admirable clearness. But though the English Kings acted constitutionally in the sense that their acts were in accordance with the letter of law and were covered by precedents the subjects always claimed that they were free to assert their fundamental rights and to wrest them from the King by force or insurrection. The doctrine of law and order received a rude shock when King John was obliged to put his signature to the Magna Charta on the 15th of June 1215. The 61st clause of the Charter is important for our purpose securing as it did to the subject the liberty of rebellion as a means for enforcing the due observance of the Charter by the Crown. Adams, a celebrated writer of the English constitutional history, says that the conditional right to rebel is as much at the foundation of the English Constitution today as it was in 1215.

But though the doctrine of law and order had received a rude shock, it did not altogether die; for in the intervening period the Crown claimed and asserted the right to raise money, not only by indirect taxes but also by forced loans and benevolences; and frequently exercised large legislative functions not only by applying what are known as suspending and dispensing powers but also by issuing proclamations. The Crown claimed, as Hallam says, "not only a kind of supplemental right of legislation to perfect and carry out what the spirit of existing laws might require but also a paramount supremacy, called sometimes the King's absolute or sovereign power which sanctioned commands beyond the legal prerogative, for the sake of public safety, whenever the Council might judge that to be in hazard."

By the time of the Stuarts the powers claimed by the Crown were recognised by the courts of law as well founded, and, to quote the words of Adams, "the forms of law became the engines for the perpetration of judicial murders." It is necessary to remember that it was the process of law and order that helped to consolidate the powers of the Crown; for it was again and again laid down by the Court of Exchequer that the power of taxation was vested in the Crown, where it was "for the general benefit of the people." As Adams says, "the Stuarts asserted a legal justification for everything done by them," and, "on the whole, history was with the King."

But how did the Commons meet this assertion of law and order? They were strict non-cooperators both within and outside the Parliament. Within the Parliament they again and again refused to vote supplies unless their grievances were redressed. The King retorted by raising customs duties on his own initiative and the courts of law supported him. The Commons passed a resolution to the effect that persons paying them "should be reputed betrayers of liberties of England and enemies to the same." There was little doubt that revolution was on the land; and King Charles finding himself in difficulty gave his Royal Assent to the Bill of Rights on the 17th of June 1926. The Bill of Rights constitutes a triumph for non-cooperators; for it was by their refusal to have any part or share in the administration of the country that the Commons compelled the King to acknowledge their rights. The events that followed between 1629 and 1640 made the history of England. In spite of the Bill of Rights the King continued to raise customs duties, and Elliot and his friends were put on their trial. They refused to plead, and the result was disastrous for the arbitrary power of the King. The King levied Ship Money on the nation. The chief constables of various places replied that the sheriffs had no authority to assess or tax any man without the consent of the Parliament. On the refusal on the part of the people to pay the taxes their cattle was distrained, and no purchaser could be found for them. The King took the opinion of the Exchequer Court on the question whether "when the good and safety of the kingdom in general is concerned, and the whole kingdom is in danger,"—mark how the formula has been copied verbatim in the Government of India Act—"may not the King. .. .command all the subjects of his kingdom, to provide and furnish such number of ships, with men, victuals and munitions, and for such time as he shall think fit, for the defence and safeguard of the kingdom from such peril, — "again the formula! — " and by law compel the doing thereof in case of refusal and refractoriness. And whether in such a case the King is not the sole judge, both of the danger, and as to when and how the same is to be prevented." The judges answered in the affirmative and maintained the answer in the celebrated cases which Hampden brought before them.

I desire to emphasise one point, and that is, that throughout the long and bitter struggle between the Stuarts and Parliament, the Stuarts acted for the maintenance of law and order, and there is no doubt that law and history were on their side. On the eve of the civil war, the question that divided the parties was this: Could the Crown in the maintenance of law and order claim the passive obedience of the subject, or was there any power of resistance in the subject, though that resistance might result in disorder and in breaches of law? The adherents of Parliament stood for the power and the majesty of the people, the authority and "independency of Parliament," individual liberty, the right to resist, and the right to compel abdication and secure deposition of the Crown; in a word, they stood for Man against the coercive powers of the State. The adherents of the Crown stood for indefeasible right, a right to claim passive obedience and secure non-resistance on the part of the subject through the process of law and order; in a word, they stood for state coercion and compulsory cooperation against individual liberty.

The issue was decided in favour of Parliament, but, as it must happen in every war of arms, the victory for individual liberty was only temporary. Though the result of Civil War was disastrous from the point of view of individual liberty and though it required another revolution, this time a non-violent revolution, to put individual liberty on a sure foundation, "the knowledge that subjects had sat in rude judgement on their King, man to man, speeded the slow emancipation of the mind from the shackles of custom and ancient reverence."

The revolution of 1688 — a bloodless revolution — secured for England that rule of law which is the only foundation for the maintenance of law and order. It completed the work which the Long Parliament had begun and which the execution of Charles I had interrupted. But how was the peaceful revolution of 1688 brought about? By defiance of authority and by rigid adherence to the principle that it is the inalienable right of the subject to resist the exercise by the executive of wide, arbitrary or discretionary powers of constraint.

The principle for which the revolution of 1688 stood was triumphantly vindicated in the celebrated case of Dr. Sacheverell. In the course of a sermon which he had preached, he gave expression to the following sentiment:

> "The grand security of our Government and the very pillar upon which it stands, is founded upon the steady belief of the subject's obligation to an absolute and unconditional obedience to the supreme power in all things lawful and the utter illegality of resistance on any pretence whatsoever."

This is the doctrine of passive obedience and non-resistance — the doctrine of law and order which is proclaimed today by every Bureaucrat in the country, foreign or domestic, and which is supposed to be the last word on the subject's duty and Government's rights. But mark how they solved the problem in England in 1710. The Commons impeached Dr. Sacheverell for giving expression to a view so destructive of individual liberty, and the Lords, by a majority of votes, found him guilty. The speeches delivered in the course of the trial are interesting. I desire to quote a few sentences from some of those speeches. Sir Joseph Jakyll said in the course of his speech that "as the law is the only measure of the Prince's authority, and the people's subjection, so the law derives its being and efficiency from common consent; and to place it on any other foundation than common consent, is to take away the obligation; this notion of common consent puts both Prince and people under, to observe the laws.

My Lords, as the doctrine of unlimited non-resistance was impliedly renounced by the whole nation in the revolution, so diverse Acts of Parliament were afterwards passed, expressing their renunciation... .and, therefore, I shall only say that it can never be supposed that the laws were made to set up a despotic power to destroy themselves, and to warrant the subversion of a Constitution of a Government which they were designed to establish and defend." Mr. Walpole put the whole argument in a nutshell when he said: "The doctrine of unlimited, unconditional passive obedience was first invented to support arbitrary and despotic power and was never promoted or countenanced by any Government that had not designs, some time or other, of making use of it." The argument against the doctrine of law and order could not be put more clearly or forcibly: for his argument comes to this, the doctrine is not an honest one, if law and order is the process by which absolutism consolidates its powers and strengthens its hand. I will make one more quotation, and that is from the speech of Major-General Stanhope: "As to the doctrine itself of absolute non-resistance it should seem needless to prove by argument that it is inconsistent with the law of reason, with the law of nature, and with the practice of all ages and countries. And indeed, one may appeal to the practice of all churches and all states and of all nations in the world, how they behaved themselves when they found their civil and religious Constitutions invaded and oppressed by tyranny."

This, then, is the history of the freedom movement in England. The conclusion is irresistible that it is not by acquiescence in the doctrine of law and order that the English people have obtained the recognition of their fundamental rights. It follows from the survey that I have made, firstly, that no regulation is law unless it is based on the consent of the people; secondly, where such consent is wanting, the people are under no obligation to obey; thirdly, where such laws are not only not based on the consent of the people but profess to attack their fundamental rights, the subjects are entitled to compel their withdrawal by force or insurrection; fourthly, that law and order is, and has always been, a plea for absolutism; and lastly, there can be neither law nor order before the real reign of law begins.

I have dealt with the question at some length, as the question is a vital one, and there are many Moderates who still think that it is the duty of every loyal subject to assist the Government in the maintenance of law and order. The personal liberty of every Indian today depends to a great extent on the exercise of wide, arbitrary or discretionary powers by persons in authority. Where such powers are allowed, the rule of law is denied. To find out the extent to which this exploded doctrine of law and order influences the minds of sober and learned men, you have only to read the report of the committee appointed to examine the repressive laws. You will find in the report neither the vision of the patriot nor the wisdom of the statesman: but you will find an excessive worship of that much advertised, but much misunderstood pharse "law and order." Why is Regulation 111 of 1818 to be amended and kept on the Statute Book? Because for the protection of the frontiers of India and the fulfilment of the responsibility of the Government of India in relation to Indian States, there must be some enactment to arm the Executive with powers to restrict the movements and activities of certain persons who, though not coming within the scope of any criminal law, have to be put under some measure of restraint. Why are the Indian Criminal Law Amendment Act, 1908 and the Prevention of Seditious Meetings Act, 1911 to be retained on the Statute Book? For the preservation of law and order. They little think, these learned gentlemen responsible for the report, that these Statutes, giving, as they do, to the Executive, wide, arbitrary and discretionary powers of constraint, constitute a state of things wherein it is the duty of every individual to resist and to defy the tyranny of such lawless laws.

These Statutes in themselves constitute a breach of law and order, for, law and order is the result of "the rule of law; and where you deny the existence of the rule of law, you cannot turn round and say: "It is your duty as law-abiding citizens to obey the law."

We have had abundance of this law and order during the last few years of our national history. The last affront delivered to the nation was the promulgation of an Executive order under the authority of the Criminal Law Amendment Act making the legitimate work of Congress volunteers illegal and criminal. This was supported by our Moderate friends on the ground that it is the duty of the law-abiding subject to support the maintenance of law and order.

The doctrine, as I said before, has travelled all the way from the shores of England. But may I ask: Is there one argument advanced today by the bureaucracy and its friends which was not advanced with equal clearness by the Stuarts? When the Stuarts arrogated to themselves a discretionary power of committing to prison all persons who were on any account obnoxious to the Court, they made the excuse that the power was necessary for the safety of the nation, and the power was resisted in England, not because it was never exercised for the safety of the nation, but because the existence of the power was inconsistent with the existence at the same time of individual liberty. When the Stuarts claimed the right to legislate by proclamations and by wide exercise of suspending and dispersing powers, they did so on the express ground that such legislation was necessary for public safety. That right was denied by the English nation, not because such legislation was not necessary for public safety, but because such right could not co-exist with the fundamental right of the nation to legislate for itself. Is the power of the Governor-General to certify the passage of a Bill is essential for safety or tranquillity or interest of British India any different from the power claimed by the Stuarts? There is indeed a striking resemblance between the power conferred on the Governor-General and the Governors of the provinces and the powers claimed by the Tudors and the Stuarts. When the Stuarts claimed the right to raise revenue on their own initiative, they disclaimed any intention to exercise such right except *"when the good and safety of the kingdom in general is concerned and the whole kingdom is in danger"*.

That right was resisted in England, not because the revenues raised by them were not necessary for the good and safety of the kingdom, but because that right was inconsistent with the fundamental right of the people to pay such taxes only as were determined by the representatives of the people for the people. Is the power conferred on the Governor to certify that the expenditure provided for by a particular demand not assented to by the Legislature is essential to the discharge of his responsibility for the subject any different from the power claimed by the Stuarts? It should be patent to everybody that we do not live under the rule of law, and the history of England has proclaimed that it is idle to talk of the maintenance of law and order when large discretionary powers of constraint are vested in the Executive. The manhood of England triumphantly resisted the pretensions of "law and order." If there is manhood in India today, India will successfully resist the same pretensions advanced by the Indian bureaucracy.

I have quoted from English history at length because the argument furnished by that history appeals to most people who are frightened by popular movements into raising the cry of "law and order," and who think that the development of the great Indian nation must follow the lines laid down in that history. For myself I oppose the pretensions of "law and order," not on historical precedent, but on the ground that it is the inalienable right of every individual and of every nation to stand on truth and to offer a stubborn resistance to the promulgation of lawless laws. There was a law in the time of Christ which forbade the people eating on the Sabbath, but allowed the priests to profane the Sabbath. And how Christ dealt with the law is narrated in the New Testament.

> "At that time Jesus went on the Sabbath day through the corn; and his disciples were an hungered, and began to pluck the ear of corn, and to eat. But when the Pharisees saw it, they said unto him, Behold, thy disciples do that which is not lawful to do upon the Sabbath day.
>
> "But he said unto them, Have ye not read what David did, when he was an hungered and they that were with him?
>
> "How he entered into the house of God and did eat the shewbread which was not lawful for him to cat, neither for them which were with him, but only for the priests?
>
> "Or have ye not read in the law, how that on the Sabbath days the priests in the temple profaned the Sabbath, are blameless?".

The truth is that law and order is for Man, and not Man for law and order. The development of nationality is a sacred task and anything which impedes that task is an obstacle which the very force and power of nationality must overcome. If,. therefore, you interpose a doctrine to impede the task, why, the doctrine must go. If you have recourse to law and order to establish and defend the rule of law then your law and order is entitled to claim the respect of all law-abiding citizens but as soon as you have recourse to it not to establish and defend the rule of law but to destroy and attack it, there is no longer, any obligation on us to respect it, for a Higher Law, the Natural Law, the Law of God compels us to offer our stubborn resistance to it. When I find some thing put forward in the sacred name of law and order which is deliberately intended to hinder the growth, the development, and the self-realisation of the nation, I have no hesitation whatever in proclaiming that such law and order is an outrage on man and insult to God.

But though our Moderate friends are often deluded by the battle-cry of law and order, I rejoice when I hear that cry. It means that the bureaucracy is in danger and that the bureaucracy has realised its danger. It is not without reason that a false issue is raised; and the fact that false issue has been raised fills me with hope and courage. I ask my countrymen to be patient and to press the charge. Freedom has already advanced when the alarm of law and order is sounded: that is the history of bureaucracies all over the world.

In the meantime it is our duty to keep our ideal steadfast-We must not forget that we are on the eve of great changes, that world forces are working all round us and that the battle of freedom has yet to be won.

Nationalism: the Ideal

What is the ideal which we must set before us? The first and foremost is the ideal of nationalism. Now what is nationalism? It is, I conceive, a process through which a nation expresses itself and finds itself, not in isolation from other nations, not in opposition to other nations, but as part of a great scheme by which, in seeking its own expression and therefore its own identity, it materially assists the self-expression and self-realisation of other nations as well. Diversity is as real as unity. And in order that the unity of the world may be established it is essential that each nationality should proceed on its own line and find fulfilment in self-expression and self-realisation. The nationality of which I am speaking must not be confused with the conception of nationality as it exists in Europe today. Nationalism in Europe is an aggressive nationalism, a selfish nationalism, a commercial nationalism of gain and loss. The gain of France is the loss of Germany and the gain of Germany is the loss of France. Therefore French nationalism is nurtured on the hatred of Germany and German nationalism is nurtured on the hatred of France. It is not yet realised that you cannot hurt

Germany without hurting humanity, and in consequence hurting France; and that you cannot hurt France without hurting humanity, and in consequence hurting Germany. That is European nationalism; that is not the nationalism of which I am speaking to you today. I contend that each nationality constitutes a particular stream of the great unity, but no nation can fulfil itself unless and until it becomes itself and at the same time realises its identity with humanity. The whole problem of nationalism is therefore to find that stream and to face that destiny. If you find the current and establish a continuity with the past, then the process of self-expression has begun, and nothing can stop the growth of nationality.

Throughout the pages of Indian history, I find a great purpose unfolding itself. Movement after movement has swept over this vast country, apparently creating hostile forces, but in reality stimulating the vitality and moulding the life of the people into one great nationality. If the Aryans and the non-Aryans met, it was for the purpose of making one people out of them. Brahmanism with its great culture succeeded in binding the whole of India and was indeed a mighty unifying force.

Buddhism with its protests against Brahmanism served the same great historical purpose; and from Magadha to Taxila was one great Buddhistic Empire which succeeded not only in broadening the basis of Indian unity, but in creating, what is perhaps not less important, the greater India beyond the Himalayas and beyond the seas, so much so that the sacred city where we have met may be regarded as a place of pilgrimage of millions and millions of people of Asiatic races. Then came the Mohammedans of diverse races, but with one culture which was their common heritage. For a time it looked as if here was a disintegrating force, an enemy to the growth of Indian nationalism, but the Mohammedans made their home in India, and, while they brought a new outlook and a wonderful vitality to the Indian life, with infinite wisdom they did as little as possible to disturb the growth of life in the villages where India really lives. This new outlook was necessary for India; and if the two sister streams met, it was only to fulfil themselves and face the destiny of Indian history. Then came the English with their alien culture, their foreign methods, delivering a rude shock to this growing nationality but the shock has only completed the unifying process so that the purpose of history is practically fulfilled. The great Indian nationality is in sight. It already stretches its hands across the Himalayas, not only to Asia but to the whole of the world—not aggressively, but to demand its recognition, and to offer its contribution. I desire to emphasise that there is no hostility between the ideal of nationality and that of world peace. Nationalism is the process through which alone will world peace come. A full and unfettered growth of nationalism is necessary for world peace, just as a full and unfettered growth of individuals is necessary for nationality. It is the conception of aggressive nationality in Europe that stands in the way of world peace; but once the truth is grasped that it is not possible for a nation to inflict a loss on another nation without at the same time inflicting a loss on itself, the problem of humanity is solved. The essential truth of nationality lies in this, that it is necessary for each nation to develop itself, express itself and realise itself, so that humanity itself may develop itself, express itself and realise itself. It is my belief that this truth of nationality will endure, although, for the moment, unmindful of the real issue, the nations are fighting amongst themselves; and, if I am not mistaken, it is the very instinct of selfishness and self-preservation which will ultimately solve the problem—not the narrow and the mistaken selfishness of the present, but a selfishness universalised by intellect and transfigured by spirit, a selfishness that will bring home to the nations of the world that in the efforts to put down their neighbours lies their own ruin and suppression.

We have, therefore, to foster the spirit of nationality. True development of the Indian nation must necessarily lie in the path of Swaraj. A question has often been asked as to what is Swaraj. Swaraj is indefinable and is not to be confused with any particular system of government. There is all the difference in the world between Swaraj and Samrajya. Swaraj is the natural expression of the national mind. The full outward expression of that mind covers, and must necessarily cover, the whole life history of a nation. Yet it is true that Swaraj begins when the true development of a nation begins, because, as I have said, Swaraj is the expression of the national mind. The question of nationalism, therefore, looked at from another point of view, is the same question as that of Swaraj. The question of all questions in India today is the attainment of Swaraj.

Nonviolent Noncooperation

I now come to the question of method. I have to repeat that it has been proved beyond any doubt that the method of non-violent non-cooperation is the only method which we must follow to secure a system of government which may in reality be the foundation of Swaraj. It is hardly necessary to discuss the philosophy of non-cooperation. I shall simply state the different viewpoints from which this question may be discussed. From the national point of view the method of non-cooperation means the attempt of the nation to concentrate upon its own energy and to stand on its own strength. From the ethical point of view, non-cooperation means the method of self-purification, the withdrawal from that which is injurious to the development of the nation, and therefore to the good of humanity. From the spiritual point of view, *Swaraj* means that isolation which in the language of *Sadhana* is called "pratyahar"—that withdrawal from the forces which are foreign to our nature—an isolation and withdrawal which is necessary in order to bring out from our hidden depths the soul of the nation in all her glory. I do not desire to labour the point, but from every conceivable point of view, the methods of non-violent non-cooperation must be regarded as the true method of following in the path of *Swaraj*.

Force and Violence

Doubt has, however, been expressed in some quarters about the soundness of the principle of non-violence. I cannot refuse to acknowledge that there is a body of Indian opinion within the country as well as outside according to which non-violence is an ideal abstraction incapable of realisation, and that the only way in which *Swaraj* can ever be attained is by the application of force and violence.. I do not for a moment question the courage, sacrifice and patriotism of those who hold this view.

I know that some of them have suffered for the cause which they believe to be true. But may I be permitted to point out that, apart from any question of principle, history has proved over and over again the utter futility of revolutions brought about by force and violence? I am one of those who hold to non-violence on principle. But let us consider the question of expediency. Is it possible to attain *Swaraj* by violent means? The answer which history gives is an emphatic "No." Take all the formidable revolutions of the world.

French Revolution

The history of the French Revolution is the history of a struggle at the first instance between the Crown and the Nobility on one side and the Representative Assemblies with armed Paris on the other. Both took to violence, one to the bayonet and the other to the pike. The pike succeeded because the bayonet was held with uncertain hands. And then, as is usual after the victory gained with violence, the popular party was sharply divided between two sections — the Girondins and the Jacobins. Again there was an appeal to force. The Girondins asked the provinces to rise in arms, the Jacobins asked Paris to rise in arms. Paris being nearer and stronger, the Girondins were defeated and sent to the guillotine — the Jacobins seized the power. But it did not take them many months to fall out among themselves. First Robespierre and Danton sent Herbert and Chaumette to the guillotine, then Robespierre sent Danton to the guillotine. Robespierre in his turn was guillotined by Collot, Billaud and Tallien. These men, again, were banished by others to the far-off South America. If there was a slight difference of views between the Girondins and the Jacobins, there was practically none between the different sections of the Jacobins. The whole question was which of the various sections was to rule France. Force gave way to stronger force and at last under Napoleon France experienced a despotism similar to if not worse than the despotism of Louis XIV. As regards liberty there was not more liberty in France under the terrible Committee of Public Safety and Napoleon than under Louis XIV or Louis XV. The law of Prairial was certainly much worse than *Lettres de Cachet*. And the people —? On the *Pont au Change, on the Place de Greve,* in long sheds, Merrier, at the end of the Revolution, saw working men at their repast. One's allotment of daily bread had sunk to an ounce and a half. "Plates containing each three grilled herrings, sprinkled with shorn onions, wetted with a little vinegar;

to this add some morsel of boiled prunes, and lentils swimming in a clear sauce; at these frugal tables I have seen them ranged by the hundred; consuming, without bread, their scant messes, far too moderate for the keenness of their appetite, and the extent of their stomach." "Seine water," remarks Carlyle grimly, "rushing plenteous by will supply the deficiency." One cannot forget the exclamation of Carlyle in this connection:

> "O Man of Toil, Thy struggling and thy daring, these six long years of insurrection and tribulation, thou hast profited nothing by it, then? Thou consumest thy herring and water, in the blessed gold-red of evening. O why was the Earth so beautiful be crimsoned with dawn and twilight, if man's dealings with man were to make it a vale of scarcity, of tears—not even soft tears? Destroying of Bastilles, discomfiting of Brunswicks, fronting of Principalities and Powers, of Earth and Tophet, all that thou hast dared and endured—was it for a Republic of the Salons? Aristocracy of Feudal Parchment has passed away with a mighty rushing; and now, by a natural course, we arrive at Aristocracy of the Moneybag. It is the course through which all European Societies are, at this hour, travelling. Apparently a still baser sort of Aristocracy. An infinitely baser—the basest yet known."

Even today France is plodding her weary way towards Swaraj.

Revolutions in England

The history of England proves the same truth. The revolution of the barons in 1215 took away or purported to take away the power from the King; but the power fell into the hands of the aristocracy, and democracy did not share in the triumph of the barons. Thus the Great Charter, as a great historian has observed, was not a Charter of Liberty, but of liberties. The revolution in the reign of Charles I produced a new dictator who suppressed freedom. The work which the Long Parliament began was interrupted by the revolution which followed the execution of the King, and it required another revolution, this time a bloodless revolution, to complete the work. I deny that the work is yet complete. The continual class war and the obvious economic injustice do not proclaim that freedom which England claimed for herself. I maintain that no people has yet succeeded in winning freedom by force and violence. The truth is that love of power is a formidable factor to be reckoned with, and those who secure that power by violence will retain that power by violence. The use of violence degenerates them who use it, and it is not easy for them, having seized the power, to surrender it. And they find it easier to carry on the work of their predecessor, retaining their power in their own hands. Non-violence does not carry with it that degeneration which is inherent in the use of violence.

Revolutions in Italy and Russia

The Revolutions in Italy and Russia illustrate the same principle. The Italian Revolution inspired by Mazzini and worked out by Garibaldi and Cavour did not result in the attainment of *Swaraj*. The freedom of Italy is yet in the making, and the men and women of Italy are today looking forward to another revolution. If it results in a war of violence, it will again defeat its purpose, but only to allow freedom and non-violence to triumph in the end.

The recent revolution in Russia is very interesting study. The shape which it has now assumed is due to the attempt to force Marxian doctrines and dogmas on the unwilling genius of Russia. Violence will again fail. If I have read the situation accurately, I expect a counter-revolution. The soul of Russia must struggle to free herself from the Socialism of Karl Marx. It may be an independent movement, or it may be that the present movement contains within itself the power of working out that freedom. In the meantime, the fate of Russia is trembling in the balance.

Nonviolent Noncooperation, the Only Method

I believe in revolutions, but, I repeat, violence defeats freedom. The revolution of non-violence is slower but surer. Step by step the soul of the nation emerges and step by step the nation marches on in the path of *Swaraj*. The only method by which freedom can be attained, in India at any rate, is the method of non-violent non-cooperation. Those who believe this method to be impracticable would do well to ponder over the *Akali* movement. When I saw the injuries of the wounded at Amritsar and heard from their lips that not one of them had even wished to meet violence by violence in spite of such grave provocation, I said to myself: "Here was the triumph of non-violence."

Non-violence is not an idle dream. It was not in vain that Mahatma declared: "Put up thy sword into the sheath," Let those who are "of the truth" hear his voice as those others heard a mightier voice two thousand years ago.

The attempt of the Indian nation to attain *Swaraj* by this method was, however, met by severe, repression. The time has come for us to estimate our success as well as our failure. So far as repression is concerned, it is easy to answer the question. I have not the least doubt in my mind that the nation has triumphed over the repression which was started and continued to kill the soul of the movement.

Success of Nonviolent-Noncooperation

But the, question, which agitates most minds, is as to whether we have succeeded in our work of non-violent non-cooperation. There is, I am sorry to say, a great deal of confusion of thought behind the question. It is assumed that a movement must either succeed or fail, whereas the truth is that human movements—I am speaking of genuine movements—neither altogether succeed nor altogether fail. Every genuine movement proceeds from an ideal, and the ideal is always higher than the achievement. Take the French Revolution. Was it a success? Was it a failure?

To predicate either would be a gross historical blunder. Was the non-cooperation movement in India a success? Yes, a mighty success when we think of the desire for *Swaraj* which it has succeeded in awakening throughout the length and breadth of this vast country. It is a great success when we think of the practical result of such awakening, in the money which the nation contributed, in the enrolment of members of the Indian National Congress and in the boycott of foreign cloth. I go further and say that the practical achievement also consists of the loss of prestige suffered by educational institutions and the Courts of Law and the Reformed Councils throughout the country. If they are still resorted to, it is because of the weakness of our countrymen. The country has already expressed its strong desire to end these institutions. Yet it must be admitted that from another point of view, when we assess the measure of our success in the spirit of arithmetic, we are face to face with "the petty done" and "the undone vast.' There is much which remains to be accomplished. Non-violence has to be more firmly established. The work of non-cooperation has to be strengthened, and the field of Non-cooperation has to be extended. We must be firm but reasonable. The spirit of sacrifice has got to be further strengthened, and we must proceed with the work of destruction and creation more vigorously than before. I say to our critics: I admit we have failed in many directions, but will you also not admit our success where we have succeeded?

Charge of Corrupting the Youth

We have been denounced by the Moderates for having corrupted the youth of the country. It has been asserted that we have taught sons to disobey their fathers, the pupils their teachers, and the subjects the Government. We plead guilty to the charge, and we rely upon every spiritual movement as argument in our support. Christ himself was tried for having corrupted the people, and the answer which he gave in anticipation is as emphatic as it is instructive:

> "Think not that I am come to send peace on earth: I come not to send peace, but a sword."
>
> "For I am come to set a man at variance against his father, and the daughter against her mother, and the daughter-in-law against her mother-in-law."

Charge of Hypocrisy

It has been said that with love on our lips we have been preaching the gospel of hatred. Never was such a vile slander uttered. It may be we have failed to love, it may be we lost ourselves, some of us, in hatred, but that only shows our weakness and imperfectness. Judge us by our ideal, not by what we have achieved. Wherever we have fallen short of that ideal put it down to our weakness. On behalf of the Indian National Congress I deny the charge of hypocrisy. To those who are ever anxious to point out our defects, I say with all humility: "My friends, if we are weak, come and join us and make us stronger. If the leaders are worthless, come and join us to lead and the leaders will stand aside. If you do not believe in the ideal, what is the use of always criticising us in the light of that ideal?" We need no critic to tell us how far we have fallen short of that ideal. Evidence of weakness has met me from every direction in which I have looked; but in spite of our defects of human weakness, of human imperfection, I feel bold enough to say that our victory is assured and that the bureaucracy knows that our victory is assured.

How to Apply the Method of Nonviolent-Noncooperation?

But though the method of non-violent non-cooperation is sure and certain, we have now to consider how best to apply that method to the existing circumstances of the country. I do not agree with those who think that the spirit of the nation is dead, that non-violent non-cooperation is no longer possible. I have given the matter my earnest thought, and I desire to make it perfectly clear that there is absolutely no reason for entertaining any feelings of doubt or despair. The outward appearance of the people today is somewhat deceptive. They appear to be in a tired condition and a sense of fatigue has partially overcome them. But beneath all this exterior of quietude, the pulse of the nation beats as strongly as before and as hopefully as at the beginning of this movement. We have to consolidate the strength of the nation. We have to devise a plan of work which will stimulate their energy so that we can accelerate our journey towards Swaraj. I shall place before you one by one the items of work which, in my opinion, the Indian National Congress should prescribe for the nation.

Declaration of the Rights of Different Communities

It should commence its work for the year by a clearer declaration of the rights of the different communities in India under the Swaraj Government. So far as the Hindus and the Mohammedans are concerned, there should be a clear and emphatic confirmation of what is known as the Lucknow Compact, and along with that there should be an emphatic recognition of each others rights, and each should be prepared to undergo some kind of sacrifice in favour of the other. Let me give an instance to make my meaning clear. Every devout Musalman objects to any music in front of a mosque, and every devout and orthodox Hindu objects to cows being slaughtered. May not the Hindus and the Musalmans of India enter into a solemn compact so that there may not be any music before any mosque and that no cows may be slaughtered? Other instances may be quoted. There should be a scheme of a series of sacrifices to be suffered by each community so that they may advance shoulder to shoulder in the path of *Swaraj*. As regards the other communities such as Sikhs, Christians and Parsees, the Hindus and the Mohammedans who constitute the bulk of the people should be prepared to give them even more than their proportional share in the Swaraj administration. I suggest that, the Congress should bring about real agreement between all these communities by which the rights of every minority should be clearly recognised in order to remove all doubts which may arise and all apprehensions which probably exist. I need hardly add that I include among Christians not only pure Indians, but also Anglo-Indians and other people who have chosen to make India their home. Such an agreement as I have indicated was always necessary, but such an agreement is specially necessary in view of the work which faces us today.

Foreign Propaganda

I further think that the policy of exclusiveness which we have been following during the last two years should now be abandoned. There is in every country a number of people who are selfless followers of liberty and who desire to see every country free. We can no longer afford to lose their sympathy and cooperation. In my opinion, there should be established Congress Agencies in America and in every European country. We must keep ourselves in touch with world movements and be in constant communication with the lovers of freedom all over the world.

Great Asiatic Federation

Even more important than this is the participation of India in the great Asiatic Federation, which I see in the course of formation. I have hardly any doubt that the Pan-Islamic movement, which was started on a somewhat narrow basis, has given way or is about to give way to the great Federation of all Asiatic people.

It is the union of the oppressed nationalities of Asia. Is India to remain outside this union? I admit that our freedom must be won by ourselves but such a bond of friendship and love, of sympathy and cooperation between India and the rest of Asia, nay, between India and all the liberty-loving people of the world is destined to bring about world peace. World peace to my mind means the freedom of every nationality, and I go further and say that no nation on the face of the earth can be really free when other nations are in bondage. The policy which we have hitherto pursued was absolutely necessary for the concentration of the work which we took upon ourselves to perform, and I agreed to that policy wholeheartedly. The hope of the attainment of *Swaraj* or a substantial basis of Swaraj in the course of the year made such concentration absolutely necessary. Today that very work demands broader sympathy and a wider outlook.

Culture of Bengal

[Excerpts from speech as President of the Bengal Provincial Conference delivered on the 23rd of April 1917 *at Bhowanipore]*

...It was in this period of gloom and depression that the English tradesman came to India. He raised his Empire in a world of ruins, and by his rapid extension of power gave proof of his wonderful energy and vitality. To us it happened as it happens to all the weak. We accepted the English Government and with that we accepted the English race — their culture, their civilization, their luxury and their licence. And even as some benighted traveller, missing the easy and well-beaten track, may follow some far and circuitous route, so we, in the blindness of our misfortune drifted away from the ancient landmarks of our soil — its history, its culture, its law and its philosophy and went in passionate pursuit of the Literature, Science and Philosophy of the English people. Perhaps this infatuation for things foreign has lessened in force but we cannot claim that it has disappeared altogether.

The trumpet of Science which Ram Mohan sounded at the threshold of national life—we heard it or we thought that we heard it; in any case we began repeating its formulas. But we cared little for that profound study of the *Shastras* in which Ram Mohan had immersed himself; we overlooked altogether the fact that

Ram Mohan had sought to find the path of our salvation in the midst of our national culture and civilization. Time passed; schools and colleges came to be founded, and our bent towards Western Civilization became more marked still. Then, after long years, Bankim Chandra came and set up the image of our Mother in the motherland. He set up the image, and inspired it with life; and it was he who beheld and recognised the

Mother first. He called unto the whole people and said:

"Behold, this is our Mother; worship her and establish her in your house." The song which he sang was of this Mother "well-watered, well-fruited, cool with the south breeze; green with the growing corn". But we were deaf to the song that he sang, we were blind to the image that he saw; and hence Bankim lamented and said, "I am crying alone in the wilderness."

More time passed. The trumpet of Swadeshism began to sound in 1905. The people of Bengal began once more to understand and realise themselves. Rabindranath sang: "The soil of Bengal, the water of Bengal make it true O Lord."' And as if in response to the poet's song, the soil and water of Bengal began to justify themselves.

There are many wise, grave and reverent seigniors among us who think — so I have heard — that the Swadeshi agitation was a colossal blunder. Western education has given rise to a kind of soulless culture in our midst — a culture that is powerless for good but is ambitious of much. People who boast of this culture seek to measure all things by rule and scale; they are pundits of mathematics and they reduce all questions to the level of mathematical problems. But the flood of life defies mathematics, it sweeps away scale and balance. The Swadeshi movement came like a tempest; it rushed along impetuously like some mighty flood. When the soul awakes, it awakes without calculation; when man is born, he is born without calculation. Man comes into life because he must; and the soul rises to consciousness because it must. And the great flood of life which we designate as the Swadeshi movement it submerged us, it enabled us to come once more in contact with the living, vital soul of Bengal. Under its reviving influence we steeped ourselves once again in that stream of culture and civilization which has been flowing perennially through the heart of Bengal; we were enabled once more to catch glimpses of the true continuity of our national history. The soul of Buddhism, of Saivism, of Saktaism and of Vaishnavism the Swadeshi movement helped us to understand it all; it reminded us of the song of Chandi Das and Vidyapati; it enabled us to appreciate more fully the radiant glory of Chaitanya's great life. The strains of Jnan Das, Govinda Das, Lochan Das and the old *kaviwaras* began once more to echo in our hearts; Ramprasad's devotional music enraptured us again; we understood the significance of Ram Mohan's deep discipline; we recognised the image which Bankim worshipped and about which he sang: "Thou art culture, and thou art law; thou art heart and thou art soul and thou art the breath of life in the body. In the arms thou art strength; in the heart thou art devotion; and it is thy image, Mother, which we build in all our shrines." Bankings song went through our ears and thrilled our hearts. We understood once again what it was that Ramakrishna sought and found; and we understood how it was that Keshab Chandra could leave the outer world of argument and enter the inner world of the heart. The speech of Vivekananda filled our souls; we understood that the Bengali might be a Hindu or Mohammedan or Christian but he continued to be a Bengali all the same; that he has a distinct type, a distinct character and a distinct law of his own. In this world of men, the Bengali has a place of his own a claim, a culture and a duty. We understood that the Bengali, if he means to realise himself, will have to be a true Bengali. In the wonderful variety of God's infinite creation the Bengali represents a distinctive type, and Bengal is the image and embodiment of that type; nay, more, it is the life and soul of that type. And with the dawn of this consciousness in our souls, the Mother, radiant in her glory, revealed her infinite, her universal beauty before us. Our hearts were flooded with this beauty We beheld that the Mother was one and yet many; distinctive and yet universal. Others may discuss and argue about this beauty; I am content to die in ecstasy over the wonder and charm of it.

The Swadeshi movement came without calculation and went without calculation; but the time for calculation has come now.

The Mother has revealed her presence; and now we must proceed to her worship; and for this worship we shall have to reckon and calculate, to draw up lists and procure materials. A great flood-tide has swept over the soil of the land; but the soil will have to be tilled and made to bring forth its hidden grains of gold; only, be confident that the gold is bound to come.

So, the main problem for our consideration is this how to develop fully and adequately the newly awakened national life of Bengal.

Each nation must develop its latent manhood as a nation, are it is possible to rouse within them the sense of true amity and brotherliness. . . As the family cannot grow unless each individual within it grows at the same time; as society cannot grow unless each component family-group develops within it; and as the nation cannot grow unless each community embraced by it grows along with it; so humanity at large cannot advance unless each different nation develops its distinctive type of character and civilization.

Whatever may be the blood that flows within our veins, be it Aryan or non-Aryan — and like Satyakama of old, the Bengalee will never seek to conceal the truth — the Bengali cannot forget that he is a Bengali first and last, that he has grown up on the soil and atmosphere of Bengal and that his daily intercourse is with this soil and atmosphere of his land. A true, permanent and fundamental relation underlies this physical intercourse; and the nationality of Bengal is founded upon this true, permanent and fundamental relation.

Even the commercial and cultural intercourse that we may have with other countries will help to enrich and develop this distinctive type of nationality; for it is the special virtue of nationality that it can give as well as receive. As for the inevitable conflict between different nationalities of which some people make so much it is impossible to deny that the development of the nation-idea leads on to a certain amount of necessary clash and conflict. But, after all, must we abolish nationality because nations enter into war with one another? Following the same train of reasoning, will it be said that we must abolish individual existence because individuals are perpetually quarrelling with one another?

Such argument is foolish. Man will develop his humanity, will find out the path to harmony, in spite of all differences and conflicts; and the same truth holds good in the case of nations as well. It is in and through the hundred wars and conflicts of today that the nations of the world will march on towards that temple of harmony and peace which Providence has fixed for them all.

But though there will be no fusion between the East and the West and no mechanical or electric union between them, yet I, together with many others, believe in the possibility of a deeper union between these two entities. Now, what will be the nature of this union? This question may be considered from two points, the point of view of nationality and the point of view of government and administration. Considered from the second standpoint, it may be said that the Bengalees and the English will both preserve the distinctive type of their national character, yet, in affairs of higher administration and Government, there is bound to come about an ultimate union between the two.

To sum up what I have said before: In order to advance the true welfare of our country, we shall have to look to our newly awakened national life; we shall have to look to the continuity of our national history; we shall have to adopt such measures for the improvement of those conditions as may be consonant with our national life and the continuity of our national history. Mimic Anglicism has become an obsession with us; we find its black footprint in every walk and endeavour of our life. We substitute meeting houses for temples; we perform stage-plays and sell pleasures in order to help charities. We hold lotteries in aid of our orphanages; we give up the national and healthful games of our country and introduce all sorts of foreign importations. We have become hybrid in dress, in thought, in sentiment and culture and are making frantic attempts even to be hybrids in blood. What wonder, then, that in this new pursuit of Western ideals we should forget that money is only a means to an end and not an end in itself? But we must beware even now and listen to the wise warning of Bankim — a warning all too-unheeded when it was first uttered.

Combined and harmonious work — this then must be our motto. But what must be our plan? With your permission, I shall give you the outline of a scheme, such as has suggested itself tc me. Government has divided our provinces among district — and for the purpose of our work it will be best to go on the basis of these territorial divisions. Our first step will be to organise all the villages of each district into a number of village-groups or unions. Where one village is sufficiently large and populous, that by itself will constitute one union or group. In the case of smaller villages, several of them will be combined to form one group or union. Then a census must be; taken of the adult males of each village union; these will form the primary village assemblies; and they will elect from among themselves a Panchayat or executive body of five members. This Panchayat or executive body will have the sole administration of the village-group in its hands. It will look to sanitation; it will arrange for water supply; it will establish night-schools; it will arrange for industrial and agricultural education; in short, the domestic economy of the village-group will be entirely in the hands of the Panchayat. Besides, in each village-group there will be a public granary; each agricultural proprietor will contribute to this granary according to the extent of his land; and in years of drought and scarcity, the resources of this public granary will be drawn upon to feed the people.

In case of petty disputes, civil or criminal, the Panchayat will be the sole deciding authority; but in the case of larger disputes, they will report to the district civil and criminal courts; and their reports will be treated as the sole plaints or complaints in such cases.

We demand our right. Only come forward and respond in unison. We demand this right and I am sure no sovereign power can resist the united demand of a united people. Only come forward and repeat your demand in chorus !

Demand for Punjab Wrongs, Khilafat, Swaraj, etc.

We are on the eve of great changes, and the world forces are upon us. The victory of Kemal Pasha has broken the bond of Asia, and she is all astir with life. It is Prometheus who "spoke within her" and her "thoughts arc like the many forests of vale through which the might of whirlwind and of rain had passed." The stir within every European country for the real freedom of the people has also worked a marvellous transformation in the mentality of subject races. That which was more or less a matter of ideal has now come within the range of practical politics. The Indian nation has found out its bearings. At such a time as this, it is necessary for us to reconsider and to restate our demands. Our demands regarding the Punjab wrongs have got to be restated, because many of them have already been realised; our demands regarding *Khilafat* have got to be reconsidered because some of them have already been worked out, and we hope that before the Lausanne Commission has finished its work very little of it will remain unrealised. Our demand for *Swaraj* must now be presented in a more practical shape. The Congress should frame a clear scheme of what we mean by a system of government which may serve as a real foundation for *Swaraj*. Hitherto, we have not defined any such system of government. We have not done so advisedly, as it was on the psychological aspect of *Swaraj* that we concentrated our attention. But circumstances today have changed. The desire is making us impatient. It is therefore the duty of the Congress to place before the country a clear scheme of the system of government which we demand. *Swaraj*, as I have said, is indefinable and is not to be confused with any particular system of government. Yet the national mind must express itself and although the full outward expression of *Swaraj* covers the whole life history of a nation, the formulation of such a demand cannot be any further delayed.

Scheme of Government and Village Organisation

It is hardly within the province of this address to deal with any detailed scheme of any such government. I cannot, however, allow this opportunity to pass without giving you an expression of my opinion as to the character of that system of government. No system of government which is not for the people and by the people can ever be regarded as the true foundation of Swaraj. I am firmly convinced that a parliamentary government is not a government by the people and for the people. Many of us believe that the middle class must win *Swaraj* for the masses. I do not believe in the possibility of any class movement being ever converted into a movement for *Swaraj*. If today the British Parliament grants provincial autonomy in the provinces with responsibility in the Central Government, I, for one, will protest against it, because that will inevitably lead to the concentration of power in the hands of the middle class. I do not believe that the middle class will then part with their power. How will it profit India, if in place of the White bureaucracy that now rules over her, there is substituted an Indian bureaucracy of the middle classes. Bureaucracy is bureaucracy, and I believe that the very idea of *Swaraj* is inconsistent with the existence of a bureaucracy. My ideal of *Swaraj* will never be satisfied unless the people cooperate with us in its attainment. Any other attempt will inevitably lead to what European Socialists call the "bourgeois" government.

In France and in England and in other European countries it is the middle class who fought the battle of freedom, and the result is that power is still in the hands of this class. Having usurped the power they are unwilling to part with it. If today the whole of Europe is engaged in a battle of real freedom it is because the nations of Europe are gathering their strength to wrest this power from the hands of the middle class. I desire to avoid the repetition of that chapter of European history. It is for India to show the light to the world — *Swaraj* by non-violence and Swaraj by the people.

To me the organisation of village life and the practical autonomy of small local centres are more important than either provincial autonomy or central responsibility; and if the choice lay between the two, I would unhesitatingly accept the autonomy of the local centres. I must not be understood as implying that the village centres will be disconnected units. They must be held together by a system of cooperation and integration. For the present, there must be power in the hands of the Provincial Governments and the Indian Government; but the ideal should be accepted once for all, that the proper function of the central authority, whether in the Provincial or in the Indian Government is to advise, having a residuary power of control only in case of need, and to be exercised under proper safeguards. I maintain that real *Swaraj* can only be attained by vesting the power of government in these local centres, and I suggest that the Congress should appoint a committee to draw up a scheme of government which would be acceptable to the nation.

The most advanced thought of Europe is turning from the false individualism on which European culture and institutions are based to what I know to be the ideal of the ancient village Organisation of India. According to this thought modern democracy of the ballot box and large crowds has failed, but real democracy has not yet been tried. What is the real democracy of modern European thought?

The foundation of real democracy must be laid in small centres—not gradual decentralisation which implies a previous centralisation—but a gradual integration of the practically autonomous small centres into one living harmonious whole. What is wanted is a human state, not a mechanical contrivance. We want the growth of institutions and organisations which are really dynamic in their nature and not the more static stability of a centralised state.

This strain of European thought found some expression in the philosophy of Hegel, according to whom "human institutions belong to the region, not of inert externality, but of mind and purpose, and are therefore dynamic and self-developing."

Modern European thought has made it clear that from the individual to the "unified state," it is one continuous process of real and natural growth. Sovereignty (Swaraj) is a relative notion. "The individual is sovereign over himself"—attains his Swaraj—"in so far as he can develop, control and unify his manifold nature". From the individual we come to "integrated neighbourhood" which is the real foundation of the unified state which again in its turn gives us the true ideal of the world-state. This integrated neighbourhood is great deal more than the mere physical continuity of the people who live in the neighbourhood area. It requires the evolution of what has been called neighbourhood "consciousness." In other words, the question is: "How can the force generated by the neighbourhood life become part of our whole civic and national life?" It is the question which now democracy takes upon itself to solve.

The process prescribed is the generation of the collective will. The democracy which obtains today rests on an attempt of securing a common will by a process of addition. This really means a war of wills, the issue being left to be decided by a mere superiority of numbers. New democracy discountenances this process of addition, and insists on the discovery of detailed means and methods by which the different wills of a neighbourhood entity may grow into one common collective will. This process is not a process of addition but of integration and the consciousness of the neighbourhood thus awakened must express the common collective will of that neighbourhood entity. The collective wills of the several neighbourhood centres must by a similar process of integration be allowed to evolve the common collective will of the whole nation. It is only thus, by a similar process of integration, that any league of nations may be real and the vision of a world-state may be realised.

The whole of this philosophy is based on the idea of the evolution of individual. The idea is to "release the powers of the individual." Ordinary nations of state have little to do with true individualism, *i.e.*, "with the individual as consciously responsible for the life from which he draws his breath and to which he contributes his all. According to this school of thought, "representative government, party organisation, majority rule, with all their excrescences are deadwood. In their stead must appear the organisation of non-partisan groups for the begetting—the bringing into being—off common ideas, a common purpose and the collective will." This means the true development and extension of the individual self.

The institutions that exist today have made machines of men. No Government will be successful, no true Government is possible which does not rest on the individual. "Up to the present moment," says the gifted authoress of the NEW STATE, "we have never seen the individual yet. The search for him has been the whole long striving of our Anglo-Saxon history. We sought him through the method of representation and failed to find him. We sought to reach him by extending the suffrage to every man and them to every woman and yet he eludes us. Direct Government now seeks the individual." In another place the same writer says: "Thus group organisation releases us from the dominion of mere numbers, thus democracy transcends time and space. It can never be understood except as a spiritual force. Majority rule rests on numbers: democracy rests on the well grounded assumption that society is not a collection of units, but a network of human relations. Democracy is not worked out at the polling booths; it is the bringing forth of a genuine collective will, one to which every single being must contribute the whole of his complex life as one which every single being must express the whole of at one point. Thus the essence of democracy is creation. The technique of democracy is group organisation." According to this school of thought no living state is possible without the development and the extension of the individual self. State itself is no static unit. Nor is it an arbitrary creation. "It is a process; a continual self-modification to express its different stages of growth in which each and all must be so flexible that continual change of form is twin-fellow of continual growth." This can change of form is twin-fellow of continual growth." This can only be realised when there is a clear perception that individuals and groups and the nation stand in no antithesis. The integration of all these into one conscious whole means and must necessarily mean the integration of the wills off individuals into the common and collective will of the entire nation.

The general trend of European thought has not accepted the ideal of this new democracy. But the present problems which are agitating Europe seem to offer no other solution. I have very little doubt that this ideal which appears to many practical politicians as impracticable will be accepted as the real ideal at no distant future. "There is little yet," I again quote from the same author, "that is practical in practical politics."

The fact is that all the progressive movements in Europe have suffered because of the want of a really spiritual basis and it is refreshing to find that this writer has seized upon it. To those who think that the neighbourhood group is too puny to serve as a real foundation of self-government, she says: "Is our daily life profane, and only so far as we rise out of it, do we approach the sacred life? Then no wonder politics are what they have become. But this is not the creed of men today; we believe in the sacredness of our life; we believe that Divinity is forever incarnating in Humanity, and so we believe in Humanity and the common daily life of all men."

There is thus a great deal of correspondence between this view of life and the view which I have been endeavouring to place before my countrymen for the last 15 years. For the truth of all truths is that the outer "leela" of God reveals itself in history. Individual, society, nation, humanity are the different aspects of that very "leela" and no scheme of self-government which is practically true, and what is really practical can be based on any other philosophy of life. It is the realisation of this truth which is the supreme necessity of the hour. This is the soul of Indian thought, and this the ideal towards which the recent thought of Europe is slowly but surely advancing.

To frame such a scheme of government regard must, therefore, be had to:

- the formation of local centres more or less on the lines of the ancient village system of India;
- the growth of larger and larger groups out of the integration of these village centres;
- the unifying state should be the result of similar growth;
- the village centres and the larger groups must be practically autonomous; and
- the residuary power of control must remain in the Central Government but the exercise of such power should be exceptional and for that purpose proper safeguard should be provided, so that the practical autonomy of the local centres may be maintained and at the same time the growth of the Central Government into a really unifying state may be possible. The ordinary work of such Central Government should be mainly advisory.

As a necessary corollary to what I have ventured to suggest as the form of government which we should accept, I think that the work of organising these local centres should be forthwith commenced. The modern sub-divisions or even smaller units may be conveniently taken as the local centres, and large centres may be conveniently formed. Once we have our local areas—"the neighbourhood group"—we should foster the habit of corporate thinking and leave all local problems to be worked out by them.

There is no reason why we should not start the Government by these local centres today. They would depend for their authority on the voluntary cooperation of the people, and voluntary cooperation is much better than the compulsory cooperation which is at the bottom of the bureaucratic rule in India. This is not the place to elaborate the scheme which I have in mind; but I think it is essentially necessary to appoint a committee with power not only to draw up a scheme of government but to suggest means by which the scheme can be put in operation at once.

Boycott of Councils

The next item of work to which I desire to refer is the boycott of Councils. Unhappily the question has become part of the controversy of Change or No-change. To my mind the whole controversy proceeds on a somewhat erroneous assumption. The question is not so much as to whether there should be a change in the programme of the work; the real question is whether it is not necessary now to change the direction of our activities in certain respects for the success of the very movement which we hold so dear. Let me illustrate what I mean. Take the Bardoli Resolution. In the matter of boycott of schools and colleges the Bardoli Resolution alters the direction of our activity, which does not in any way involve the abandonment of the boycott. During the *Swaraj* year the idea was to bring the students out of Government Schools and colleges, and if national schools were started they were regarded as concessions to the "weakness" of those students. The idea was, to quote the words of Mahatma Gandhi, "political" and not "educational." Under the Bardoli Resolution, however, it is the establishment of schools and colleges which must be the main activity of national education. The idea is "educational," and if it still be the desire of the Congress to bring students out of Government schools and colleges, it is by offering them educational advantages: Here the boycott of schools and colleges is still upheld, but the direction of our activities is changed. In fact, such changes must occur in every revolution, violent or non-violent, as it is only by such chances that the ideal is truly served.

In the next place, we must keep in view the fact that according to unanimous opinion of the members of the Enquiry Committee, civil disobedience on a large scale is out of the question because the people are not prepared for it.

I confess that I am not in favour of the restrictions which have been put upon the practical adoption of any system of civil disobedience, and in my opinion, the Congress should abolish those restrictions. I have not yet been able to understand why, to enable a people to civilly disobey particular laws, it should be necessary that at least 80 per cent of them should be clad in pure *Khadi*. I am not much in favour of general mass civil disobedience. To my mind, the idea is impracticable. But the disobedience of particular laws which are eminently unlawful, laws which are the creatures of "law and order," laws which are alike an outrage on humanity and an insult to God—disobedience of such laws is within the range of practical politics and in my opinion, every attempt should be made to offer disobedience to such laws. It is only by standing on truth that the cause of *Swaraj* may prevail. When we submit to such laws, we abandon the plank of truth. What hope is there for a nation so dead to the sense of truth as not to rebel against lawless laws, against regulations which injure their national being and hamper their national development?

I am of opinion that the question of the boycott of Councils which is agitating the country so much must be considered and decided in the light of the circumstances I have just mentioned. There is no opposition in idea between such civil disobedience as I have mentioned and the entry into the Councils for the purpose, and with the avowed object of either ending or mending them. I am not against the boycott of Councils. I am simply of opinion that the system of the Reformed Councils, with their steel frame of the Indian Civil Service covered over by a dyarchy of deadlocks and departments, is absolutely unsuitable to the nature and genius of the Indian nation. It is an attempt of the British Parliament to force a foreign system upon the Indian people. India has unhesitatingly refused to recognise this foreign system as a real foundation for Swaraj. With me, as I have often said, it is not a question of more or less; I am always prepared to sacrifice much for a real basis of *Swaraj*, nor do I attach any importance to the question as to whether the attainment of full and complete independence will be a matter of seven years or ten years or twenty years. A few years is nothing in the life history of a nation. But I maintain that India cannot accept a system such as this as a foundation of our Swaraj. These Councils must therefore be either mended or ended. Hitherto we have been boycotting the Councils from outside. We have succeeded in doing much—the prestige of the Councils is diminished, and the country knows that the people who adorn those chambers are not the true representatives of the people. But though we have succeeded in doing much, these Councils are still there. It should be the duty of the Congress to boycott the Councils more effectively from within. Reformed Councils are really a mask which the bureaucracy has put on. I conceive it to be our clear duty to tear this mask from off their face. The very idea of boycott implies, to my mind, something more than mere withdrawal.

The boycott of foreign goods means that such steps must be taken that there may be no foreign goods in our markets. The boycott of the Reformed Councils, to my mind, means that such steps must be taken that these Councils may not be there to impede the progress of Swaraj. The only successful boycott of these Councils is either to mend them in a manner suitable to the attainment of *Swaraj* or to end them completely. That is the way in which I advise the nation to boycott the Councils. A great deal of discussion has taken place in the country as to whether the boycott of Councils—in the sense in which I mean it—is within the principle of non-violent Non-cooperation. I am emphatically of opinion that it does not offend against any principle of non-cooperation which has been adopted and applied by the Indian National Congress. I am not dealing with logical or philosophical abstractions. I am only dealing with that which the Congress has adopted and calls non-cooperation.

In the first place, may I point out that we have not up to now non-cooperated with the bureaucracy? We have been merely preparing the people of this country to offer non-cooperation. Let me quote the Nagpur Resolution on non-cooperation in support of my proposition. I am quoting only the portions which are relevant to this point:

> "Whereas in the opinion of the Congress the existing Government of India has forfeited the confidence of

> the country, and, whereas the people of India are now determined to establish Swaraj. . . .now this Congress. . . .declares that the entire or any parts of the scheme of non-violent non-cooperation, with the renunciation of voluntary association with the present Government at one end, and the refusal to pay taxes at the other, should be put into force at a time to be determined by either the Indian National Congress, or the All-India Congress Committee and that, in the meanwhile to prepare the country for it, effective steps should continue to be taken in that behalf."

Then follows the effective steps, such as national education, boycott of law courts, boycott of foreign goods, etc., which must be taken "in the meanwhile." It is clear therefore that the Congress has not yet advocated the application of Non-cooperation but has merely recommended certain steps to be taken, so that, at some time or other, to be determined by the Congress, the Indian nation may offer non-cooperation.

In the second place, let us judge of the character of this principle, not by thinking any of logical idea or philosophical abstraction, but by gathering the principle from the work; it is clear to my mind, that the Congress was engaged in a two-fold activity. In everything that the Congress commanded there is an aspect of destruction as there is an aspect of creation. The boycott of lawyers and law courts means the destruction of existing legal institutions; and the formation of Panchayats means the creation of agencies through which justice may be administered. The boycott of schools and colleges means the destruction of the Department of Education; and the establishment of national schools and colleges means the creation of educational institutions for the youth of India. The boycott of foreign goods followed as it was by the burning of foreign cloth means the destruction of the foreign goods already in the country and the preventing, in future, of foreign goods coming into the country. But, on the other hand, the spinning wheel and the looms mean creative activity in supplying the people with indigenous cloth. Judged by this principle, what is wrong about the desire either to convert the Councils into institutions which may lead us to *Swaraj*, or to destroy them altogether? The same two-fold aspect of creation and destruction is to be found in the boycott of Councils in the way I want them to be boycotted.

It has also been suggested that it offends against the morality and spirituality of this movement. Let us take the two points separately. As regards the question of morality apart from the ethics of Non-cooperation, it has been urged that entering the Councils for the purpose of ending the Councils is unfair and dishonest. The argument implies that the Reformed Councils belong entirely to the bureaucracy and the idea is that we should not enter into other people's property with a view to injure it. To my mind, the argument is based on a misconception of facts. Inadequate as the Reforms undoubtedly are, I do not for a moment admit that the Reforms Act was a gift of the British Parliament. It was to quote the words of Mahatma Gandhi, "a concession to popular agitation." The fact is that it is the resultant of two contending forces, the desire of the people for freedom and the desire of the bureaucracy to oppose such desire.

The result is that it has travelled along lines neither entirely popular nor entirely bureaucratic. The people of India do not like these Reforms, but let us not forget that the bureaucracy does not like them either. Because it is the result of two contending forces pulling in different directions, the Reforms have assumed a tortured shape. But so far as the rights recognised are concerned, they are our rights—our property—and there is nothing immoral or unfair or dishonest in making use of the rights which the people have extorted from the British Parliament.

If the fulfilment of the very forces which have succeeded in securing the Reforms require that the Councils should either be mended or ended, if the struggle for freedom compels the adoption of either course, what possible charge of immorality can be levelled against it? I admit if we had proposed to enter the Councils stealthily with the avowed object of cooperation but keeping within our hearts the desire to break the Councils, such a course would undoubtedly have been dishonest. European diplomacy, let us hope, has been abolished by the Indian National Congress under the leadership of Mahatma Gandhi. If we play now, we play with all our cards on the table.

But some people say that it is immoral from the point of view of Non-cooperation, because it involves an idea of destruction. The work of Non-cooperation, according to these patriots —I have the highest reverence for them—is only to build our national life, ignoring altogether the existence of the bureaucracy. It may be an honest ideal, and logically speaking, it may be the inner meaning of Non-cooperation; but the Non-cooperation which the Congress has followed is not so logical. I claim that if the principle of Non-cooperation is to be advanced as a test of my programme, let it be the same principle which the Congress has accepted, adopted and applied. As I have already said, that principle countenances destruction as well as creation. As a matter of fact, circumstanced as we are with the bureaucracy to the right and the bureaucracy to the left; bureaucracy all round us, it is impossible to create without destroying, nor must it be forgotten that if we break, it is only that we may build.

It has also been suggested that the very entry into the Councils is inconsistent with the ideal of Non-cooperation. I confess I do not understand the argument. Supposing the Congress had sanctioned an armed insurrection, could it be argued that entry into the fort of the bureaucracy is inconsistent with the principle of Non-cooperation? Surely the charge of inconsistency must depend on the object of the entry. An advancing army does not cooperate with the enemy when it marches into the enemy's territory. Cooperation or Non-cooperation must therefore depend on the object with which such entry is made. The argument, if analysed, comes to this that whenever the phrase "entry into Councils" is used, it calls up the association of cooperation, and then the mere idea of this entry is proclaimed to be inconsistent with Non-cooperation. But this is the familiar logical fallacy of four terms. Entry into the Councils to cooperate with the Government and entry into the Councils to non-cooperate with the Government are two terms and two different propositions. The former is inconsistent with the idea of Non-cooperation, the latter is absolutely consistent with the very idea.

Next let us understand the opposition from the point of view of the spirituality of our movement. The question of spirituality is not to be confused with the dictates of any particular religion.

I am not aware of the injunctions of any religion against entering the Councils with a view either to mend them or end them. I have heard from many Mohammedans that the Holy Quran lays down no such injunction. Other Mohammedan friends have told me that there may be some difficulty on that ground, but that is a matter with regard to which I am not competent to speak. The *Khilafat* must answer that question with such assistance as they may obtain from the *Ulemas*.

It is needless to point out that should the *Ulemas* come to the conclusion that under the present circumstances it would be an offence against their religion to enter the Councils, the Congress should unhesitatingly accept their decision, because no work in this country towards the attainment of Swaraj is possible without the hearty cooperation of both Hindus and Mussalmans. But I am dealing with that spirituality which does not affect any particular creed or any particular religion. Judged from the standpoint of such spirituality, what objection can there be in removing from our path by all legitimate means any obstacle to the attainment of Swaraj? We burned foreign cloth without a scruple, and the spirituality of the movement did not receive a shock when we burned them. It is as well to start with a clear conception as to what that spirituality is. Apart from any creedal or doctrinal injunction and apart from any question of morality, the basis of spirituality must be the attainment of freedom and of Swaraj.

What is the duty which every human being owes not only to Humanity, but also to his God? It is the right to fulfil oneself. It is the duty of living in the light of God. Shortly after my release from imprisonment I said in a public speech that all our national activities should be based on truth. Ever since that day questions and conundrums have been put to me. I have been asked to define what is truth. It has also been suggested that because I dared not tell the truth that I took refuge under the general expression. I still insist that our national activities must be based on truth. I repeat that I do not believe in politics, or in making watertight compartments of our national life which is an indivisible organic whole. I repeat that as you cannot define life, you cannot define truth. The test of truth is not logical definition. The test of truth lies in its all compelling force in making itself felt. You know truth when you have felt it. God cannot be defined, nor can truth, because truth is the revelation of God. Two thousand years ago, a jesting judge asked the same question of the Son of God. He made no answer by word of mouth; but he sacrificed himself and Truth was revealed. When I speak of spirituality, I speak of the same truth. I look upon history as the revelation of God. I look upon human individual personality, nationality and humanity each contributing to the life of the other as the revelation of God to man. I look upon the attainment of freedom and Swaraj the only way of fulfilling ourselves as individuals, as nations. I look upon all national activities as the real foundation of the service of that greater humanity which again is the revelation of God to man. The Son of God brought to the world not peace but a sword—not the peace of death and immorality and corruption but the "separating sword" of truth. We have to fight against all corruption and all immorality. It is only thus that freedom can be attained. Whatever obstacles there may be in the path of Swaraj, either of the individual or of the nation, or humanity at large, these obstacles must be removed by the individual if he desires his freedom, by the nation if that nation desires to fulfil itself, by all the nations of the world if the cause of humanity is to prosper. That being the spirituality of the movement as I understand it, I am prepared to put away all obstacles that lie between the Indian nation and the attainment of its freedom, not stealthily but openly, reverently in the name of Truth and God. Judged from this ideal of spirituality, the entry into the Councils for the purpose I have stated is necessary to advance the cause of truth. Everything in connection with the controversy must be judged by that standard.

At present the question before the country put by those members of the Civil Disobedience Enquiry Committee who are in favour of Council Entry is simply that the members of the Congress should stand as candidates. It is unnecessary therefore to go into other questions raised, such as in the matter of taking oath, the probability or otherwise of securing a majority, and so on. With regard to the question of oath, all that I need say at present is this, that apart from the dictates of any particular religion which I do not propose to deal with, the question does not present any difficulty at all. The oath is a constitutional one. The King stands for the Constitution. Great changes in the Constitution have taken place in England under that very oath. Now, what is the oath? It binds those who take it—first, not to make any use of powers which are not allowed by the Reforms Act; secondly, to discharge their duties faithfully. So far as the first point is concerned, there is nothing in my suggestion which militates against it. So far as the second point is concerned, I am aware that a forced interpretation has been:

> Sought to be put upon it, namely, that a member taking the oath is bound to discharge his duties faithfully to the bureaucracy. All that I need say is, that there is no constitutional authority of any kind to justify that interpretation. To my mind, the words mean a faithful discharge of a members duties to his constituency by the exercise of powers recognised under the Reforms Act. I do not therefore understand what possible objection there may be to take the oath. But there again the question does not arise at present.

Various other questions have been asked as to whether it is possible to secure a majority, and as to what we should do supposing we are in a majority. I think it possible that having regard to the present circumstances of the country, the non-cooperators are likely to get the majority. I am aware of the difficulty of the franchise, I am aware of the rules which prevent many of us from entering the Councils; but making every allowance for all these difficulties, I believe that we shall be in the majority. But here also the question doesn't arise till we meet in the Congress of 1923 when the matter may be discussed not on suppositions but on actualities.

As regards the question as to what we should do if we have the majority, the answer is clear. We should begin our proceedings by a solemn declaration of the existence of our inherent right, and by a formal demand for a Constitution which would recognise and conserve those rights and give effect to our claims for the particular system of government which we may choose for ourselves. If our demands are accepted, then the fight is over. But, as I have often said, if it is conceded that we are entitled to have that form of government which we may choose for ourselves, and the real beginning is made with that particular form of government in view, then it matters nothing to me whether the complete surrender of power is made to us today, or in five years or even in twenty years. If, however, our demand is not given effect to, we must non-cooperate with the bureaucracy by opposing each and every work of the Council. We must disallow the entire Budget. We must move the adjournment of the House on every possible occasion; and defeat every Bill that may be introduced.

In fact we must so proceed that the Council will refuse to do any work unless and until our demands are satisfied. I am aware of the large powers of certification which Governors can exercise under the Reforms Act. But Government by certification is just as impossible as Government by veto. Such procedure may be adopted on a few occasions. The time must soon come when the bureaucracy must yield or withdraw the Reforms Act. In either case it is a distinct triumph for the nation, and either course, if adopted by the bureaucracy, will bring us nearer to the realisation of our ideal.

Another question is often asked: Suppose we end these Reformed Councils—what then? Could not the same question be asked with regard to every step the Congress has hitherto undertaken in the way of breaking, of destroying institutions. If we had succeeded in destroying the Educational Department, might not somebody ask: What then, If we had succeeded in destroying the legal institutions, might not the question be put with equal relevance? The fact is, destruction itself will never bring us Swaraj. The fact further is that no construction is possible without destruction. We must not forget that it is not this activity or that activity which by itself can bring Swaraj. It is the totality of our national activity in the way of destruction and in the way of creation that will bring Swaraj. If we succeed in demolishing these Reformed Councils, you will find the whole nation astir with life. Let them put other obstacles in our way; we shall remove them with added strength and greater vitality.

It has also been suggested that the bureaucracy will never allow the Non-cooperators to enter the Councils—they will alter the rules to prevent such entry. I cannot conceive of anything better calculated to strengthen the cause of Non-cooperation than this. If any such rule is framed I should welcome it and again change the direction of our activity. The infant nation in India requires constant struggle for its growth and development. We must not forget that a great non-violent revolution is on the land, and we shall change the direction of our activities as often as circumstances require it. Today the Councils are open and we must attack them,—tomorrow if the Councils are closed, we must be prepared to deal with the contingency when it arises. What do we do when it pours with rain? We turn our umbrella in the direction from which the water comes. It is in the same way that we must turn the direction of our activities whenever the fulfilment of our national life demands it.

The work of the Councils for the last two years has made it necessary for Non-cooperators to enter the Councils. The bureaucracy has received added strength from these Reformed Councils, and those who have entered the Councils, speaking generally, have practically helped the cause of bureaucracy. What is most necessary to consider is the fact that the taxation has increased by leaps and bounds. The expenditure of the Government of India has grown enormously since the pre-war year 1913-14. In that year the total expenditure of the Government of India amounted to Rs. 79 crores and 37 lakhs in 1919-20, it rose to Rs. 138 crores, and in 1920-21, the first year of the reformed system of administration, it stood at Rs. 149 crores. The expenses of the current year are likely to be even higher. To meet the successive increases in expenditure, additional taxation was levied in 1916-17, 1917-18, 1919-20, 1921-22, and 1922-23. We may prepare ourselves for proposals for further additional taxation in the ensuing year. In spite of the levy of additional taxation, seven out of the last nine years have been years of deficit.

The increase in military expenditure is chiefly responsible for the present financial situation. In 1913-14, the expenses of this department amounted to about Rs. 31½ crores, in 1919-20, after the conclusion of the War, they mounted up to Rs. 87½ crores, and in 1920-21, they stood at Rs. 88½ crores. As Sir M. Visvesvaraya remarks, the expenses under the head "Civil Administration" also have shown a perpetual tendency to increase. As a part and parcel of the Reform Scheme, the emoluments of the members of the Indian Civil Service, the Indian Educational Service, the Indian Medical Service and of all the other services recruited in England have been enormously increased; and to maintain some kind of fairness, the salaries of the subordinate services which are manned by Indians have also been increased.

The financial situation in the provinces is not much better. Under the financial arrangements of the Reform Scheme, the provinces of India, taken together, secured an accession to their resources of about 11 crores of rupees. Besides the provinces had between them in 1920-21 a total accumulated balance of Rs. 21 crores and 68 lakhs. But so great has been the increase in provincial expenditure during the last two years that even those provinces which had hoped to realise large surpluses are now on the verge of bankruptcy.

In the first year of the Reform Era, most of the provinces were faced with deficits and were just able to tide over their financial difficulties by drawing upon their balances. But, in the current year, the financial situation in many of the provinces has become worse. The Burma Budget shows a deficit of Rs. 1 crore and 90 lakhs, the Punjab Rs. 1 crore and 30 lakhs. Bihar and Orissa Rs. 51 lakhs, Madras Rs. 41 lakhs, the United Provinces Rs. 27 lakhs, the Central Provinces Rs. 37 lakhs. The deficit of the Madras Government would have been much higher had it not taken steps to increase its revenues by Rs. 77½ lakhs from fresh taxation. The Bengal statement shows an estimated surplus owing to the remission of the Provincial contribution to the Central Government and expected receipts from fresh taxation amounting to Rs. 1 crore and 40 lakhs. But it is very doubtful if the expectation will be realised, and early next year, further fresh taxes are likely to be imposed. Assam has budgeted for a deficit of Rs. 14½ lakhs after the imposition of additional taxation. Proposals for further taxation are under consideration in the Punjab, Bihar and Orissa, the Central Provinces and Assam. In the United Provinces the proposals brought forward by the Government were rejected by the Legislative Council.

I warn my countrymen against the policy of allowing these Reformed Councils to work their wicked will. There will undoubtedly be a further increase of taxation and there is an apprehension in my mind. I desire to express it with all the emphasis that I can command, that if we allow this policy of drift to continue the result will be that we shall lose the people who are with us today. Let us break the Councils if the bureaucracy does not concede to the demands of the people. If there is fresh taxation, as it is bound to be, let the responsibility be on the bureaucracy. Then you and I and the people will jointly fight the powers that be.

Labour Organisation

I am further of opinion that Congress should take up the work of labour and peasant organisation. With regard to labour, there is a resolution of the Nagpur Congress, but I am sorry to say that it has not been acted upon. There is an apprehension in the minds of some non-cooperators that the cause of Non-cooperation will suffer if we exploit labour for Congress purposes. I confess again I do not understand the argument. The word "exploitation" has got an ugly association, and the argument assumes that labour and peasants are not with us in this struggle for Swaraj. I deny the assumption. My experience has convinced me that labour and the peasantry of India today are, if anything, more eager to attain *Swaraj* than the so-called middle and educated classes. If we are "exploiting" boys of tender years and students of colleges, if we are "exploiting" the women of India, if we are "exploiting" the whole of the middle classes irrespective of their creed and caste and occupation, may I ask what justification is there for leaving out the labourers and peasants? I suppose the answer is that they are welcome to be the members of the Congress Committees but that there should not be a separate organisation of them. But labour has got a separate interest and it is often oppressed by the foreign capitalists, and the peasantry of India is often oppressed by a class of men who are the standard bearers of the bureaucracy. Is the service of this special interest in any way antagonistic to the service of nationalism? To find bread for the poor, to secure justice to the class of people who are engaged in a particular trade or avocation—how is that work any different from the work of attaining Swaraj? Anything which strengthens the national cause anything which supports the masses of India is surely as much a matter of *Swaraj* as any other item of work the Congress has in mind. My advice is that the Congress should lose no time in appointing a committee, a strong workable committee, to organise labour and peasantry of India. We have delayed the matter already too long. If the Congress fails to do its duty, you may expect to find organisations set up in the country by labourers and peasants detached from you, dissociated from the cause of *Swaraj* which will inevitably bring, within the arena of the peaceful revolution, class struggles and the war of special interests. If the object of the Congress be to avoid that disgraceful issue let us take labour and the peasantry in hand, and let us organise them both from the point of view of their own special interest and also from the point of view of the higher ideal which demands satisfaction of their special interest and the devotion of such interest to the cause of Swaraj. Here again we have to make use of the selfishness of labourers and peasants, as we know that the fulfilment of that very selfishness requires just and proper contribution to the life of the nation.

Work Already Taken Up

I now turn to the work which the Congress has already taken up. I may at once point out that it is not my desire that any work which the Congress has taken up should be surrendered. The change of direction which I advocate and the other practical changes which I have mentioned are not by way of surrendering any thing that is already on the plank—but it is simply by way of addition.

Boycott of Schools and Colleges

I am firmly of opinion that the boycott of schools and colleges should be carried on as effectively as before. I differ from the Civil Disobedience Enquiry Committee when they propose the abandonment of the withdrawal of boys from such schools and colleges. The question to my mind is of vital importance. It is on the youth of the country that the cause of *Swaraj* largely depends and what chance is there for a nation which willingly, knowingly sends its boys, its young men to schools and colleges to be stamped with the stamp of slavery and foreign culture? I do not desire to enter into the question more minutely. I have expressed my views on the subject so often that I find it unnecessary to repeat them. I, however, agree with the recommendations of the Enquiry Committee that national schools and colleges should also be started.

Boycott of Law Courts and Lawyers

With regard to the question of the boycott of lawyers and legal institutions, I agree with the main recommendations of the Committee. Many questions have been raised as to whether the right of defence should be allowed or not, and on what occasions, and for what purposes. I have never been in love with formal rules and I think it impossible to frame rules which will cover all the circumstances which may arise in particular cases. All that I desire to insist on, is the keeping in view of the principle of the boycott of the courts.

Hindu-Muslim Unity

With regard to the question of Hindu-Muslim unity, untouchability and such matters, I agree with the recommendation of the Enquiry Committee. I desire to point out, however, that true unity of all sections of the Indian nation can only be based on a proper cooperation and the recognition by each section of the rights of the others—that is why I propose that there should be a compact between the different sections, between the different communities of India. We will do little good to the section known as Untouchables if we approach them in a spirit of superiority. We must engage them in the work before us and we must work with them side by side and shoulder to shoulder.

Khaddar

I now come to the question of Khaddar which I regard as one of the most important questions before us. As I have already said, I am opposed to the manufacture of Khaddar on a commercial basis. I said among other things when I seconded the Bezwada Resolution on the 31st of March 1921 proposed by Mahatma Gandhi:

> "Our reason in asking the people to take to the Charkha was not based upon any desire to enter into any competition with foreign capitalist production either from without or from within. Our idea is to enable

> the people to understand and fashion for themselves their economic life and utilise the spare time of their families and opportunities with a view to create more economic goods for themselves and improve their own condition."

The idea is to make the people of this country self-reliant and self-contained. This work is difficult but essential and should be carried on with all our strength. I would much rather that a few families were self-contained than factories were started on a large scale. Such factories represent a short-sighted policy, and there is no doubt that though it would satisfy the present need it will create an evil which it would be difficult to eradicate. I am naturally opposed to the creation of a new Manchester in India of which we have had sufficient experience. Let us avoid that possibility, if we can.

It is often stated that Khaddar alone will bring us Swaraj. I ask my countrymen in what way is it possible for Khaddar to lead us to Swaraj? It is in one sense only that the statement may be true. We must regard Khaddar as the symbol of Swaraj. As the Khaddar makes us self-contained with regard to a very large department of our national life, it is hoped that the inspiration of Khaddar will make the whole of our national life self-contained and independent. That is the meaning of the symbol. To my mind, such symbol worship requires the spreading out of all non-cooperation activities in every possible direction. It is thus and only thus that the speedy attainment of *Swaraj* is possible.

Conclusion

It remains to me to deliver to you a last message of hope and confidence. There is no royal road to freedom, and dark and difficult will be the path leading to it. But dauntless is your courage, and firm your resolution; and though there will be reverses, sometimes severe reverses, they will only have the effect of speeding your emancipation from the bondage of a foreign Government. Do not make the mistake of confusing achievement with success. Achievement is an appearance, and appearances are often deceptive. I contend that, though we cannot point to a great deal as the solid achievement of the movement, the success of it is assured. That success was proclaimed by the bureaucracy in the repeated attempts which were made, and are still being made, to crush the growth of the movement, and to arrest its progress, in the refusal to repeal some of the most obnoxious of the repressive legislations, in the frequent use that has been made of the arbitrary or discretionary authority that is vested in the executive government, and in sending to prison our beloved leader who offered himself as a sacrifice to the wrath of the Bureaucracy. But though the ultimate success of the movement is assured, I warn you that the issue depends wholly on you, and on how you conduct yourselves in meeting the forces that are arrayed against you. Christianity rose triumphant when Jesus of Nazareth offered himself as a sacrifice to the excessive worship of law and order by the Scribes and Pharisees.

The forces that are arrayed against you are the forces, not only of the bureaucracy, but of the modern Scribes and Pharisees whose interest it is to maintain the bureaucracy in all its pristine glory. Be it yours to offer yourselves as sacrifices in the interest of truth and justice, so that your children's children may have the fruit of your sufferings. Be it yours to wage a spiritual warfare so that the victory when it comes, does not debase you nor tempt you to retain the power of government in your own hands. But if yours is to be a spiritual warfare, your weapons must be those of the spiritual soldiers. Anger is not for you, hatred is not for you; nor for you is pettiness, meanness or falsehood for you is the hope of dawn and the confidence of the morning, and for you is the song that was sung of Titan—chained and imprisoned but the Champion of Man—in the Greek fable:

> To suffer woes which Hope thinks infinite: To forgive wrongs darker than death or night; To defy Power, which seems omnipotent: To love, and bear; to hope till Hope creates From its own wreck the thing it contemplates; Neither to change, nor falter, nor repent; This, like the glory. Titan, is to be Good, great and joyous, beautiful and free; This is alone Life, Joy, Empire and Victory."

Bande Mataram

Hindu-Muslim Mass Meeting at Calcutta

[In the course of his presidential address at the Hindu-Mohammedan Mass meeting held at Calcutta in October 1917 to protest against the internment of Messrs. Mohammed Ali and Shakut Ali, Mr. C. R. Das said:]

The difficulty is the European Association. We are used to the tricks of the European Association. In the days of the Ilbert Bill Agitation, we saw what the Anglo-Indians can do. But then, public opinion had hardly been born in this country. Today, again, when the British Government has recognised the policy of self-government we hear the same uproar. These people who come here to make money, who come here penniless and when they retire, take away thousands and thousands—these people pretend to talk in the name of India when they say that these gentlemen, these honoured gentlemen should not be released because they knew that if they are released, they will strengthen the party which seeks Self-Government, because they know that when Mr. Mohammed Ali comes out, when Babu Sham Sunder Chakravarty comes out, they will fight shoulder to shoulder for the cause of Self-government in this country. And if Self-government is granted what about the policy of these merchants? If Self-Government is granted the authority of Magistrates and Collectors in every district will be lessened — and then what would happen to these gentlemen who write letters to Collectors saying, — my dear so and so, will you see this clone and will you see that done? It is a notorious fact that in this country and I have heard complaints from many Indian Merchants engaged in the coal trade that they cannot get waggons at a time when English merchants are fully supplied with waggons. These are the advantages which they get by this country being ruled not by the people of this country but by a bureaucracy. That really is the reason of this Anglo-Indian agitation.

I must refer to the speeches made by these knights of Anglo-India against the interests of this country and against the policy of Self-Government. I will first of all refer to the foolish speech of Arden Wood. This gentleman is reported to have said: "If racial feeling is to be dominant in Indian politics the time will come, when we, the British will either have to leave India or reconquer it." Now, gentlemen, it is difficult to take this speech seriously. They may leave India if they find it unprofitable to stay in India. They may stay in India if they find it profitable to do so but the tall talk of reconquering India is a comical statement. It reminds me of the bravery of the valiant Pistol and Corporal Nymph. If this gentleman does not know, he ought to know that India was never conquered. India was won by love and won by promise of good government. India was never conquered and God willing, it will never be conquered for all time to come. India will impress her ideal, her civilization, and her culture upon the whole world. The work has commenced today. It will go on increasing till the world will listen to the message of India.

Some of the other speakers made very angry speeches. One gentleman is reported to have said that if there is a government by the people and for the people then there will be no security for life and "prosperity". Mark the word prosperity. I do not know whether the printer's devil is responsible for this but if he is, this devil has got a perfect knowledge of the internal affairs. The apprehension of this speaker is that if there is Self-government, there will be no security or prosperity. Whose prosperity may we ask? Is it the prosperity of India, is it the prosperity of the teeming millions of our country or is it the prosperity of Sir Archy Birkmyre? Whose prosperity? If the granting of Home Rule to this country means the poverty of Sir Archy Birkmyre, let it be so, but still Self-government must be granted. India does not live for Sir Archy Birkmyre or the petty traders who come here and rob us of our money. India lives for herself—she has lived for herself for centuries and she will live in herself and for herself for all time to come. There is another statement made by this angry speaker, which takes my breath away. He says that this agitation of the European Association is to assert the rights of the British in India. The rights of the British in India! These little-minded traders who at a time when the Government enjoins a calm atmosphere hold a meeting and proceed straight away to denounce the whole country; and abuse the people and all the ideals for which they fight and in which they live and move and have their being—these men claim the right to represent the British. The British indeed! When His Majesty's ministers say that there should be Home Rule, there should be Self-Government, that the people of this country should be granted equal partnership with the people of England in the Empire, who are these traders who claim to represent British interests in India? Gentlemen, I will not take you through the many comical statements made by this entertaining band of players, Jones-Birkmyre Company. They are used to many tricks. I will refer to some of the 'Statesman' newspaper, which used to pose as the Friend of India at one time. I think it has given up all that pretence now. This "Statesman" came out one day with a furious article on the Extremists of Bengal and praised the Moderates and the next day it said that there did not seem to be any difference between the Extremists and the Moderates. Well, the reason for that is quite clear. There is in fact, no difference.

This distinction was invented by the "Statesman" newspaper some years ago. We can frankly tell the Anglo-Indian community that there are no Extremists among us, no Moderates. The Hindus and Mohammedans of Bengal are all Nationalists—they are neither Extremists nor Moderates. I may tell you who are the Extremists. It is those Anglo-Indian Agitators who are the worst Extremists. You talk of a calm atmosphere ! Who broke that calm? It is you Anglo-Indian agitators. It is Sir Hugh Bray, it is the Lieutenant-Governor of the Punjab, it is the speakers who spoke at the meeting of the European Association. These people broke the calm. I ask them to consider the position and beware.

The days of the Ubert Bill agitation have gone by. These are the days of rising Democracy in this country. We will no longer tolerate that sort of vapourings, that kind of abuse. If, inspite of that, they persist in their wicked agitation, we shall soon know how to deal with them. We are fighting in the best interests of the Empire, we are fighting for the ideal expressed by the King's ministers, we are fighting for carrying out that very policy which has been declared in England by His Majesty's ministers, and by His Excellency the Viceroy in this country. If you dare stand against that, we will know how to deal with you. Be assured, we Indians do not deny your legitimate share whatever may be the extent of that share in the Government of this country. We know what you mean when you say that Self-government is no good, because Self-government would be against the interests of the teeming millions of India. We know the hollowness of that hypocrisy. But we can tell these gentlemen, so far us I am concerned, at any rate, I am perfectly clear, — that we shall accept no Self-government, no Home Rule unless it recognises and includes within it the teeming millions of India.

When I ask for Home Rule, for Self-Government, I am not asking for another bureaucracy, another oligarchy in the place of the bureaucracy that there is at present. In my opinion, bureaucracy is bureaucracy, be that bureaucracy of Englishmen or of Anglo-Indians or of Indians. We want no bureaucracy, we want Home Rule, we want Self-government by the people and for the people. We want Self-government in which every individual of this country, be he the poorest ryot or the richest zemindar—will have his legitimate share. Every individual must have some voice. We want Home Rule broad based on the will of the people of India. Now gentlemen, this is our objective. Do they still say or can they, in reason, say, that we are not asking Home Rule on behalf and in the interests of the teeming millions of India? If they say we have got no right to ask for it in their interest, my answer is we have a thousand times greater right to ask for them than you who never know them or care for them. India has always been tolerant towards those people, whatever their religious creed or faith may be, who have made India their Home—every one of them is my brother and I embrace him with open arms. The history of India has made it abundantly clear. We have the Parsis in India. They adopted India as their home and today we embrace them as our brothers. We have had hosts of Mohammedan invaders who came to this country as conquerors but they made this country their home and today we embrace them with open arms. If these Anglo-Indians want to make India their home, let them do so and we will work hand in hand with them in the interest of the Indian Empire. But if they come here to make money and all their interests, it is how best to make it. I say they are no friends of India, they have got no right to call themselves Indians, they have got no legitimate right to oppose the granting of self-good to the people of India. I say to them. "Come here if you want. Make money if you can. Go away in peace if you want to do so.'

I said that our difficulty is the mischievous working of the European association. Let us be united, gentlemen. Let us assist the Government against this selfish and unreal agitation. I feel sure the victory is ours.

Speech at a Public Meeting in Mymensingh

[A large meeting of the people of Mymensingh was held in Oct. 1917 at the Surjakanta Hall, under the presidency of Balm Anathbandhu Guha to formulate a scheme of responsible Government for India, when Mr. C. R. Das addressed as follows:]

Mr. Chairman, and gentlemen,—I thank you heartily for calling upon me to address you tonight. This is my first visit to Mymensingh. Before I arrived here, I really did not know that I had so many friends amongst you. My friend Mr. Guha has referred to my unselfish activities. I am sure I do not deserve that praise. But this I will claim for myself that whenever the interest of the country required my services, I have never lagged behind. I might not have always adopted the right course—I might have been wrong, every one of us is often wrong but I have always honestly tried to place the interest of the country above all considerations. With me work for my country is not imitation of European politics. It is part of my religion. It is part and parcel of all the idealism of my life. I find in the conception of my country the expression also of divinity. With me nationality is no mere political conception, borrowed from the philosophy of the west. With me a nation has to grow because a nation must grow. God's universe teems with varieties of life. Every nation is one unit of such life. Every nation must grow to the evolution of life.. The nation to which I belong must also grow, only we must help in its growth. I value this principle of nationality as I value the principle of morality and religion. The service of country and nationality is service of humanity. Service of humanity is worship of God.

Bengal has a Message to Deliver

Tonight, I wish to say a few words to you about the present political situation in our country. Do not imagine gentlemen, that your political situation is detached from other matters which belong to our country. Political activity is part and parcel of your culture; it is the practice of your patriotism; it is the expression of your religion. I never believe in watertight compartments of human culture. There are people of this country, who try to divide the whole field on human life into so many compartments or divisions. With them politics is one thing, religion, education—these things have nothing to do with politics. With them religion is a different branch altogether. Neither politics nor education has anything to do with it. They forget that human soul is one, they forget that the individuality of human beings is one complex whole covering many activities. As the individual soul is one so the national soul is one. I do not desire to deal with the political situation of today in any narrow spirit or in a spirit which is borrowed from the politics of Europe,—much as I venerate European culture, much as I love and much as I acknowledge my indebtedness to the education which I had in Europe, I cannot forget that Bengal stands for something higher than that. I cannot forget that our nationality must not rest content with borrowing things from European politics and I repeat what I said elsewhere, that Bengal has a message to give to the world. When you will find that infant nationality has grown and we have developed according to our light, our country will deliver that message and the world will listen.

Predominant Note in the Political Situation

Now, gentlemen, what is the predominant note in the political situation of today. I refer to the many attempts which are being made to introduce in this country some kind of Self-government. Some people call it Self-government, others call it Home-Rule, others again *Swaraj*—but we need not quarrel with words, they all mean the same thing. I would much rather you should give your attention to the thing itself than the name with which you want to call that thing. Now, what is it which is necessary in the interest of our race not only in the interest of our race (but in the interest of the world at large) for no race can have its self-interest fulfilled in the highest degree without at the same time contributing to the interest of the Empire and of the human race. So I ask you to consider what is necessary for you to have by way of self-government. It is abundantly clear that the highest authorities in England have come to the conclusion—our politicians and many other persons who have devoted their time and energy to the cause of the country have also come to the conclusion—that we must have some form of Government which may be described as Government by the people and for the people.

What Our Politics Consists in?

Now gentlemen, I desire to point out one thing clearly here. It has been said by Anglo-Indian newspapers and Anglo-Indian agitators that our politics consists in abusing the Government. Well, I deny that charge in toto. Our politics consists in this that we want some kind of Government which may be described as responsible Government, according to the principles of constitutional law. We want some sort of Government in which the Government officials will be responsible to the people whom they govern. We have no quarrel with individuals. If a civilian official does some wrong in some place we feel we have to criticise his actions. But my objection will not be met by replacing the whole of the Civil Service by Bengalees. My quarrel is not with individuals, my quarrel is with the system—it is an evil system. It might have been necessary at one time. It has done its work and it is no longer necessary. It hampers our growth at the present moment—anything which stands against our growing nationality. I have no hesitation in describing that as an evil. The time has come when this system should be cast away as a 'creed outworn.'

What Kind of Government We Want?

Gentlemen, if you have once made up your mind that you want some kind of Government which will be responsible to the people, the next point to consider will be, what kind of Government is it that you want. We cannot forget that we live in the midst of an Empire, the largest and the most glorious Empire in the history of the human race. We cannot forget that our interests are bound up intimately with the interest of England. We cannot forget that our interests are also bound up with the interest of Australia and South Africa. All of us live and grow under the sway of the same Empire, If you consider the geographical magnitude of this Empire, the different races, the different creeds, the different cultures, the different religions which this Empire represents, you will find that here is a glorious opportunity for federating so many human races, with so many distinct interests, distinct nationalities, different cultures, different religions and in that way for contributing to the ultimate federation of the whole human race. That is the philosophy of nationalism today. Therefore first of all, we must get a government which will be autonomous in so far as it will be government by the people and for the people. The different provincial governments are to be connected together by some sort of central government and then again that central government is to be connected up with the different parts of this vast Empire. That is the sort of Government for which the time has come for which to make a definite scheme.

Enunciation of Policy

The proclamation of 1858, impliedly promised some such free autonomous representative government. Years rolled by, we passed through many changes, we had many different promises on different occasions, but these promises had never been redeemed. The other day, His Majesty the King-Emperor came to this country and from his lips, we had the message of hope. Though we have been disappointed over and over again, the time has come when these promises must be redeemed. In connection with the political situation of the present moment, I ask you to consider first the statement of the Secretary of State for India, which was published on the 20th August last (1917). I invite your particular attention to the words of that statement. I will read out to you certain portions which are significant of what is to come.

["The policy of His Majesty's Government etc. etc. is that of increasing the association of Indians in every branch of administration and the gradual development of self-governing institutions with a view to the progressive realisation of responsible government in India, as an integral part of the British Empire"], etc.

I draw your particular attention to the words "Progressive realisation of responsible government in India, as an integral part of the British Empire." That is the ideal which the Secretary of State has sketched out. What is the deduction from this? What is it that we have got to hope for from this statement? It is this: that there will be several representative institutions and that these institutions will be responsible institutions and that these institutions will form the Government of India, which will be an integral part of the British Empire. Now, what does that mean? It means that there should be autonomous governments in every province that these provincial governments are to be responsible and autonomous, that is to say, responsible not to the Government of India, not to anything which is above them, but to the people, the electors who would elect the representatives to these autonomous legislative bodies. That is the doctrine of responsible self-government as it is understood in politics and in constitutional law. Now, therefore, you get these provincial governments which are responsible to the people, i.e. the members being elected by the people and you get these autonomous governments connected with the Government of India and again the Government of India connected with the Empire. How that connection will be served has been described by certain political thinkers in England but I do not desire to deal with it because before it is declared as the policy of Government, we have no right to take those utterances as part of any statement by the Government. Having sketched out this ideal, the Secretary of State goes on to say: "They have decided that substantial steps in this direction should he taken as soon as possible, etc."

Therefore, gentlemen, you get two things perfectly distinct in this statement and I appeal to you that, you should not lose sight of these two, *viz.* the ideal of responsible government which will be representative in the highest sense of the word and which will be connected with the Empire and secondly, some steps should be taken immediately in that direction. That is the declaration of policy made by His Majesty's Government. We have, therefore, a right to expect that some definite steps will be taken soon towards the practical attainment of that ideal.

Viceroy on Self-government

The next thing to which I wish to refer is the speech of His Excellency the Viceroy, delivered on the 5th of September. I will only refer to that part of it which deals with this ideal of self-government. His Excellency says:

> "I now turn to the third task, viz, constitutional reforms. At the very first Executice Council, which I held as Viceroy and Governor-General, I propounded two

> questions to my Council: (1) What is the goal of British Rule in India? (2) What are the steps on the road to that goal? We came to the conclusion which, I trust most Hon. Members will agree, was inevitable, that the endowment of British India, as an integral part of the British Empire, with self-government was the goal of British Bute, and His Majesty's Government have not put forward in precise terms their policy, which we may say that we as the Government of India regard in substance as practically indistinguishable from that which we put forward, etc., etc."

Having said what the goal is, His Excellency proceeds to say that the first road to that goal is in the domain of local self-government, village, rural, town or municipal.

The second road is in the domain of more responsible employment of Indians under the Government. Referring to the third, His Excellency says:

> *["He come now to our third road, which lay in the domain of Legislative Council. At Hon. Members will readily appreciate, there is no subject on which so much difference of opinion crists, and with regard to which greater need is required for careful investigation and sober decision. I may say frankly that we, as the Government of India, recognise fully that an advance must be made on this road simultaneously, with the advances on the other two, etc. etc.]"*

I draw your attention to this. We, therefore, have got the right to hope that not only will this work of local self-government commence but simultaneously, along with that, work in the other two domains must also commence His Excellency says:

> "And His Majesty's Government, in connection with the goal which they have outlined in their announcement have decided that substantial steps in the direction of the goal they define-should be taken as soon as possible."

I say, therefore, gentlemen, that we have got a right to expect that in the near future some substantial steps should be taken for granting to the people of this country that government which is responsible, which is representative and which is an integral part of the British Empire.

How Difficulties Began?

After these declarations were made, difficulties began. On the one hand, it filled us with hope that many of us, I must confess, did not examine this statement minutely and critically and had only a vague impression as to what was going to be done and were unduly suspicious, but on the whole, it has made us hope for the realisation of that which we have been fighting for, for the last 50 years. On the other hand, it gave rise to despair in other people. I would ask you to mark the dates. The statement of the Secretary of State was made on the 20th of August. On the 13th of September the memorable pronouncement was made by His Excellency the Viceroy. On the 20th September, Sir Hugh Bray and Mr. Hogg spoke in the Indian Legislative Council; and they at once made it clear that it was nonsense to think of any kind of Self-government so far as India is concerned. I ask you to note that fact because I shall ask you to consider what followed, in the light of that interesting event which took place on the 20th September. I am referring to the speeches made by Sir Hugh Bray and Mr. Hogg. Now, Sir Hugh Bray, apart from criticising the political activities of the people of this country — I will not retaliate by abuse for abuse — made it perfectly clear by saying this: "It is not we who wanted a change in the method of Government." So, Sir Hugh Bray does not want a change in the method of Government. The European Association, 6 days after, declared that they did not want a change in the method of Government in this country.

Is it a Wild Inference?

Is it a wild inference to draw from these two significant events that these people did not want a change in the method of Government in this country, because they know the present system of Government is the most profitable to them? If any one draws that inference, is he to be characterised as a violent speaker? I say the dates and the speeches speak for themselves. It is idle to say afterwards "we were not against changes, we wanted our interest to be safeguarded." The fact is they did not want a change and why should they? It I had been an Anglo-Indian merchant, I should not have wanted a change. They say that they have sunk capital in this country. I do not know the exact extent of that capital. My impression is — I speak from my impression and I am subject to correction, but I think I am right — that for whatever capital they invested, they have taken out a great deal more in the shape of profits. But granting, that they have sunk capital in this country, what right does it give them to dictate to the people of this country that the method of this particular Government is not to be changed. British capital has been invested in America, France and Germany. Does any British Merchant ever dream that they have got the right to dictate to the American, French, or German Government about the method of their particular Government? Why is it that the sinking of capital should have such a different effect on the soil of this country? The reason is perfectly clear. In America, they would not stand such nonsense, in France they will be asked to keep quiet. But it is only in this country that these merchants who have sunk capital—I am assuming that they have and that it still remains unrealised—can put forward the claim that the Government of this country should be run in their interest and not in the interest of the people of India. They see the absurdity of their position and because they see the utter absurdity of this illogical and extravagant claim which they make in furtherance of their self-interest they have to say that they are the real representatives of India. They say, "We are speaking not only on our behalf but on behalf of the teeming millions of this country. You are professional agitators," I do not understand what they mean by "professional agitators' '—nobody pays me or Mr. Surendra Nath Banerjea or any of my friends for making speeches. However, what they mean is this: that the speakers belong to a particular profession? I happen to belong to law. Many of my friends who have to make speeches belong to the medical profession or some other profession. But these speakers of the European Association also belong to some profession or trade. Sir Archy Birkmyre has also his trade to ply, the other merchants I suppose make their profits, Mr. Jones of the

"Statesman" gets his wages—and even the fire-eater of the Lamartinaire College must draw his pay. Mr. Pugh I do not think forgets to send in his bills of costs. That is not what they mean. They have got to find out some ground of abuse. Therefore they say "Oh those professional agitators, these wicked agitators, do not listen to them for one single moment. The teeming millions of this country do not want them." No, gentlemen, our countrymen do not want us. They want Mr. Jones of the "Statesman" and the other celebrities who exhibited their eloquence at that meeting! These worthies next proceeded to demonstrate the utter absurdity of any idea of self-government for us.

Charge of Illiteracy

Mr. Jones in his speech says that out of a total of 315 millions of people in this country only a very few know how to read and write. I take it that he asks us to infer from that people who do not know how to read and write are worthless—they have got no conscience of their own they do not know what is good and what is bad—they cannot choose between Mr. Jones and Mr. Surendra Nath Banerje. Well, I deny that proposition. I do not know what it is in Europe but so far as the teeming millions of our country are concerned, I have very often come across men who are called illiterate, but I can assure you that great many of them are shrewd men of business. They are certainly competent to judge as to who could look after their interest better whether it is Sir Archy Birkmyre or any one of us. They are certainly in a position to judge that. But if they are illiterate, may we ask why have they remained so? What has the Government done, if at the close of a hundred and fifty years, so many in this country have remained illiterate, and in such a state that they cannot choose their own representatives? That itself is the surest condemnation of the present method of Government. It has got to be changed and I can assure you if some kind of self-government is granted to us in the near future within the next twenty years there will not be one single illiterate man in this country. I throw out this challenge: let them put us in that position, give us power to work out our own good and I am sure that before many years are over the people in this country will be better than people of most countries. The illiteracy of Our people is one of the strongest grounds upon which we put our claim for Home Rule. We say that we are not being allowed to develop. We say that our infant nationality is being choked. We are the inheritors of a great culture. We are the stewards of a spirituality which must be presented to the world. We must rekindle that fire. That which is dormant must be brought to life and light. Self-government alone can do that. Gentlemen, be he European or Indian, who stands for self-government in this country stands for Humanity and God. Our Anglo-Indian friends have this glorious opportunity. The other day in Calcutta I criticised their speeches. Today I wish to refer to some of the statements made by Mr. Jones of the "Statesman".

Friendly Antics of the "Friend of India"

You remember, gentlemen, we had some differences in the Reception Committee. We have made them up. I do not wish in the least degree to refer to any of these disputes, but these are disputes which must occur in every healthy community, in every political organisation, which is not absolutely lifeless. As soon as these disputes occurred, the "Statesman" was in high glee. What did it say? "Oh the extremists, you have been found out; oh, the good moderates, do not mix with the extremists, we will embrace you. Don't you make that mistake" Articles were written crying down the extremists and heaping abuse upon them. If any Indian speaker had used half those expressions, he would at once have been denounced by the Statesman" as a wild agitator. But the "Statesman" is not wild, it is very tame and in that tame way, it tried to accentuate the differences between the two parties.

Our disputes were settled as they must be settled. If they had not been, both parties would have accepted the decision of the All-India Congress Committee. Directly the disputes were settled, the "Statesman" thought of the stories of Alphonso and it tried to be jocular. In one of the stories, the "Statesman" said, it is said that kids do not eat up wolves but it is the wolves who eat up kids; and the wolves of the extremists have eaten up the kids of the moderates.

However, the revelation came upon Mr. Jones not after many years but in the course of a few days that there were no Moderates in India. I entirely agree with him; only I wish to add a rider that there are no Extremists either. We are all Nationalists. After a few days the question of the internment of Mr. Mohammed All arose and I had the honour of presiding over a meeting in Calcutta of both Hindus and Mohammedans to protest against the internments. The next day, the "Statesman' published long accounts of Bakr-Id riots and said that Hindus and Mohammedans in this country could never unite. That is the policy of the "Statesman." Do you believe that the "Statesman" newspaper ever thought that there was any possible distinction between the people whom it characterised as Extremists and those whom it characterised as Moderates?

Does the "Statesman" not know that the interests of Mohammedans and the interests of Hindus are identical? of course, it knows but it chooses not to say so because it has got its own interests to serve. I wish to call some gems from Mr. Jones' speech.

Gems from Mr. Jones' Speech

He says: "Because I am satisfied that in this country the struggle will be very hard, possibly fruitless "—oh, the pathos !—it breaks my heart—"and that our real course of action lies in bringing the cant home to the people of England and impostures with which they have been stuffed." Cant and imposture with which the British people have been stuffed—that is the general proposition I quote from Mr. Jones:

> "The next imposture, the next abuse of political terms is connected with these words Legislative Councils.' There are Legislative, Councils in the Colonies which are really and truly Legislative Assemblies corresponding to our Parliament."

Nobody has any doubt about that!

> "Now, a Legislative Council in India is a very different thing."

Exactly so. That is our grievance, we complain that our Legislative Councils are shams. They are without power, without responsibility. But let us see how he makes that out to be an imposture;

> "But the trick played is to confuse the two and to make out to the British people that a Legislative Council in India is just such a representative body as one of these Colonial Parliaments."

Mr. Jones' Logic

Have you ever heard anything like that? Yet this is said by Mr. Jones. He says that we Indians have said in England that our Legislative Councils are exactly like those in the Colonies. Is not it too rediculous for words? We say that our Legislative Councils are shams because they are not representative. We ask for such a grant of Home Rule that our Legislative Councils may be like those in Australia. But Mr. Jones says that we have deceived the English people by saying that our Legislative Councils are truly representative bodies. Does he think that he was doing some conjuring trick?

Well that is the sort of imposture with which he fed his audience. I will give you one other sample and finish with Mr. Jones. You have read those speeches and noticed that when the name of the Secretary of State was mentioned by one of the speakers the audience hissed aloud.

If any speech could bring the Government into discredit and contempt, it was the speech of Mr. Jones. These people who become violently immoderate in speech and sentiment when their selfish interests are attacked are the people who lecture us to be moderate in our expressions. I ask you to say if I am not right in calling these agitators as extremists. I said elsewhere there are no moderates or extremists among us, but the real extremists are those people who by their actions and by their words have betrayed the Government of this country and also the people of this country.

Our Attitude Loyal Throughout

Our whole attitude on the question of self-government is to hold to the banner of the moires. Our attitude has been loyal through out and as I read out to you the statements of the Secretary of State and the Viceroy you have found that our demands are based on the words and the spirit of those statements. We are for the Empire, they are for selfish interests of their own. We are for a great ideal, they are for their money. That is the difference between the Anglo-Indian agitators and ourselves. Well, gentlemen, do not be troubled by these agitators. Let them go on in their way. They ought to realise that the days of the Ilbert Bill agitation are dead and gone and buried for ever. They have no right to dictate anything to the Government.

A Word to Anglo-Indian Extremists

The Government of the country has openly declared its policy and the people of this country are in sympathy with that policy; they will try to assist the Government in carrying out that scheme. And if these Anglo-Indian Extremists should come in the way, they should be told once for all that India is not their home. India is our home—our fathers have lived here for thousands of years. The dust of this country is sacred to us. Every incident of its history is part of our Scripture. Who are you who have come here to make profits who are you to stand between us and the Government?

Under the Banner of the Empire

I say again the message of hope which His Majesty the King-Emperor gave us is about to be redeemed. The banner of the Empire is uplifted. Let us close our ranks; let us be united. Let us put forward a definite, and reasonable and sufficient scheme. Let us not be timid. Let us not be foolhardy. Let us fight this battle for the honour of this country and for the glory of the Empire.

Great Meeting at Dacca

[A meeting of the citizens of Dacca was held in the spacious room of the Bar Library on the 11th October 1917. Babu Ananda Chandra Ray, Dacca presided, when Mr. C. R. Das spoke as follows:]

Mr. Chairman, and gentlemen, I thank you very much for calling upon me to address you tonight on the question, which of all questions is agitating the mind of all of our countrymen today. Whatever the Anglo-Indians may say, I believe, I am speaking the truth when I say that there is hardly an educated man in the country who is not today thinking of Self-Government. And I say further, that every educated man in this country has a right to think of Self-Government. If you consider the history of the public events for the last five years, you cannot but come to the conclusion that the time has come when the educated community of this country, taking such assistance from their uneducated brethren as they can, must think out clearly and rationally as to what form of Self-Government they might expect and they insist upon.

His Majesty's Message of Hope

Gentlemen, I begin with the King-Emperor's Message of Hope which His Majesty personally delivered to this country before he left the shores of India and his voice still rings in our ears. We did not know then what that message was but this we know that the great question which had been agitating the mind of our countrymen for many years had also left some impression on the minds of our rulers. Gentlemen, after that, many proposals have been put forward for the introduction of some kind of Home Rule or Self-Government in this country.

Mr. Montagu's Statement

But it was only the other day, I believe on the 20th of August, that the statement of the Secretary of State was published. I do not know, gentlemen, whether you have read that message clearly and carefully. You will find in that statement an indication that the Message of Hope which was delivered by His Majesty personally is about to be fulfilled. You will remember that the Secretary of State says in that statement that some kind of responsible government is to be granted to this country. Gentlemen, I will not deal with that in detail, as I had dealt with it yesterday at Mymensingh.

Viceroy's Speech

But I cannot help repeating one thing before you, viz, that precisely the same message, the same indication is to be found in the speech of His Excellency the Viceroy which was delivered in early September. There, His Excellency clearly lays down that there are three ways in which the work of Self-Government in this country must be commenced.

The first method is the institution of Local Self-Government. Now when any question of local self-government is discussed, and we are apt to ignore its importance; it does not catch our imagination; we do not attach that interest to it which the question deserves. And whatever the kind of self-government you succeed in obtaining—and I am sure we will obtain some substantial measure of self-government—be sure that our national work for the next 20 years to come will be in the field of local self-government more than any other.

The second road, His Excellency said, must be the filling up of the public offices in this country with more Indians and the third road was by the introduction of some kind of responsible Legislative Councils—and gentlemen, to allay your suspicions—I must confess, we are somewhat suspicious at times— His Excellency said clearly that all this work is to be carried on simultaneously.

So, gentlemen, according to His Excellency, you will not be relegated merely to Local self-government for many years to come but along with the development of local self-government you may expect, according to the message of His Excellency, a Legislative Council which is at once representative and responsible.

"Responsibility" in Politics

Do not forget, gentlemen, that the word, "responsibility" has got a technical meaning in politics. It does not imply merely moral responsibility. It means that the Government must be responsible to the people of the country, to the electors, i.e. the Legislative Councils will be elected by the people of the country—whatever the extent of the franchise may be, that is a matter of detail which has got to be discussed and no doubt considered carefully. But whatever be the electorate, it is that electorate which will elect members of the Legislative Councils and the Executive Councils will be either elected or taken from the Legislative Councils and the Executive Councils will be responsible not to any outside authority but to the Legislative Councils from which they will be taken and thus ultimately to the people. These are the indications that I find in the statement of the Secretary of State as also in the message of the Viceroy.

Self-government from Many View-points

I say therefore, that the people of this country has got the right now, to expect some kind of responsible self-government in this country and the time has come when we must shake off our apathy and devote our entire energies to the consideration of the question as to the precise form of self-government that we want in this country. The question is a very difficult one and has got to be discussed from a great many points. We have got to consider it from the point of view of our nationality, I mean provincial nationality. We have got to consider this question from a wider outlook. We cannot forget that we live and have been living for many years in the midst of an Empire. We cannot forget that the different provinces in India are gradually coming closer to one another and a new nationality which expresses not only the different provinces but the whole of India is growing up in our midst and we cannot forget that our interests, even our selfish interests, our hopes, our ambitions are indissolubly connected with the interest of the Empire. These are all the considerations before us. When we sit down to frame a scheme, we cannot lose sight of any one of these points.

Provincial Autonomy

If you consider what is the kind of self-government which is exactly necessary for us, what is the first point which suggests itself to you ! I will tell you what suggests itself to me. The first thing is provincial autonomy. I desire to explain that expression clearly as far as I understand it, because that expression has been used by many Government officials and by great thinkers in Europe. But I desire you to approach this question not at all from the European point of view, so far as conception is concerned, but from our own national standpoint.

What is the exact meaning of provincial autonomy? I say that the meaning of that expression is that people who have for hundreds and hundreds of years been living in Bengal, have come under the sway of a particular culture, have been animated by a particular genius and the provincial government which will be established in Bengal must give the fullest expression to that ideal. I mean that the Hindus have, for several centuries been living in

Bengal and amongst them there have grown up a very great culture which has made itself felt in the domain of science, philosophy, religion, literature and Art. It has got a cast of its own; it has got a spirit of its own; it has got a distinct individuality.

When I am speaking of the Hindus of Bengal, I am at once reminded of the Mohammedans of Bengal. They have also lived in Bengal; they have lived with us, by our side and have been surrounded by the same environments and whatever our religious difference may be, there can hardly be any question that their interests and our interests, in point of education, in point of culture, and in point of nationality are the same. When I am speaking of provincial autonomy, I am not forgetting any community or the members of any particular religion. I want to include the whole of them and I say, taking the whole of them, there is a distinct individuality of Bengal. It is on that individual nature that we must take our stand.

Now, gentlemen, provincial government must be so formed that it will not lose the particular interest which that individuality requires. The people of Bengal must realise that the whole of their political enfranchisement must be based upon their ancient ideals and traditions enlarged no doubt, developed no doubt, modernised no doubt, but still based on those ancient ideals.

Borrowing Ideals from Europe

I am not one of those who will borrow all our ideals from Europe. All my life, I have protested against it, I protest against it again and I shall protest against it so long as I live. I am not unmindful of the great culture of Europe. I am not slow in recognising my indebtedness to it but I cannot forget my own individuality. I cannot forget the spirit of Bengal, which pervades every thought that I entertain, every hope that I cherish, every fear that I have, and so long as I live, I promise before you today that I will devote my life to work out the salvation of the ideal of Bengal. The soul of Bengal had been sleeping for years but directly Self-Government is given to us, that soul, while living in an atmosphere of freedom, will make its enormous claim to give the fullest expression to its ideal. I feel sure that the Government cannot but grant us that opportunity—as I hope, the Government will. Gentlemen, I believe that Bengal has a message to give I feel sure that the Day is not distant when the message of Bengal will be delivered and the world will listen.

Ideal to be Worked Out

Now, gentlemen, this is the ideal of provincial autonomy and how has this ideal to be worked out in practice? We must not rest content with expressing our ideal. We must at once sit down to work to execute that ideal. How do you propose to do it? Different schemes have been put forward. There is the scheme of the 19 members, there is the scheme of the Congress and the Muslim League. There is the scheme of the late Mr. Gokhale. I do not desire to criticise those schemes because it is the universal desire of all our leaders that every district ought to form its own committee to frame its scheme and there should be a conference in Calcutta, where the representatives from all these districts will meet to discuss and deliberate on those schemes, and finally the scheme which is to be presented to the Congress and the League and to the Secretary of State, should be adopted.

Parochial Politics

I do not propose to discuss that in detail at all, but I desire to impress upon you that whatever the scheme you may be pleased to frame, you must not lose sight of what is called parochial politics. From time immemorial the village has been the unit of our national life. You must consider the reconstruction of our village life, you must consider the education of our villagers. You must consider the question as to how they may be represented in the district association, which will be formed with representatives sent by them and you must so frame your scheme—I am merely telling you as to what my individual opinion is—you must so frame it that the interest of what is called parochial government may not in any way suffer from what may be called the interest be so connected with the province that it may not be felt as an obstruction but as a real and integral part of the province. Then in considering the representation to the Legislative Council, you will try to so frame your scheme that the interest of the poorest villager as well as that of the richest zemindar may be equally represented; and the interest of the minority may not be neglected.

Charge of Illiteracy

Gentlemen, it has been said, and often said by Anglo Indians that the great majority of our people are so ignorant, are so illiterate that they cannot be trusted with votes. I do not know, gentlemen, what conclusion you will arrive at, but so far as my own view is concerned, I do not at all agree with that. I do not think that illiteracy and want of education are exactly the same thing. As I know my villagers, I know this that they may be trusted, with the duty of electing persons to represent them in the Legislative Councils. You are more in touch with the villagers than I am—I have seen some of it, but I feel sure that you have got a far more intimate knowledge. I ask you to say whether this is correct that our villager is so ignorant, though he may not be able to read or write, that he does not know between a bad man and a good man, between a man who will be able to represent his interests properly and a man who will not. I do not think so. And in any scheme which you may draw up, you must make that perfectly clear. I am speaking of this because there is a danger. I do not desire that the mistakes of English history should be repeated in this country. There is no necessity for it. There is no necessity for starting with a very limited franchise and then extending it or having to extend it by civil war afterwards. The history of the Reform Bill in England ought not to be repeated in this country. So, your scheme should be so framed that it must carry within itself the possibility of improvement.

Central Government

That is, roughly speaking, my idea of the provincial government. I said that the first thing which should strike us is provincial autonomy. But do not forget that there is a wider interest to consider. These provincial governments must be bound together by a Central Government. I believe it was John Bright who said that the future of India was the United States of India. So far as idea is concerned, it is a grand idea and the idea of provincial autonomy to which I have referred is part of that ideal. But John Bright went further; he said that the several provincial governments should be connected with the British Parliament. To that view I do not assent because the result of that would be that the wider interest of Indian nationality would be overlooked. So we want a central government. What the character of that government is to be, must also be considered, i.e. how they could have most fully represented all the provincial governments.

Imperial Federated Government

Gentlemen, the third need which you must not forget is the need of another Imperial Federated Government to which all the governments of the Empire should belong — a Government to which the English Government should belong as one unit, the Indian Government should belong as another, the Governments of Africa, Australia and Canada should belong as other units. It will be a sort of federated Parliament. I ask you to consider the grand ideal which is contained in that proposal. I do think in the history of the world there ever was another instance of an Empire so vast, of an Empire in which so many different races and nationalities and creeds were represented. When you consider all this, you will find what a grand opportunity there is within the British Empire of fulfilling that yet still grander ideal of the federation of the human race. If the federation of the human race is not always to remain the poet's dream, if it is ever to be fulfilled, I feel sure that fulfilment will come through the federation of this vast Empire, to which we have the honour to belong.

Word of Advice

Well, gentlemen, that is the ideal I put before you and I ask you to consider all this in the scheme which you will frame. But there is one thing to which I desire to draw your attention and it is this: that in framing this scheme you must not be swayed by a feeling that the Government will not grant this, the Government will not grant that. What the Government will grant and what the Government will not grant, that is the business of the Government we have got only to consider what is necessary for our national well-being. We have no doubt got to consider the question of our capacity, but we have got to consider what is necessary for our national well being and if you find that certain steps are absolutely necessary for our national development, do not fail, gentlemen, to put that down in your scheme out of timidity. I ask you not to be timid. Do not be foolhardy, but there is no necessity of being afraid of putting forward the whole of your scheme before the Government. People who are afraid to ask do not deserve. Why should we be afraid to tell the Government that a certain scheme of self-government is necessary for our well-being. The Government invites your opinion. The British Government has declared its policy; the Viceroy has asked you to consider the scheme and do not, for God's sake, spoil that by timidity. Say, there are five items, all of which we want; but let us not ask 2 or 3 of these because the Government will not grant all. I say it is no business of ours and I do not think that at the present moment when the Government is full of that truly imperial idea, when the King's Ministers have declared the policy of the Government to grant to this country some kind of responsible self-government, I do not think any scheme which is reasonable, any scheme which is necessary will be refused.

What, if it is refused? Have we not to carry on this fight from year to year, supposing the whole of it is not granted today. Have we not to place that scheme before the public—have we not to fight for it year to year, giving the whole of our attention, devoting the whole of our energy to that, and go on fighting till victory is ours? I have seen a great many schemes fail because of our timidity. I ask you to be on your guard because the present is the most opportune moment, because the Government has invited your opinion and in giving your opinion do not think that we ought not to put this or that down because the Government will not accept this.

For the Whole of the Ideal

Let us fight for the whole of our ideal. Let us start with this that every cultivator here in this country has got the capacity to judge as to who his representative is going to be. Let us start with this that we can, if we only try, if we will only shake off our apathy, do the work of local self-government without the intervention of Government officials. Let us think of this that we are in a position to so form our Legislative Councils, by sending proper representatives there, that they will carry out our mandate, that they will carry out our ideal and they would elect such an executive that they will do the work which the country requires. Indicate in your scheme how the Provincial Governments will have to be connected with a Central Government. But so far as provincial autonomy is concerned, so far as the different departments of the Executive Government in Bengal are concerned, I should not hesitate to ask for the whole of those powers being transferred to the people of Bengal. Naturally, the Indian Government will retain some powers and I admit it is right that they should retain some powers now at this stage for the task of uniting the different provinces in imperial matters for the purpose of directing the foreign policy and military affairs of the country. But I insist upon you, I implore you, that whatever scheme you may frame, you will not lose sight of the idea that we are capable of governing Bengal, we are capable of carrying on the work which the Executive Council in Bengal does.

System to Blame

Gentlemen, our requirements will not be met by the introduction of a few more of our countrymen into the Civil Service. My quarrel as I said elsewhere, is not with individuals. There are Civil Servants who are honourable men, good men, true men; there may be again those who are not so good—but that would happen in every community. My quarrel is not with the individual at all. My quarrel is with the system. It is the system which is responsible for the bad government of this country. Why is the system bad? It is for this—that there is no responsibility. An English friend of mine has pointed out that. What are the Civil Servants to do? They are not responsible to the people. They have to take their orders from the Executive Council of Bengal. To whom are the members of the Executive Council responsible? Not to the people. They have got to take their orders from the Government of India. To whom is the Government of India responsible? Not to the people. They have got to take their orders from the British Parliament. Has the British Parliament got any time to devote to India? Or to make that responsibility real? No. My English friend says: they have not. They have neglected India not out of apathy but because their own interest required it —they are to discuss so many questions which are of far greater importance to England than the question of India. So you get a state of things in this country, where the Civil Service the Executive Council the Government of Bengal and the Government of India are not responsible to anybody. And under such circumstances, good government is impossible. That is why the Bureaucracy has failed and that is why that Bureaucracy has got to be removed by the introduction of some sort of responsible government—that is why the British Cabinet has suggested the introduction of responsible government.

There is no further any question of the failure of the Bureaucracy—that is accepted as a fact, accepted as a fact by people who have the right to know, by people—not ourselves—but people who have the capacity to judge, by people who have political insight and wisdom to come to a correct conclusion. We ought not to waste our energy any more in discussing the question whether this Bureaucracy has succeeded or whether it has failed. It is an accepted fact that it has failed.

The question now is what is the Government that we ought to have. What is the exact character of the representation which we ought to obtain and, gentlemen, I also ask you to consider another thing carefully. In framing the scheme, do not be carried away by mere clamour. It does not matter at all whether your Legislative Council consists of 100 members or whether it consists of 300 members. It does not matter at all whether the Executive Council will contain two more Indians. What is necessary to consider is how to make the Legislative Council responsible to the people, how to make the Executive Council responsible to the Legislative Council and how to make this responsible government express the true ideal of the people of Bengal.

Speech at Home Rule Meeting at Barisal

A largely attended meeting, presided over by Babu Nibaran Chandra Das Gupta, was held at the Raja Bahadur's Haveli Barisal on 14th October 1917, when Mr. C. R. Das spoke as follows:

Mr. Chairman and gentlemen, I thank you very much for the kind words that have been said of me this afternoon. I wish I could say that I fully deserve all the kind things which have been said about me by your worthy Chairman. But I will not waste your time by expressing my modesty. I accept this welcome in all humility. I feel in a way tonight which I never felt before.

Memory of Barisal Conference Recalled

When I stand here before you, I feel I am standing on sacred soil. To every Nationalist of Bengal, Barisal is a place of pilgrimage. Here it was that our friend and guru Babu Aswini Kumar Dutt (cheers) has passed the best years of his life in the service of the people of this country and in awakening within them the spirit of nationality in the true light of spirituality. Here it was, gentlemen, that we met at one of the most memorable conferences that took place in Bengal, I mean the Provincial Conference in which we came into conflict with the Executive. I cannot efface from my mind the memory of that meeting. The song of Bande Mataram had been sung before in Bengal but never in that significant way as it was done on that memorable occasion. I remember the conference vividly, the march from this very place to the hall of the conference the illegal orders that were passed, the illegal arrests that were made, and the voice of the people triumphing over all those illegal attempts on the part of the Executive. Gentlemen, that surely was a landmark in the history of Nationalism and if I have come before you to might to speak of the most momentous question which is agitating the whole country, it is only meet that you should remember the struggles, the glorious fight, the unselfish work and activities our leaders which have brought us to this state.

Self-government and Home Rule Mean the Same Thing

Now, gentlemen, the question of all questions, which we desire to discuss and consider is the question of Self-Government or Home Rule or Swaraj. Both these are mere names. Bombay may call it Swaraj; Madras may call it Home Rule and again Bengal may call it Self-Government—but ail these expressions mean the same thing, the same ideal. Once we understand the ideal clearly there will be no further differences as to what it means and what it implies.

History of the Growth of National Consciousness in Bengal

But before we try to understand the ideal of Self-Government it is as well to take a bird's eye view of the modern history of Bengal which bears upon that momentous question. I shall not weary you by a detailed analysis of that history. But I shall place before you as briefly as I can the landmarks, as it were, of that history within which Nationalism was in the making, within which our self-consciousness was growing and which has led us to the present day when the whole country is demanding in one voice, as it were, some sort of responsible self-government. If you do not understand the trend of events and incidents which have led up to this consciousness of nationalism, I am afraid you will miss much that is important to know.

Gentlemen, when we talk of the modern history of Bengal, we have to begin with Rajah Ram Mohan Roy (cheers). He was from that point of view, the founder of modern Bengal although I admit that the life work of this great man has got to be re-estimated, revalued, re-understood and reinterpreted. There is no doubt that he was the first who held before us the ideal of freedom. He was the first to sound the note of freedom in every department of life and in all different cultures that have met today in India. It may be, we have to modify that, it may be we have to analyse that more carefully and more in details for the purpose of scientific study but it is enough for our purpose to say that he inaugurated many reforms—you might call that reforming activity. He inaugurated the reforms which again, in turn, gave rise to reaction which, again, gave rise to further reforms which made the nation turn on itself till at last, it began to be self-conscious. I do not admit that in the days of the Rajah the nation was self-conscious, but he put before us just the sort of thing which would have helped the immediate awakening of the national consciousness. We cannot but pay homage to that great genius, who, first of all, sounded the note of freedom in politics as well as in other spheres of life. After the death of Rajah Ram Mohan Roy, the work of reform was naturally taken up by the Brahmo Samaj and although a section of our educated people followed the movement, it was principally led by the Brahmo Samaj.

That movement was nothing but sounding the same note of freedom, though the ideal of freedom and culture was borrowed from European culture and civilization. With Ram Mohan Roy it was the extension and the Europeanisation of our cultural systems.

The same ideal was applied by the Brahmo Samaj to different parts, different provinces of our society.

Bankim Discovers the Soul of Bengal

Side by side and almost in parallel lines with that, was another activity which is to be found in the literature of Bengal and principally I refer to the writings of Bankim. You will find that whereas our activity in the domain of reforms followed the European ideals and was a great deal more and more European in its tendencies, the writing of Bankim Chandra Chatterjee shows a different tendency altogether — and, as I am reminded, also in the writings of Bhudeb—in their writings an attempt was made, though it was not perfect by any means, still an attempt, an honest and sincere attempt was made to discover the soul of Bengal. In that period of our literary history you will find the glorification of Bengal.

Bengal was held up as mother and with him, Durga was nothing but the personification, as it were, of Bengal; and in other writings of his you will find an attempt is made to depict though in a somewhat superficial way our national life, to dive deep into the history of our people, into the instincts and culture of our people and find out that which is truly Bengali and not that which is imported from Europe. All this was in the literature, brewing as it were, and growing in the literature of Bengal but the activities, political and social, were of a different character. I do not know whether it is the result of that literature but gradually it gave rise to an agitation which it is difficult to describe—I mean the reactionary agitation of Sashadhar and his friends. That was a blind movement, an irrational movement it may be, but none the less it was a landmark in the history of the progress of Nationalism. There also you will find the nation began to turn on itself, the nation began to criticise the wealth of culture which was brought from Europe.—Look at it carefully, keenly and try to judge its real value to the people of this country. It was not a rational movement—it started with a hatred of things European, irrational hatred of everything European—but none the less it was a genuine and sincere movement. I desire to be very brief because I am afraid I am tiring you out (Cries of No. No).

Message of the Great Swami

That movement again, in its turn gave rise to the movement of the late Swami Vivekananda. All that was narrow in the movement of Sashadhar was widened, a more liberal note was sounded. The national spirit of which the first note was heard in the movement of Sashadhar, was developed by Swami Vivekananda and in his hands it became a trumpet, I am not saying that the message of the Swami was the final word in our nationalism. It was somewhat abstract in so far as it was more Indian than Bengali. But it was tremendous—something with an undying glory all its own. If you read his books, if you read his lectures, you are struck at once with his patriotism, love of country, not that abstract patriotism which came to us from Europe but of a different nature altogether a more living thing, something which we feel within ourselves when we read his writings.

Swadeshi Movement

I now pass on to another phase of this national history, that is, the great Swadeshi movement. It really began in 1902. It was intensified in 1905; it went on and I believe, it is still going on. That movement was inaugurated by the same spirit of nationalism made broader, perhaps a little selfish—all national claims begin in national selfishness but made more real. Bengal, for the first time, in those clays, realised the great soul within her. At that time we became fully conscious so far as Bengalis concerned. We turned to the country, the whole of Bengal became to us the symbol of the soul of Bengal. Many of you, gentlemen, must have lived through that period, must have taken part in the many activities of that period and I ask you to say if you ever felt the pulse of the people of Bengal beat so clearly as you did in those days. (Hear, hear) I say before that movement all other movements were more or less borrowed because before that the soul of Bengal was hidden from us. For the first time in the history of our national life that soul began to reveal herself and we were struck with the glory and majesty of it. This period of our national life is remarkable for the writings of Rabindra Nath Tagore (Cheers) and of Bipin Chandra Pal, of D.L. Roy (Cheers) and many others. But at that time our idea of nationalism was centred in Bengal. We never looked beyond Bengal, we were looking at Bengal, we were drinking of Bengal, as it were; and of course, we were enraptured, as all lovers are. Now, gentlemen, the nationalism of today is wider than that. We have lived to grow and we discover that although the soul of Bengal must direct all our activities that although the soul of Bengal must find its fullest expression in every work in which we engage yet there is a wider outlook which cannot be neglected.

Awakening of the Consciousness of Mohammedans

Before I come to deal with that I should draw your attention to another significant fact and that is, the gradual awakening of the consciousness of the Mohammedan community of Bengal (cheers). At the time of the Swadeshi agitation we were held apart. The self-consciousness which grew within us—the soul of Bengal which revealed herself to us, did not reveal herself to the Mohammedans and we found that they were banded together against this national activity; but, gentlemen, do not be disappointed. You have to view the awakening of the political consciousness of the Mohammedans in Bengal in its true historical perspective, otherwise you will lose sight of much that is important. If you will allow me, I will tell you very briefly something about that history. The literature which would show the wonderful activities of the Mohammedans of Bengal has not yet been unearthed but I have not the least doubt that one day you will find that literature in which both Hindus and Mohammedans joined, Hindus writing in Urdu and Bengali Mohammedans writing in Sanskrit—I have seen one or two such manuscripts and I am sure there are many such—and when all that literature is unearthed, you will find a wonderful history of Bengali civilization. In the days of Raja Ram Mohan Roy when English education was introduced in this country, the Mohammedans did not accept it. I am not sorry for that. The Mohammedans did not accept it and they were waiting for a ruder shock. They had forgotten what their forefathers had done in the way of national development. They did not accept English education and at the same time they were divorced from the culture which their fathers had advanced. The result was that whereas the Hindus got on in life, got into government employment, got many things which people value in life, the Mohammedans were left without it and gradually there came to be a sort of estrangement between the two nationalities at the time of the Swadeshi movement. They kept away from that movement and even fought with their might and main against it. Now, gentlemen, I told you I am not sorry for that. I do not remember how I felt it then but now I see that the very attitude which the Mohammedans had taken that very opposition was the result of their national awakening. We used to deprecate the work of the late Nawab Salimullah in those days because he had organised the Mohammedan opposition to the Swadeshi movement in Bengal. I do not do that now because whatever the form of that activity might have been, Nawab Salimulla succeeded in organising the Mohammedans (cheers). The spirit of nationality spoke amongst the Mohammedans at that time. Once the name is roused I do not care how it is roused. Let it be roused once and then all its narrowness will pass away. All that is true forms part of the national consciousness. What is the result today? I went to Dacca and the Mohammedans invited me to an informal conference. When I went there what did I find? Not that estrangement but an intense anxiety on their part to side with the Hindus to combine with the Hindus, (cheers) to fight shoulder to shoulder with the Hindus for working out the real salvation of Bengal (Loud applause). If the Swadeshi Movement was the first step in our national self-consciousness so far as Hindus are concerned, I say it was equally the first step of Mohammedan self-consciousness. Its appearance was against the nation, but its reality was in our favour.

Message of Nationality

Gentlemen, the message of nationality, as I said before has a wider outlook today. We cannot forget that we are living within an Empire, perhaps the vastest, the largest and the most glorious Empire in the history of mankind. We cannot forget that however truly national we may be—and we ought to be national—under no circumstances should we be divested of our own Individuality and I say the Hindus and Mohammedans of Bengal, living together side by side for so many generations, imbibing each other's culture, surrounded by the same atmosphere, the same climate, influenced by the same culture, the two together form the real Bengali nation.

Although we should not lose our own individuality, the spirit of isolation is not the best thing in national lite and philosophy.

We Must Reach Out to the World

We ought to stand on our own individuality in all the glory which that individuality implies but at the same time we must emerge from that and with the fullest consciousness of ourselves we should reach out to the world. That is the true philosophy of our nationality, and if we are living in an Empire today, we ought to see that we do not live self-centred, in the splendid isolation of our own individuality. We ought to give the fullest expression to our individuality but we ought to do something more than that. We ought to reach out to the world and how do we reach out to the world?. It is by taking our legitimate part in the Empire. We should hold fast to this that our individuality should be kept absolutely distinct. I should not give that up for the whole world for if we give that up, we cease to be ourselves, (hear, hear) But stand on that as we must, we must stretch out our hands across to the world. That we can only do by taking our legitimate part in the activities of this great Empire.

Provincial Autonomy the First Step

Gentlemen, the first step in the region of ideal is perfect provincial autonomy. Let us take Bengal. Any form of self-government that we can demand from this point of view must be a government which will secure the autonomy of the Bengali nation. Then you must not forget that apart from the individuality of Bengal, India as a whole has got a special individuality of its own.

Indian Nationality-the Second Step

We cannot forget that the different nationalities of India, although there are differences between them, although they differ from each other in many respects, yet spiritually and historically they are bound up as so many links in the chain of one living national individuality. We ought not to forget that Bengal, Madras, Bombay and the Punjab are all dominated by one great central culture. The epics of Ramayana and Mahabharata are epics of not only the Punjab, of Bombay, of Madras but also of Bengal and the rest of India. The great religious institutions are common—I am speaking of the Hindus only— to all the provinces. Each province has got a speciality of its own, I admit, but over and above that, all these different provinces are bound together in one common culture. If we are to hold fast to our provincial individuality, we must also see that the great individuality of India is not lost. At one time the idea was to develop the different provinces, making the provinces autonomous and to connect these different autonomous provinces with the British Parliament. That will not work out our ideal—that ideal will not allow the great Indian nationality to develop and much as I love Bengal and much as I love my own individuality, my own provincial individuality, I should be sorry indeed if any kind of Self-Government is sought to be introduced into this country which will greatly injure that great ideal of Indian Nationality. If the whole of the Hindu races are bound up in that way you must also realise that the whole of the Mohammedan races all over India is also similarly bound up together and you must not forget that the two great cultures must meet together, and the result will be a great culture which is not purely Hindu, not purely Mohammedan but something which is made up of the contact of these two great races. And that is the ideal of Indian Nationality which must be preserved and developed to the fullest extent. If you ask me if I get Provincial Self-Government in Bengal, why I should trouble myself about this Indian Nationality.

India Moving towards Unity

In answer I say if I have understood the lesson of Indian history correctly, I consider that from ages past there was a movement of unifying the whole of India and I think through the many vicissitudes of Indian history, in the time of the Hindus, in the time of Mohammedan rule and now English rule, throughout the many vicissitudes that one idea stands out prominently, viz., with each success, with every failure, India was growing more and more and becoming herself. I do not believe that in the old times in the ancient history of our country, there ever was one united India—India was never one whole under the Hindus at any time. I hold in great reverence and veneration all the activities of ancient India. India was great, but the great Indian nationality was in the making. We have profited by what was done in the ancient days, we have inherited all their culture but it is for us to widen that culture for the evolution of the great Indian nation. That day, gentlemen, is fast approaching. I ask you to consider critically the history of India.

Was India Ever One Whole?

Can you point your finger to any period of Indian history in which there was an united India? I have failed to discover it. Take the Magadh Empire—that great Empire which was built up and which perished in course of time. That Empire did not bring out Indian unity to the fullest extent. Take the Mohammed an Empire—it did not—it strove for that and I fully appreciate that, that is the tendency of the Indian history from the earliest time to the present day. (A voice: in the time of Asoke?) Even in the time of Asoke there was not one whole united India; it was the domination of one country over the rest of India. The great Indian nationality of which I am speaking was not born then. I am not for belittling the glory of the culture of India under those Empires— I have the deepest veneration for them and I say the purpose of Indian history is that throughout the ages, through every success, through every failure, through every battle which was won, through every battle which was lost, the history of India was working out her destiny and turning out the great Indian nation. Today we see the vision of that glory (cheers). That which could not come to pass under the Hindu Kings, that which was not brought about under the Mohammedan, gentlemen, it is for us to consider now whether we who represent modern India, whether it will be our glorious task to accomplish that; if we fail—what of that?— others will come after us who will achieve this. But achieved it must be (Hear, Hear). The message of India must be given to the world. The history of India is working out– is bringing out gradually the soul of India and the time will come– -we may not live then our children may not live then—but I say the day will come when India will stand before the whole world in all her glory of spirituality. The unity of the Hindus and the Mohammedans and of all sects and creeds will be bound together in one great cultural ideal and will influence the civilization of the world (Prolonged cheers). Well, gentlemen, as I am dealing with Self-Government, the point of practical importance which arises is this: that in a scheme of self-government not only should there be perfectly autonomous provincial governments but along that such a scheme should be made that all these provincial governments may be united in one central Indian Government because in this our desire for provincial autonomy, we are apt to forget the spirit of the history of India. That is the spirit of nationalism today.

Federal Government of the Empire—the Third Step

But what of the nationalism of tomorrow?—You have to think of the whole human race, and gradually, some sort of a federal government must be established. It may not be in a few years. It may be a long time yet but some sort of Government must be established which may be called the Federal government of the whole Empire, a government to which the British Parliament will send their representatives, a government to which the Indian Government, after it is federated and after it is nationalised and after it is made responsible, will also send her representatives,—a government to which Australia will send her representatives—a government to which Africa will also send her representatives.

Federation of All Nations-the Goal

That is the future federal government of the British Empire and I say that as an Heal, we should cling to that and cling to that because we must not forget that the ultimate goal of human activity in every country is what the poet has described, a Parliament of nations, the federation of the world. That is an ideal which has got to be worked out. The time is coming when a definite scheme should be framed to work out as far as possible this great ideal.

Declaration of the Secretary of State

Gentlemen, many of you may have read the declaration of Policy issued by the Secretary of State the other clay and may also have read the speech of His Excellency the Viceroy made with reference to that. Reading these two statements together, it is clear that the time has come when every educated man in this country should set about earnestly to frame a scheme for the introduction of self-government keeping in mind the ideal which we have before us and keeping in mind also the standard of practical politics. Now, gentlemen, if you have to frame a scheme like that, you will of course take into consideration the first point, viz. of provincial autonomy, i.e. of each province. Let us think of Bengal at the present moment. Bengal must have a government which is representative that is to say, the people of Bengal will be the electors and they will elect their representatives to this Government and the Legislative Council is to regulate and control the Executive. The Government officials that there are at the present moment, will be under the control of that Executive Department or in other words, every office and the government itself will be responsible to the people of this country. That is the first point you will have to consider. You will have to consider how you can bring about these things, the particular method according to which this must be worked out. Now, gentlemen, the second thing that you have to consider is how to federate these different provinces and connect them with the Central Government. These are the two important points which you have got to think about at the present moment and I invite your attention to a scheme which you must formulate amongst yourself. I have given you what my views are but you are not bound by these; you must form a committee of competent men to frame such a scheme and I think all the representatives of the districts should meet in Calcutta some time in November to discuss the scheme of self-government. We shall then adopt one scheme for Bengal in which the interests of the Hindus and the interests of Mohammedans will all be considered and we, the Hindus and Mohammedans of Bengal will present this scheme to the Secretary of State when he arrives here in November or in December.

Difficulties Ahead

Gentlemen, I have told you what the ideal is according to my view, and I ask you to set about working it out. But you must not be negligent of the difficulties that lie in your way. And the first and foremost of these difficulties is the agitation of the Anglo-Indians who have formed themselves into the European Association for the purpose of trying their best to defeat the noble object of the Government of India (Shame, shame). Gentlemen, so far as the Government is concerned, it has declared its policy openly and clearly and if the European Association sets itself against this noble desire of the Government of this country it would be our clear duty to stand against the mischievous activity of this Association. (Hear, hear.) Gentlemen, I have dealt with their speeches and the absurdly exaggerated claims which they have made, at other places. I do not desire to repeat them again but you will find that these speeches are all couched in violent language and sobriety and judgement is conspicuous by its absence in almost all the utterances made at that meeting in Calcutta.

Racial Rancour

They have started this agitation by vilifying our leaders and attacking both the ideal and the method of the Home Rule movement of this country and I charge that the result of that is racial rancour, which I say, it ought to be the endeavour of every honest citizen, be he Indian or be he European, or be he Anglo-Indian, to avoid Gentlemen, I desire to give you just one or two specimens of that. This is how Sir, Archy Birkmyre speaks of the activities of the people. I quote from his speech:

"We should have been content to treat this agitation (i.e. our agitation) with the contempt it deserves, but we are confronted with the alarming fact that the Government is hauling down its colours before these lawless agitators." Gentlemen, this statement professes contempt not only for the activities of the people, the unselfish and honest activities of the leaders of the people of this country but it also professes contempt for their own Government, (Cries of shame) as it refers to the actions of the Government, the noble actions of the Government in these words:

> "But we are confronted with the alarming fact that the Government is hauling down its colours before these lawless agitators."

Are We Lawless Agitators?

Gentlemen, our agitation is described as the agitation of lawless people. I read through these speeches very carefully and I challenge any one of the speakers to find out a single utterance in Mrs. Besant's speeches on the question of Home Rule, in her many pamphlets on this subject which may be characterised as violent.

I challenge them to find out a single sentiment in any one of these utterances of Mrs. Besant which stands for lawlessness. I have read them carefully; these Anglo Indian agitators have not. I have read them carefully and I say that Mrs. Besant has laid down clearly and emphatically that the agitation for Home Rule must be carried on lawfully and by the use of argument not by the use of methods which are against law. She has laid that down so often in her speeches that anybody who refers to that agitation as lawless has no excuse for such ignorance.

Who is Violent—We or You?

I will now give you another bit from the same speaker:

> "Most of you are aware of the quality or the language used by the Indian agitator when he wishes to libel British rule."

The quality of language used by the Indian agitator indeed! Well, gentlemen, you have read the speeches of these Anglo-Indian agitators and you have read the speeches of Indians who have addressed the country from time to time on the question of Home Rule. I ask you to compare the tone of these speeches and I ask you to say who are violent—they or we? I will give you one choice bit from Mr. Wiggett. He says:

> "Can any one here say that in releasing Mrs. Besant the Government of India has exercised that power in a matter that we have a right to expect. ... It is a direct invitation to further noisy and blatant upheavals of violent passion."

Well, that is the language of moderation. I shall pass by that without a comment.

"Splenetic Bitterness of a Political Sect"

I will give you another from this, gentleman's speech. Referring to the writings of Indians on the question of Home Rule and in support of our claim for Home Rule, this gentleman says:

> "Such writings do not represent the feelings of the people of Calcutta, or anything indeed but the splenetic bitterness of a political sect."

That is very choice language, gentlemen, "splenetic bitterness of a political sect," That is very moderate language indeed! I shall pass by this also without any comment. I come now to Mr. F. W. Carter.

Our Unscrupulous Methods

Referring to our activity, he says:— "Unscrupulous methods and audacious claims of a few noisy agitators."

Mark the words—"unscrupulous methods and audacious claims. Our claims are audacious because we want to govern ourselves because we say that for the last 150 years there has been a bureaucratic form of government—bureaucracy has been tried and found wanting This is an admitted fact now, admitted by politicians in England and by politicians in India—admitted by implication in the statement of the Secretary of State and the speech of His Excellency the Viceroy. That the Bureaucracy will no longer do and because we saw that the bureaucracy must be replaced by some sort of government which is self-government and which is responsible to the people of this country. We are told of the unscrupulous methods and the audacious claims of a few noisy agitators. That again is language of moderation and calculated to create (A voice: and preserve)—yes and preserve a "calm atmosphere." The idea of these Anglo-Indian agitators is this: that when they speak of us they can use the most violent language, they can incite racial bitterness, they can say whatever they like with the most perfect impunity but if any agitators, if any Indian patriot refers in the slightest degree to the evils of bureaucratic government in this country, they are at once a noisy lot who must be punished by the government.

Adding Insult to Injury

I give you another passage from Sir Archy Birkmyre again:—

> "Of the loyalty and devotion of the fighting races of the Punjab, Sir Michael Odwyer has spoken in terms which everyone of us in this room will cordially endorse. But the spirit of the Punjab has not been manifested in other Provinces."

Gentlemen, so far as Bengal is concerned—and this speaker was speaking amidst Bengalees, so far as Bengal is concerned, I say, for anybody to charge that Bengal has not contributed to the war by money or by manpower is a libel on the whole Bengali race. I say it is adding insult to injury. When did you allow the Bengalees to wear arms? When was it for the first time that you called upon them to wear arms and to go and fight our enemy? It was only the other day. Do you expect, does any reasonable man who wants to put forward reasonable arguments expect that a whole people who has suddenly been called upon to take arms and march against an enemy, that they will at once, as if by a magic turn out a very large army? Whose is the fault? Is it the fault of Bengal that today you do not find thousands and thousands, lacs and lacs of Bengalees fighting for the Empire? Whose is the fault? You deprive them of their arms, you tell them that they are enemies (shame, shame), you declare to the world that they were never fit for military service and when suddenly you call upon them to take arms and fight, can anybody say that Bengal has not responded to the call sincerely, earnestly and if I may say, valiantly? I say a speech of this description is adding insult to injury. That is what these speakers say of the people of Bengal. Let me now place before you one or two passages which show their attitude to the government of this country when the government has resolved upon doing justice to the people of this country.

Meddling Muddlers

I quote from the speech of the Hon. Mr. Ironside. It is rather a long quotation but I am afraid that I must place this before you to bring out the quality of the Anglo-Indian agitation. I hope you will bear with me. He says:

> "At any rate, we don't want any from the House of Commons, and I would commend this remark to Mr. Montagu, for we distrust them root and branch. At this distance we watch the unhealthy game which proceeds at Westminster and to honest men it is enough to make one weep for one's country; and I think, you will agree with me, gentlemen, that we have none of it here. This is no time for meddling,

> least of all from a representative of a Ministry who one and all by their words and deeds brought the old country to the verge of internal ruin, vilified honest men and patriots, slithered into unprepared, and having made a mess of everything have hung on to their self elected posts like limpets until a second time the destruction of the Empire was nearly effected. We are not taking the same risk here. Mr. Montagu I believe, started in a department created for the definite purpose of helping to win the war. Had it been of any use, I presume, he would have stayed there but being one of a party of meddling muddlers, he has found his way back to the Indian Office".

This is language of moderation applied to the Secretary of State for India who is entrusted by the British Parliament with the government of this country. I can assure you gentlemen if anything half as violent as that had been said by any one of us, this gentleman would have been furious and would have exhibited his fury ten times more; and the "Statesman" newspaper would have said that speakers who make use of such language should be punished by the State so that their speeches may not create disaffection. But when you call the Secretary of State a meddling muddler, I suppose that is allowable. When you heap contempt upon the whole of the British Parliament, I suppose it is allowable. If only an Indian says that the bureaucratic government has been found to be wanting, it has failed in its duties, it has failed in its charge of the administration of this country, it is such violent language that the State must put down.

Anglo-Indians Teach the House of Commons

Then the same speaker goes on to say:

> "You must remember that we have to teach the House of Commons before we can gain their ear and support".

I hope the House of Commons will be enlightened by the lessons which it gets from speakers of this description. (Loud laughter).

Who Brings Govt. to Contempt?

To turn again to Mr. Wiggett—he says:

> " What an extraordinary spectacle!" referring to the release of Mrs. Beasant and the regret expressed by Sir Michael O'dwyer-of a sentimental weak-kneed Government' If this is not showing contempt for the Government I do not know what contempt is. This is not all: there is an alarming fact expressed in some of these speeches. Some of the speakers have stated that the civil servants and the military officers are entirely in sympathy with them in their resistance to any kind of self government being granted to this country.

Are the Members of the Civil and Military Services with Anglo-Indians?

Gentlemen, I shall place before you one passage from the speech of Mr. Carter and another from the speech of Sir A.V. Binning.

Mr. Carter says:

> "I appeal, therefore, to the Government on behalf of all Europeans whether engaged in trade and commerce or serving in Government employment I assure the Government that they are here in spirit"

Gentlemen, the Civil Servants were present in spirit at this meeting according to the statement of Mr. Carter! (Laughter).

And the other speaker says this:

> "Our claims, as put forward at present, will have the silent, but none the less effective, support of the Indian Civil Service and Military officers whose lot is cast in this country and who equally with us, view with grave apprehension the measures which we fear, an effort will be made to force on us"

Now, gentlemen that is absolutely startling. For myself, I refuse to believe this. I refuse to believe that the members of the civil service and the military officers who are servants of the King should so far forget themselves that they should express their sympathy with these Anglo-Indian agitators, express their views to them against the policy which has been declared by His Majesty's Government. I say, I refuse to believe this because if it were true, it discloses an alarming state of things. It shows this: that whatever the policy of the British Government may be, whatever the policy and the declaration of His Majesty's Government may be, His Majesty's servants in India may so combine and may so actively oppose people who stand up for that policy as perhaps to render that policy nugatory. I say, if it is true, it discloses an alarming state of things and I hope the Government will take note of the speeches and make an enquiry into this and if there is any truth in this statement, I ask the Government why should they allow their own servants to so conduct themselves as to represent unnecessary opposition to the declared policy of the Government. (Hear, hear).

What is Anglo-Indians' Claim?

Now, gentlemen, I have referred to the speeches to show to you how unreasonable in spirit, how violent in language those speeches were. But what is their claim? Why is it that just after the declaration of this policy by the Secretary of State in August and the speech of the Viceroy in September that they should assemble in a meeting and oppose that policy tooth and nail.

The declaration contained only this: that some sort of responsible government is to be introduced in this country—nothing beyond that. Why is it that all the Anglo-Indians gathered together and began to denounce that policy before the details are published or worked out? What is the claim which they make? I shall read to you from the speech of Sir Archy Birkmyre which puts forward what that claim is. This worthy gentleman says.

> "The greater part of the commerce of India the basis of her prosperity is controlled and financed by Britishers."

Mark the word gentlemen, "Britishers" not the Anglo-Indian community alone but the Britishers. He goes on:

> "All the progress that India has made in recent generations is due almost entirely to British direction, British capital and British enterprise. The men who are responsible for the vast interests created by the British in India cannot sit down voiceless and idle when the danger confronts us that these interests will be sacrificed to appease the political appetites of mob orators and Home Rulers"'.

Does it stand to this that the introduction of any kind of self-government in this country, however safeguarded the different interests may be, means such a disregard of the interests of these Anglo-Indian Agitators that the Government must be forced to give up its honest desire of introducing such a government.? I ask in all seriousness does the claim go so far as this?—The Anglo-Indian claim which is put forward at this meeting does it go so far as to insist that no kind of self-government, however limited it may be, however safeguarded the different interests in the country may be, that no kind of self-government is to be introduced at all into this country because these Anglo-Indians brought money in the shape of capital to this country—a statement which requires examination—because they brought capital to this country that India must forever be destitute, must forever be deprived of any measure of self-government? If this is their claim, it is so preposterously unreasonable that it requires no refutation at all. But gentlemen, the claim is curiously worded.

Do Anglo-Indians Represent the British Nation?

It is not a claim put forward on behalf of Anglo-Indians alone but it is a claim put forward on behalf of the Britishers, it is a claim by the people of England. I deny these Anglo-Indian agitators' right to represent the people of England. I deny that they have got any right to say anything on behalf of the people of England. It any plebiscite is taken today in England, I feel sure that there would be a vast majority in favour of the introduction of Self-Government to this country (Hear, hear).

Must We be Denied Home Rule because You have Brought Capital?

If this claim is based on the mere fact of their introducing capital in this country, you have to consider whether they have not been sufficiently profited by the introduction of such capital. Does it mean this then that because people bring capital to this country, because they find it profitable to do so, that they would have the right to say to the Government: you shall not introduce Self-Government in this country? Have they the right to tell the people: look here, we have brought capital to this country, therefore, you shall not have Self-Government! Gentlemen l have no desire to quarrel with these Anglo-Indian agitators. We do not regard politics from that utterly selfish point of view from which they regard it.

Their Only Claim is Adequate Representation

I am free to admit in any scheme of Self-Government which is framed and which is accepted by the people and the Government of this country, these Anglo-Indian merchants ought to be allowed to be represented, that is to say, I do not desire that any scheme should be framed which would disregard the interests of any class of people whether Hindu Mohammedan or Anglo-Indian, whatever the basis of the franchise may be. But I say that these people have got no right to dictate to the Government of India and to the people alike that they shall not have Self-Government. I ask my Anglo-Indian friends to consider this question from a little higher point of view. They must see that India cannot ever remain without Self-Government. They must see that at some time or other the voice of the people is bound to be heard and if they do their duty by this country, by which they have been profited to a very large extent, they ought to help in this work of Self-Government rather than oppose it. I call upon them again to stand on a higher platform and consider the question of Self-Government not in this way but more seriously and with more consideration for the interest of the people of this country.

Stirring up Conflicting Interests

Now, gentlemen, there is another difficulty to which I must also refer. When there are so many conflicting interests in this country it may be that particular classes of people will be instigated to stand up against Home Rule. I blame no one in particular but I am placing before you a possible difficulty. Interested people may stir up the Namasudras and tell them. "Look here, you are hated and Oppressed by the people, the Hindus of Bengal, why should you assist them and help them to bring in Self-Government because if Self-Government is granted, the Hindus are bound to oppress you all the more."? Advisers may be found who will go to my Mohammedan brethren and tell them: "you are as yet backward in education, if Self-Government is granted to Hindus why they will be more powerful than you and they will look down upon you and oppress you." Endeavours of that description unfortunately are not uncommon in this country and at such a momentous period of our history, the same attempts might be repeated. Gentlemen, it is your duty, under these circumstances, you who are educated to go to your less educated brethren, Hindus or Mohammedans and to expose before them the fallacy of any such argument.

Speech On Home Rule

There Will be no Room for Oppression in our Scheme of Self-government

You ought to tell them that self-government does not mean the Self-Government of the Hindus; Self-Government does not mean the Self-Government of the Mohammedans; Self-Government does not mean the Self-Government of the Zemindars; Self-Government means Government by all the people of Bengal in which all interests are to be represented and if there are any classes who are depressed or oppressed, they ought to be told that the sooner self-government is introduced into this country the better for them (Hear, hear); they ought to be told that we have no desire to restrict the franchise in any manner at all to the disregard of any such interest and if any kind of responsible government is introduced into this country, which is made responsible to the people, they will have the power in their hands to oppose any oppression or injustice in every possible way. They will have the power to return their friends to the Legislative Councils they will have the power to tell the people who oppose them: if you want to oppress us, if you go on in that way, it would be against the work of national development and you shall not have the power to do that. We are asking for putting the power into the hands of the people and are we to be told that these people for whom we are fighting in whose interest we are fighting for the last 30 years, that we are likely to disregard the interest of these people?

Teeming Millions Are of Us

If we are not fighting for the teeming millions of India, can anybody tell me whom we are fighting for? Am I fighting for myself? If I am selfish, why should I bother about self-government? Why can I not attend to my profession, make money and go home and sleep? Why should I go all over the country and demand Home Rule which is the only means of uplifting the teeming millions of our country if I have not their interest at heart? It anybody says that the Nationalists who are fighting for Home Rule are doing so in their own interest I fling the lie to the slanderer's teeth. I say we are engaged in a noble task and we shall not rest content unless such a kind of self-government is granted to this country which will keep alive the interest of every community, which will regard and safeguard the interest of every class of people in Bengal. We belong to the same race. They are of us. God give us strength to fight their battle! (Prolonged Cheers.)

(Amrita Bazar Patrika.)

6

Golden Words of Deshbandhu

- Freedom, in the first place, does not imply absence of all restraint. In the second place, freedom does not necessarily imply absence of the idea of dependence.
- We stand for freedom, because we claim the right to develop our own individuality and evolve our own destiny along our own lines, unembarrassed by what Western Civilization has to teach us and unhampered by the institutions which the West has imposed on us. But here a voice interrupts me, the voice of Rabindranath, the poet of India. He says, "The Western culture is standing at our door; must we be so inhospitable as to turn it away or ought we not to acknowledge that in the union of the cultures of the East and the West is the salvation of the world?"
- If Indian nationalism has to live, it cannot afford to isolate itself from other nations, but I have two observations to make on the criticism of Rabindranath: first, we must have a house of our own before we can receive a guest; and, secondly, Indian culture must discover itself before it can be ready to assimilate Western culture. In my opinion, there can be no true assimilation before freedom comes, although there may be, as there has been, a slavish imitation. The cultural conquest of India is all but complete;

it was the inevitable result of her political conquest. India must resist it. She must vibrate with national life and then we may talk of the union of the two civilizations.

- Freedom is my birthright, and I demand a recognition of that right, not by instalments nor in compartments, but whole and entire. I do not doubt that victory will be on our side, but supposing we fail; we would at least have preserved inviolate our national self-respect and dignity.
- Each nation must develop its latent manhood as a nation. It is possible to rouse within them the sense of true amity and brotherliness. As the family cannot grow unless each individual, within it grows at the same time; as society cannot grow unless each component family-group develops within it; and as the nation cannot grow unless each community embraced by it grows along with it; so humanity at large cannot advance unless each different nation develops its distinctive type of character and civilization.
- One has only to look at the faces of the sufferers as they are led to prison to realise that victory is already ours. It is not for nothing that Mohammed Ali and Shaukat Ali, courageous and resourceful, have lived and suffered; it is not for nothing that Lajpat Rai, one of the bravest of spirits that ever faced the sun, flung the order of the bureaucracy in its face, and marched boldly into the prison that awaited him.
- The doctrine has apparently made its way to this country from England. I shall, therefore, refer to English history to find out the truth about this doctrine. That history has recorded that most of the despots in England, who exercised arbitrary sway over the people proposed to act for the good of the people and for the maintenance of law and order, English absolutism from the Normans down to the Stuarts tried to put itself on a constitutional basis through the process of this very law and order.
- I desire to emphasise one point, and that is, that throughout the long and bitter struggle between the Stuarts and

Parliament, the Stuarts acted for the maintenance of law and order, and there is no doubt that law and history were on their side. On the eve of the civil war, the question that divided the parties was this: Could the Crown in the maintenance of law and order claim the passive obedience of the subject, or was there any power of resistance in the subject, though that resistance might result in disorder and in breaches of law?

- The adherents of Parliament stood for the power and the majesty of the people, the authority and "independency of Parliament," individual liberty, the right to resist, and the right to compel abdication and secure deposition of the Crown; in a word, they stood for Man against the coercive powers of the State. The adherents of the British Crown stood for indefeasible right, a right to claim passive obedience and secure non-resistance on the part of the subject through the process of law and order; in a word, they stood for state coercion and compulsory cooperation against individual liberty.
- The truth is that law and order is for Man, and not Man for law and order. The development of nationality is a sacred task and anything, which impedes that task is an obstacle, which the very force and power of nationality must overcome. If,. therefore, you interpose a doctrine to impede the task, why, the doctrine must go. If you have recourse to law, and order to establish and defend the rule of law, then your law and order is entitled to claim the respect of all law-abiding citizens but as soon as you have recourse to it not to establish and defend the rule of law but to destroy and attack it, there is no longer, any obligation on us to respect it.
- A Higher Law, the Natural Law, the Law of God compels us to offer our stubborn resistance to it. When I find some thing put forward in the sacred name of law and order which is deliberately intended to hinder the growth, the development and the self-realisation of the nation, I have no hesitation whatever in proclaiming that such law and order is an outrage on man and insult to God.

- Throughout the pages of Indian history, I find a great purpose unfolding itself. Movement after movement has swept over this vast country, apparently creating hostile forces, but in reality stimulating the vitality and moulding the life of the people into one great nationality. If the Aryans and the non-Aryans met, it was for the purpose of making one people out of them.
- Brahmanism with its great culture succeeded in binding the whole of India and was indeed a mighty unifying force. Buddhism with its protests against Brahmanism served the same great historical purpose; and from Magadha to Taxila was one great Buddhistic Empire which succeeded not only in broadening the basis of Indian unity, but in creating, what is perhaps not less important, the greater India beyond the Himalayas and beyond the seas.
- The history of the French Revolution is the history of a struggle at the first instance between the Crown and the Nobility on one side and the Representative Assemblies with armed Paris on the other. Both took to violence, one to the bayonet and the other to the pike. The pike succeeded because the bayonet was held with uncertain hands.
- It has been said that with love on our lips we have been preaching the gospel of hatred. Never was such a vile slander uttered. It may be we have failed to love, it may be we lost ourselves, some of us, in hatred, but that only shows our weakness and imperfectness. Judge us by our ideal, not by what we have achieved. Wherever we have fallen short of that ideal put it down to our weakness. On behalf of the Indian National Congress I deny the charge of hypocrisy.
- To those who are ever anxious to point out our defects, I say with all humility: "My friends, if we are weak, come and join us and make us stronger. If the leaders are worthless, come and join us to lead and the leaders will stand aside. If you do not believe in the ideal, what is the use of always criticising us in the light of that ideal?" We need no critic to tell us how far we have fallen short of

that ideal. Evidence of weakness has met me from every direction in which I have looked; but in spite of our defects of human weakness, of human imperfection, I feel bold enough to say that our victory is assured and that the bureaucracy knows that our victory is assured.

- To me the organisation of village life and the practical autonomy of small local centres are more important than either provincial autonomy or central responsibility; and if the choice lay between the two, I would unhesitatingly accept the autonomy of the local centres. I must not be understood as implying that the village centres will be disconnected units. They must be held together by a system of cooperation and integration.
- For the present, there must be power in the hands of the Provincial Governments and the Indian Government; but the ideal should be accepted once for all, that the proper function of the central authority, whether in the Provincial or in the Indian Government is to advise, having a residuary power of control only in case of need, and to be exercised under proper safeguards. I maintain that real *Swaraj* can only be attained by vesting the power of government in local centres, and I suggest that the Congress should appoint a committee to draw up a scheme of government which would be acceptable to the nation.
- The foundation of real democracy must be laid in small centres—not gradual decentralisation which implies a previous centralisation—but a gradual integration of the practically autonomous small centres into one living harmonious whole. What is wanted is a human state, not a mechanical contrivance. We want the growth of institutions and organisations which are really dynamic in their nature and not the more static stability of a centralised state.
- Modern European thought has made it clear that from the individual to the "unified state," it is one continuous process of real and natural growth. Sovereignty (Swaraj) is a relative notion. "The individual is sovereign over

himself"—attains his Swaraj—"in so far as he can develop, control and unify his manifold nature".

- From the individual we come to "integrated neighbourhood" which is the real foundation of the unified state which again in its turn gives us the true ideal of the world-state. This integrated neighbourhood is great deal more than the mere physical continuity of the people who live in the neighbourhood area. It requires the evolution of what has been called neighbourhood "consciousness." In other words, the question is: "How can the force generated by the neighbourhood life become part of our whole civic and national life?" It is the question which now democracy takes upon itself to solve.
- Our whole attitude on the question of self-government is to hold to the banner of the moires. Our attitude has been loyal throughout and as I read out to you the statements of the Secretary of State and the Viceroy you have found that our demands are based on the words and the spirit of those statements. We are for the Empire, they are for selfish interests of their own. We are for a great ideal, they are for their money. That is the difference between the Anglo-Indian agitators and ourselves.
- I am not one of those who will borrow all our ideals from Europe. All my life, I have protested against it, I protest against it again and I shall protest against it so long as I live. I am not unmindful of the great culture of Europe. I am not slow in recognising my indebtedness to it but I cannot forget my own individuality. I cannot forget the spirit of Bengal, which pervades every thought that I entertain, every hope that I cherish, every fear that I have, and so long as I live, I promise before you today that I will devote my life to work out the salvation of the ideal of Bengal. The soul of Bengal had been sleeping for years but directly Self-Government is given to us, that soul, while living in an atmosphere of freedom, will make its enormous claim to give the fullest expression to its ideal.
- I feel sure that the Government cannot but grant us one opportunity—as I hope, the Government will. Gentlemen,

I believe that Bengal has a message to give. I feel sure that the Day is not distant when the message of Bengal will be delivered and the world will listen.

- We ought to stand on our own individuality in all the glory which that individuality implies but at the same time we must emerge from that and with the fullest consciousness of ourselves we should reach out to the world. That is the true philosophy of our nationality, and if we are living in an Empire today, we ought to see that we do not live self-centred, in the splendid isolation of our own individuality.
- We ought to give the fullest expression to our individuality but we ought to do something more than that. We ought to reach out to the world and how do we reach out to the world?. It is by taking our legitimate part in the Empire. We should hold fast to this that our individuality should be kept absolutely distinct. I should not give that up for the whole world for if we give that up, we cease to be ourselves.
- I am free to admit in any scheme of Self-Government which is framed and which is accepted by the people and the Government of this country, these Anglo-Indian merchants ought to be allowed to be represented, that is to say, I do not desire that any scheme should be framed which would disregard the interests of any class of people whether Hindu, Mohammedan or Anglo-Indian, whatever the basis of the franchise may be. But I say that these people have got no right to dictate to the Government of India and to the people alike that they shall not have Self-Government. I ask my Anglo-Indian friends to consider this question from a little higher point of view.
- The Anglo-Indians see that India cannot ever remain without Self-Government. They must see that at some time or other the voice of the people is bound to be heard and if they do their duty by this country, by which they have been profited to a very large extent, they ought to help in the work of Self-Government rather than oppose it. I call upon them again to stand on a higher platform

and consider the question of Self-Government not in this way but more seriously and with more consideration for the interest of the people of this country.

- Independence, to my mind, is a narrower ideal than Swaraj. It implies, it is true, the negative of dependence; but by itself it gives us no positive ideal. I do not for a moment suggest that independence is not consistent with Swaraj. But what is necessary is not mere independence, but the establishment of Swaraj. India may be independent tomorrow in the sense that the British people may leave us to our destiny but that will not necessarily give us what I understand by Swaraj.
- India presents an interesting but a complicated problem of consolidating the many apparently conflicting elements which go to make up the Indian people. This work of consolidation is a long process, may even be a weary process; but without this no *Swaraj* is possible. Herein lies the great wisdom of Mahatma Gandhi's constructive programme. It is unnecessary for me to discuss that programme, as we are all privileged today to hear his message from his own lips. With that programme I entirely agree and I cannot but strongly urge upon my countrymen to give it not merely intellectual assent, but practical support, by working it out to the fullest extent.
- What is non-cooperation? I cannot do better than quote the eloquent words of Mr. Stokes: "It is the refusal to be a party to preventable evil; it is the refusal to accept or have any part in injustice; it is the refusal to acquiesce in wrongs that can be righted, or to submit to a state of affairs, which is manifestly inconsistent with the dictates of righteousness. And as a consequence it is the refusal to work with those, who on grounds of interest or expediency insist upon committing or perpetuating wrong."

7

Great Life at a Glance

1870, Nov. 5: Deshbandhu, Chittaranjan Das, was born in an upper middle class Vaidya family of Telirbagh in the Dacca district of Bengal. His father, Bhuban Mohan Das, was a famous solicitor of the Calcutta (Kolkata) High Court and a keen member of the Brahmo Samaj. Chittaranjan's patriotic ideas were greatly influenced by his father's.

1879: Das joined a school for education.

1886: Das passed Entrance Examination from Calcutta University.

1890: Passed Graduation from Presidency College, Calcutta. Sailed to England for ICS.

1893: Took the ICS examination, but was not selected; due to his political inclinations. However, he had qualified for Bar. Began legal practice at Calcutta High Court, as a lawyer. Later, he rose to prominence, when he pleaded for Aurobindo Ghose in Alipore Bomb Conspiracy Case.

1902: The Anushilan Samiti was established in Calcutta (Kolkata) by Pramatha Nath Mitra, a barrister and a patron of the revolutionary movements. Sri Aurobindo and Deshabandhu Chittaranjan Das were the vice-presidents and Suren Tagore the treasurer.

1907: For nearly three decades, beginning from the attempt to derail the train of Bengal Governor Andrew Fraser, the revolutionary movement raged in the province in full fury. Many of Gandhiji's leading followers in Bengal and well- known Congressmen, like Deshbandhu Chittaranjan Das and Sarat Chandra Bose had a sneaking sympathy for the revolutionaries. During the First World War, an attempt to procure German arms for the revolutionaries misfired.

1911, Sept. 18: After the demise of Maharaja Nripendra Narayan, the situation turned bad for Kumar Gajendra Narayan. He and his family members had to go on exile, following a complaint of theft. On behalf of them, Deshbandhu Chittaranjan Das came to fight the legal battle.

1915, May: When the British started arresting the revolutionaries during the First World War, Ashutosh Lahiri was also arrested and tried for hatching a conspiracy against the government. Deshbandhu Chittaranjan Das pleaded his case.

1921: The All India session of the Congress was held under the presidency of Deshbandhu Chittaranjan Das, which was attended by great illumanaries and prominent leaders of the Indian Independence Movement, such as Mahatma Gandhi, Rajendra Prasad, Anugrah Narayan Sinha, Sardar Patel, Maulana Azad, Moti Lal Nehru and Sri Krishna Sinha.

— Mar 6: At the clarion call of Deshbandhu Chittaranjan Das in a mammoth meeting at Comilla, Dhirendranath Das gave up his legal profession for three months and participated in the Nonviolent-Noncooperation Movement.

1923: Das formed Swaraj Party, along with Pt. Moti Lal Nehru and others.

1924: Das was elected Mayor of Calcutta Corporation.

— Nov. 6: Deshbandhu Chittaranjan Das had made a gift of his property at Bhowanipore to the nation, before he went to Patna. Coming back to Calcutta, Deshbandhu Chittaranjan Das did not go to that house again.

1925, Jun. 16: Deshbandhu Chittaranjan Das passed away at Darjeeling. His body was taken to Calcutta for last rites.

Bibliography

Abani Lahiri: *The Peasant and India's Freedom Movement*, Manak, 2001.

Ambastha, G.S.P.: *Freedom Movement and Role of Congress Leaders*, Classical, 1995.

Amiya Sen: *Hindu Revivalism in Bengal 1872-1905: Some Essays in Interpretation*, Oxford University Press, 1993.

Anil Kumar Jana: *Quit India Movement in Bengal: A Study of Contai Subdivision*, Indian Pub, 2004.

Bakshi, S. R. and Lipi Mahajan: *Social Reformers of India*, Deep & Deep, 2000.

Bakshi, S. R.: *Indian Freedom Fighters: Struggle for Independence*, Hardcover, 2002.

Banerjee Das and Co.: *Speeches of C. R. Das*, Calcutta, 1918.

Bennett, A, Hindle, J.: *London Review of Books: An Anthology*, Verso, 1996.

Bhattacharya, B. K.: *India's Freedom Movement: Legacy of Bipin Chandra Pal*, Deep and Deep, 2007.

Bhote, Perviz: *Twin Tribute*, The Hindu, 2000.

Busteed, H.E.: *Echoes of Old Calcutta*, Calcutta, 1908.

Chakrabarty, R.: *An Overview* in *Time Past and Time Present: Two Hundred and Twenty-five Years of the Asiatic Society*, The Asiatic Society, Kolkata, 2008.

Chandra, Bipan: *India's Struggle For Independence,* Penguin Books India (P) Ltd., New Delhi, 1989.

Chaudhuri, N.C.: *The Autobiography of an Unknown Indian,* New York Review of Books, 2001.

Chaudhuri, S.: *Calcutta: The Living City,* Oxford University Press, USA, 1995.

Das Gupta, Hemendra Nath: *Deshbandhu-Smriri,* Bengali, Calcutta, 1926.

Das, C. R. and Das, Bhagwan: *Outline Scheme of Swaraj,* Bombay, 1923.

Das, Sukumar Ranjan: *Deshbandhu Chittaranjan,* Bengali, Calcutta, 1936.

Diraviam, Leila: *Diraviam -Our Treasure,* Asian Printers, Chennai, 1999.

Dutta, Krishna: *Calcutta: A Cultural and Literary History,* Signal, 2003.

Erwin Neumayer and Christine Schelberger: *Bharat Mata: India's Freedom Movement in Popular Art,* Oxford University Press, 2008.

Ghosh, Amitav: *The Calcutta Chromosome: A Novel of Fevers, Delirium and Discovery,* Ravi Dayal Publisher, 1996.

Ghulam Husain Salim: *Riyazu-s-Salatin: A History of Bengal,* Baptist Mission Press, Calcutta, 1902.

Goyal, P. K.: *Battle of India's Freedom Movement,* Vista International, 2005.

Hari Hara Das: *The History of Freedom Movement in India (1857-1947),* National, 1998.

Indu Dave: *Indian Personality in Its Developmental Background,* Himanshu, 1991.

Iyengar, A. S.: *Role of Press and Indian Freedom Struggle: All through the Gandhian Era,* APH, 2001.

Kailash Khanna: *History of Indian Freedom Struggle,* Commonwealth Pub, 2004.

Kamat, Jyostna: *The Pioneers: Kamaladevi Chattopadhyaya*, Kamat's, 2003.

Kapoor, A. N. Gupta, V. P. and Mohini Gupta: *An Encyclopaedic Dictionary of Freedom Movement 1757-1947*, Radha, 2004.

Kaushik, A. S.: *Great Freedom Fighters of India*, Indian Pub, 2007.

Kejariwal, O.P.: *The Asiatic Society of Bengal and the Discovery of India's Past*, OUP, Delhi, 1988.

Khairul Anam, Md.: *Indian Freedom Movement and Murshidabad District 1905-1947*, Bagchi, K. P., 2008.

Krishan Mohan: *Encyclopaedic History of Indian Freedom Movement*, Book Enclave, 1999.

————: *Indian National Congress and the Freedom Movement*, Book Enclave, 1999.

————: *Political Leadership and Indian Freedom Movement*, Book Enclave, 1999.

————: *Revolt of 1857 and the Indian Freedom Movement*, Book Enclave, 1999.

————: *Revolutionary Politics and Indian Freedom Movement*, Book Enclave, 1999.

Krishna, B.: *Indian Freedom Struggle: The Pathfinders From Surendranath Banerjea to Gandhi*, Manohar, 2002.

Lion Agrawal, M. G.: *Freedom Fighters of India (4 Vols-Set)*, Isha Books, 2008.

Majumdar, R. C.: *History of the Freedom Movement in India (3 Vols-Set)*, Firma KLM, 1997.

————: *The History of Bengal*, 1988.

Manju Verma: *The Role of Women in the Freedom Movement in Punjab (1919-1947)*, Abhijeet, 2003.

Marcuse, P. van Kempen, R.: *Globalizing Cities: A New Spatial Order?*, Blackwell Publishers, 2000.

Marston, D.: *The Seven Year's War*, Osprey Publishing, 2001.

Maulana Syed Mohammad Mian: *The Prisoners of Malta (Asira'n-E-Malta): The Heart-Rending Tale of Muslim Freedom Fighters in British Period*, Manak, 2005.

Mazhar Kibriya: *Gandhi and Indian Freedom Struggle*, APH, 1999.

Mitra, A.: *Calcutta Diary*, Routledge, UK, 1976.

Mukherjee, SC: *The Changing Face of Calcutta: An Architectural Approach: Calcutta, 300*, Government of West Bengal, 1991.

Muthaiah, S.: *Women Freedom Fighters*, The Hindu, 2004.

Nanda, S. P.: *Freedom Movement and Constitutional Development in India*, Dominant, 2004.

Nitish Sengupta: *History of the Bengali-speaking People*, UBS Publishers' Distributors Pvt. Ltd., 1989.

Om Prakash: *Encyclopaedic History of Indian Freedom Movement (12 to 21 Vols)*, Anmol, 2003.

Omesh Saigal: *Shaheed Bhagat Singh: Unique Martyr in Freedom Movement*, Gyan Pub, 2002.

Pal, Bipin Chandra: *Presidential Address at the Bengal Pro-vincial Conference*, Barisal, 1921.

Parmanand Parashar: *Kashmir and the Freedom Movement*, Sarup, 2004.

Pradhan, K. B.: *Freedom Movement in India*, Arise Pub, 2007.

Prafulla Kumar Pattanaik: *The First Indian War of Independence: Freedom Movement in Orissa, 1804-1825*, APH, 2005.

Prato, Giuliana, B.: *Beyond Multiculturalism: Views from Anthropology*, Ashgate Publishing Limited, 2009.

Puri, Ina: *Raj Bhavan of Kolkata: Two Hundred Years of Grandeur*, 2003.

Rafiya Nisar: *Shaikh-Ul-Hind Maulana Mahmud Hasan and Indian Freedom Movement*, Manak Pub, 2008.

Raj Kumar: *Essays on Indian Freedom Movement*, History and Culture Series, Discovery, 2003.

Ram Sharma, S.: *Education of Women and Freedom Movement*, Discovery, 1996.

Ram, S. and Kumar, R.: *Encyclopaedia of Indian Freedom Struggle (10 Vols-Set)*, Commonwealth Pub, 2008.

——————: *Quit India Movement: 1942-1945*, Commonwealth Pub, 2008.

Ramanathan, K. V.: *The Satyamurti Letters, Vol. II: The Indian Freedom Struggle Through the Eyes of a Parliamentarian*, Dorling Kindersley for Pearson Longman an Imprint of Pearson Education, 2008.

Ramu, P. S.: *Azad Hind Fauj (I.N.A.) and The Freedom Movement*, Freedom Movement Memorial Comm, 1998.

Ratna Ghosh: *Netaji Subhas Chandra Bose and Indian Freedom Struggle (2 Vols-Set)*, Deep and Deep, 2006.

Ravindra Kumar: *Champaran to Quit India Movement*, Mittal, 2002.

Ray, Prithwis Chandra: *The Life and Times of C.R. Das*, Calcutta, 1927.

Roy, A, Alsayyad, N.: *Urban Informality: Transnational Perspectives from the Middle East, Latin America and South Asia*, Lexington Books, 2004.

Roy, A.: *City Requiem, Calcutta: Gender and the Politics of Poverty*, University of Minnesota Press, 2002.

Salim, Gulam Hussain: *Riyazu-s-Salatin: History of Bengal*, Baptist Mission Press, Persian, 1902.

Sen, A.: *Poverty and Famines*, Oxford University Press, USA, 1973.

Sen, Rajen and Sen, B.K.: *Deshbandhu Chittaranjan*, Calcutta, 1926.

Shachi Chakravarty: *Quit India Movement: A Study*, New Century Publication, 2002.

Shailesh Chandra: *90 Years of India's Struggle for Independence: 1857-1947*, Alfa Pub, 2008.

Shantinath Gupta: *Great Freedom Fighters of India*, Anmol, 2006.

Sharma, K. K.: *Encyclopaedia of Great Personalities of India (4 Vols-Set)*, Book Enclave, 2007.

Sharma, S. K.: *Eminent Indian Freedom Fighters (2 Vols-Set)*, Anmol, 2004.

Sirisa Kumar Shadangi: *The Prisons of South Orissa and the Freedom Fighters in Incarceration, 1900 - 1947*, Punthi Pustak, 2005.

Sitaramayya, Pattabhi, B.: *The History of the Indian National Congress: 1885-1935*, Allahabad, 1935.

Sumit Sarkar: *Calcutta and the Bengal Renaissance,* Sukanta Chaudhuri, Calcutta, 1995.

Sumiti Malhotra: *Thoughts of Great Personalities in 20 Century,* Raj Publishing, 2003.

Sundaram, V.: *Great Crusader for Women's Emancipation,* News Today, 2005.

Sundararaja, Saroja: *March to Freedom in Madras Presidency, 1916-1947,* Lalitha Publication, Chennai, 1989.

Surinder Singh: *The Political Memoirs of an Indian Revolutionary: Naina Singh Dhoot (1904-1989),* Manohar, 2005.

Taneja, Anup: *Gandhi, Women and the National Movement, 1920-47,* Har-Anand Publications, Delhi, 2005.

Thapar-Bjorkert, Suruchi: *Women in the Indian Nationalist Movement,* Sage Publication India (P) Ltd., New Delhi, 2006.

Thomas, Frederic, C.: *Calcutta Poor: Elegies on a City Above Pretense,* M.E. Sharpe, 1997.

Verma B. R. and Unnikrishnan K.: *Encyclopaedic Biography of Indian Freedom Fighters,* Commonwealth, 2004.

Vishnoo Bhagwan: *Indian Freedom Movement and Constitutional Acts,* Atma Ram, 1999.

Warrier, Shoba: *Quit India Movement: 60 Years,* Dr. Sarojini Varadappan, 2002.

Index

D

E

F

G

H

I

J

K

L

R

S

T

U

V

W

Z

❑❑❑